G.I. JOE

VOLUME 2

THE FALL OF G.I. JOE

WRITER: **KAREN TRAVISS**

ARTIST: **STEVE KURTH**

COLORIST: **KITO YOUNG**

LETTERERS: **TOM B. LONG**

AND **NEIL UYETAKE**

SERIES EDITOR: **JOHN BARBER**

Special thanks to Hasbro's Mike Ballog, Ed Lane, Heather Hopkins, and Michael Kelly for their invaluable assistance.

ISBN: 978-1-63140-355-2

18 17 16 15   1 2 3

Ted Adams, CEO & Publisher
Greg Goldstein, President & COO
Robbie Robbins, EVP/Sr. Graphic Artist
Chris Ryall, Chief Creative Officer/Editor-in-Chief
Matthew Ruzicka, CPA, Chief Financial Officer
Alan Payne, VP of Sales
Dirk Wood, VP of Marketing
Lorelei Bunjes, VP of Digital Services
Jeff Webber, VP of Digital Publishing & Business Development

Licensed By: Hasbro

www.IDWPUBLISHING.com
IDW founded by Ted Adams, Alex Garner, Kris Oprisko, and Robbie Robbins

Facebook: **facebook.com/idwpublishing**
Twitter: **@idwpublishing**
YouTube: **youtube.com/idwpublishing**
Tumblr: **tumblr.idwpublishing.com**
Instagram: **instagram.com/idwpublishing**

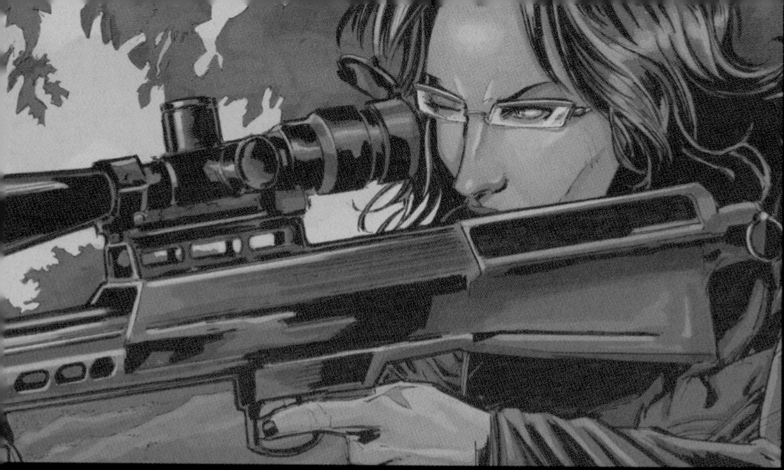

COLLECTION EDITORS
JUSTIN EISINGER
AND **ALONZO SIMON**

COLLECTION DESIGNER
CHRIS MOWRY

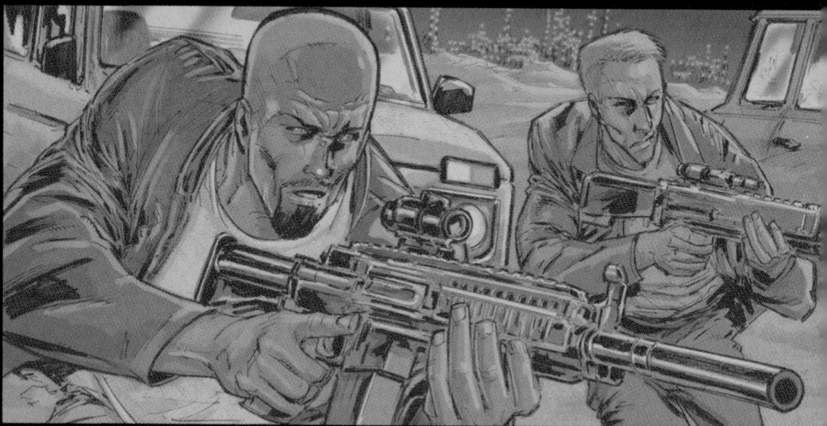

COVER ARTIST
JEFFREY VEREGGE

SPECIAL THANKS TO
MAX BROOKS

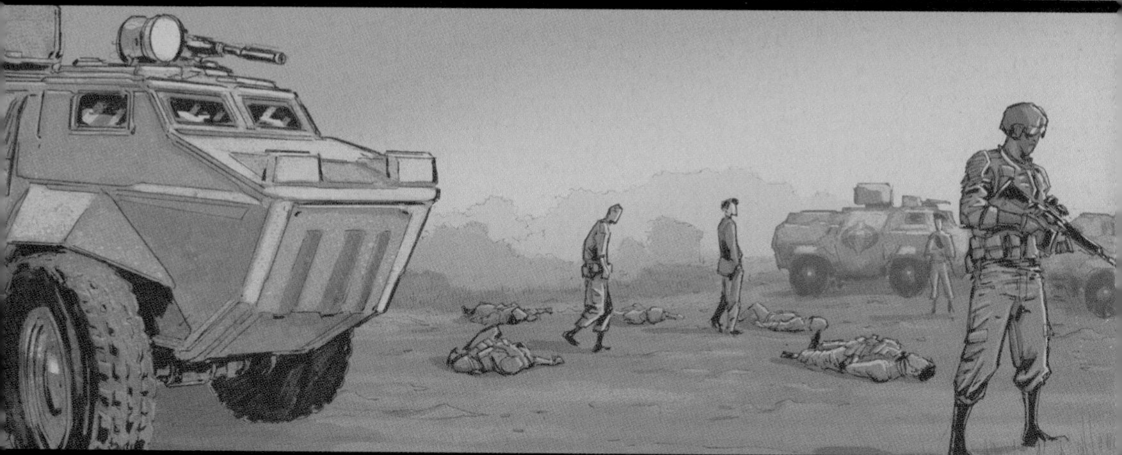

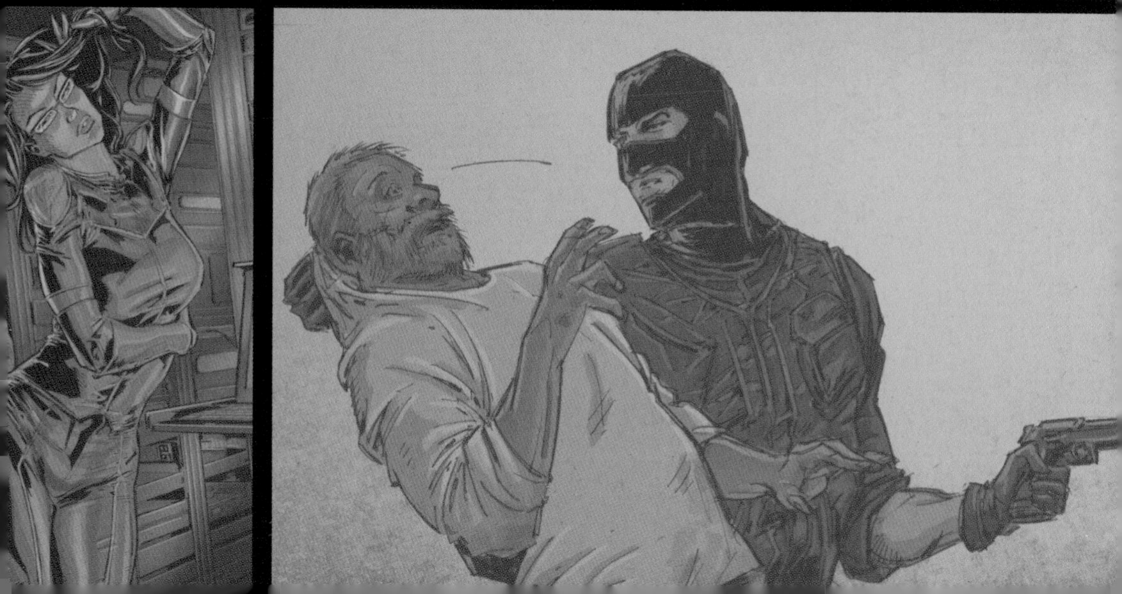

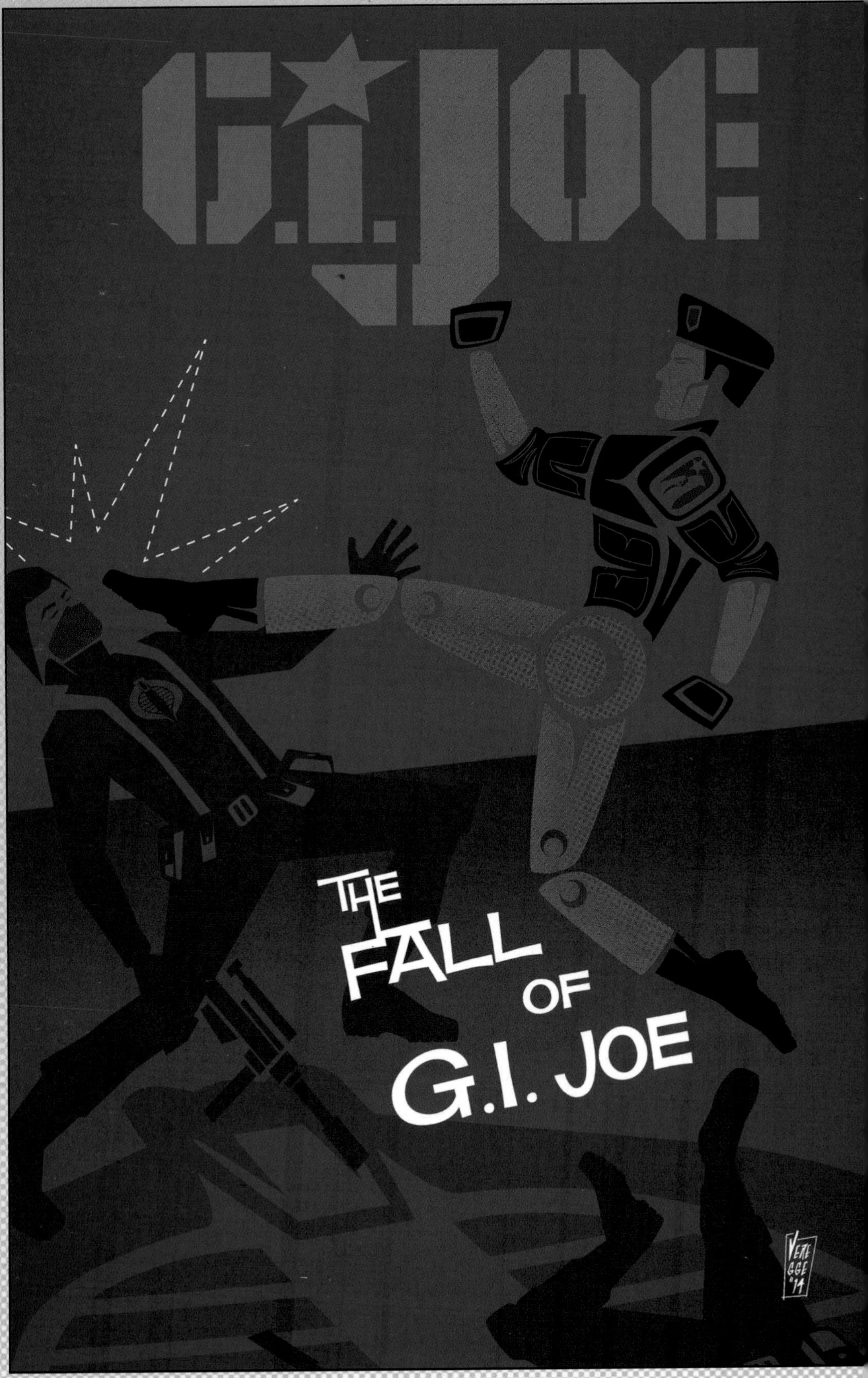
G.I. JOE
THE FALL OF G.I. JOE
VEREGGE '14

ARTWORK BY
JEFFREY VEREGGE

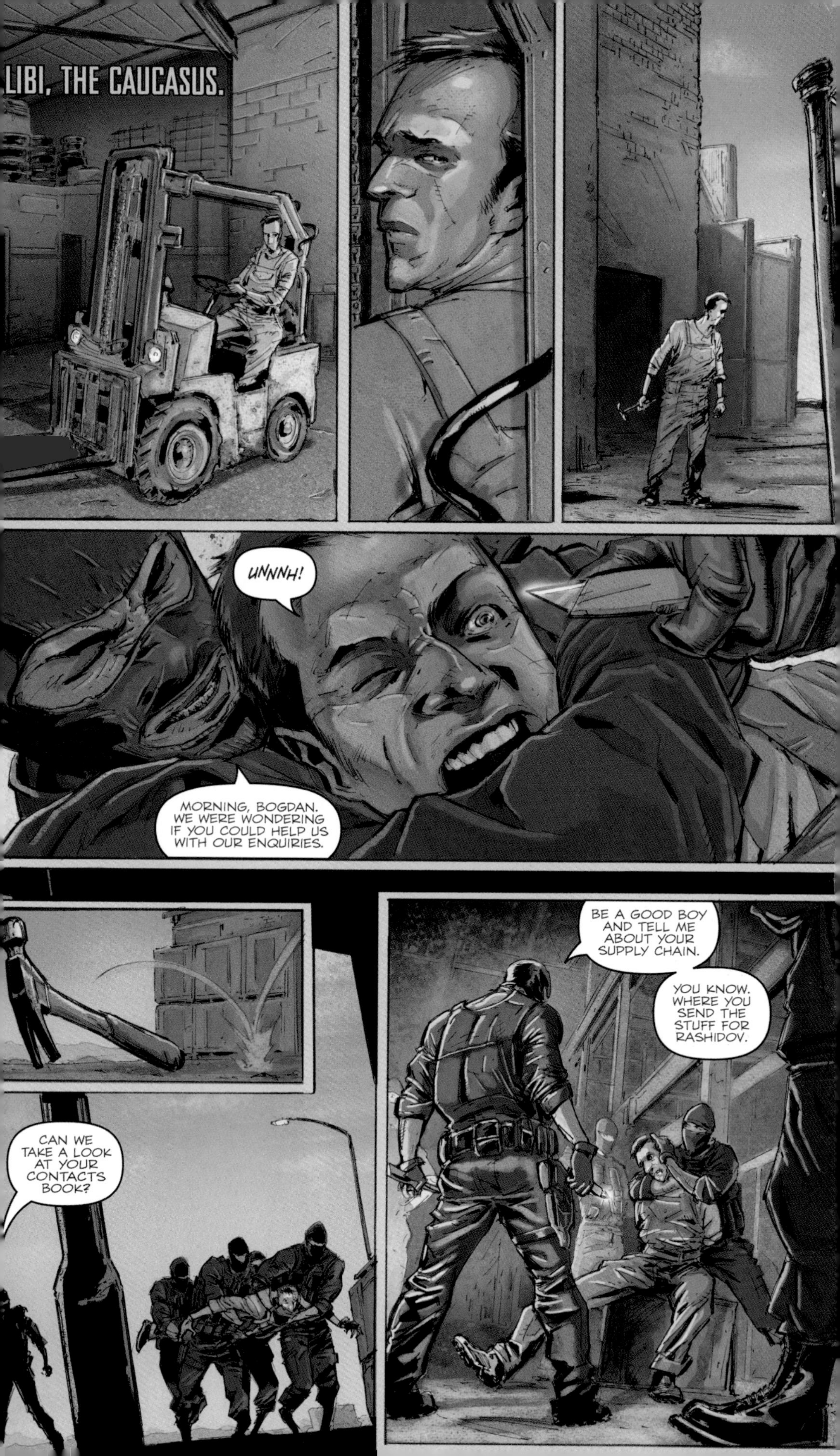
LIBI, THE CAUCASUS.
UNNNH!
MORNING, BOGDAN. WE WERE WONDERING IF YOU COULD HELP US WITH OUR ENQUIRIES.
CAN WE TAKE A LOOK AT YOUR CONTACTS BOOK?
BE A GOOD BOY AND TELL ME ABOUT YOUR SUPPLY CHAIN.
YOU KNOW. WHERE YOU SEND THE STUFF FOR RASHIDOV.

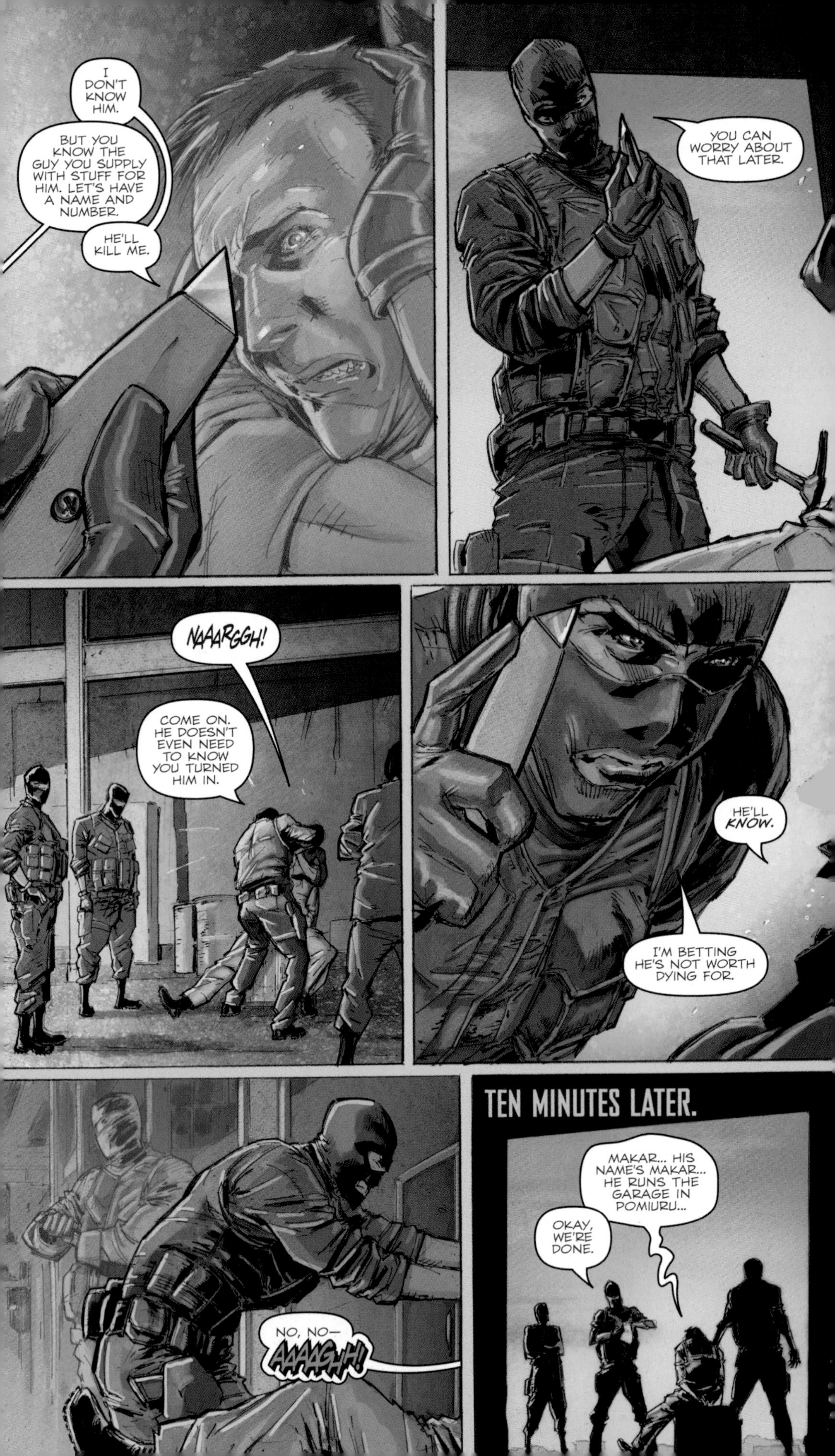
I DON'T KNOW HIM.
BUT YOU KNOW THE GUY YOU SUPPLY WITH STUFF FOR HIM. LET'S HAVE A NAME AND NUMBER.
HE'LL KILL ME.
YOU CAN WORRY ABOUT THAT LATER.
NAAARGGH!
COME ON. HE DOESN'T EVEN NEED TO KNOW YOU TURNED HIM IN.
HE'LL KNOW.
I'M BETTING HE'S NOT WORTH DYING FOR.
NO, NO—
AAAAGHH!
TEN MINUTES LATER.
MAKAR... HIS NAME'S MAKAR... HE RUNS THE GARAGE IN POMIURU...
OKAY, WE'RE DONE.

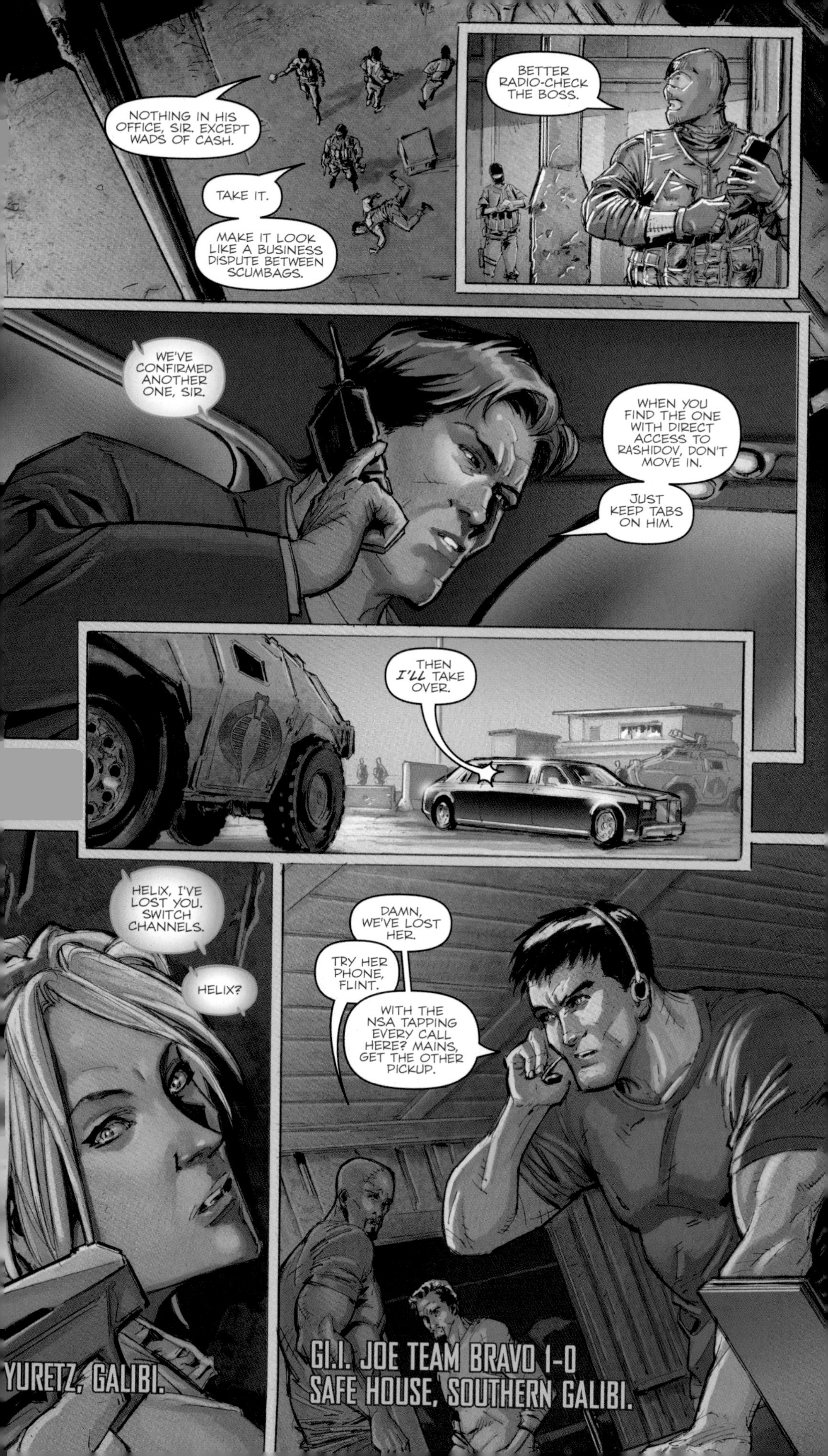
NOTHING IN HIS OFFICE, SIR. EXCEPT WADS OF CASH.
TAKE IT.
MAKE IT LOOK LIKE A BUSINESS DISPUTE BETWEEN SCUMBAGS.
BETTER RADIO-CHECK THE BOSS.
WE'VE CONFIRMED ANOTHER ONE, SIR.
WHEN YOU FIND THE ONE WITH DIRECT ACCESS TO RASHIDOV, DON'T MOVE IN.
JUST KEEP TABS ON HIM.
THEN *I'LL* TAKE OVER.
HELIX, I'VE LOST YOU. SWITCH CHANNELS.
HELIX?
YURETZ, GALIBI.
DAMN, WE'VE LOST HER.
TRY HER PHONE, FLINT.
WITH THE NSA TAPPING EVERY CALL HERE? MAINS, GET THE OTHER PICKUP.
G.I. JOE TEAM BRAVO 1-0
SAFE HOUSE, SOUTHERN GALIBI.

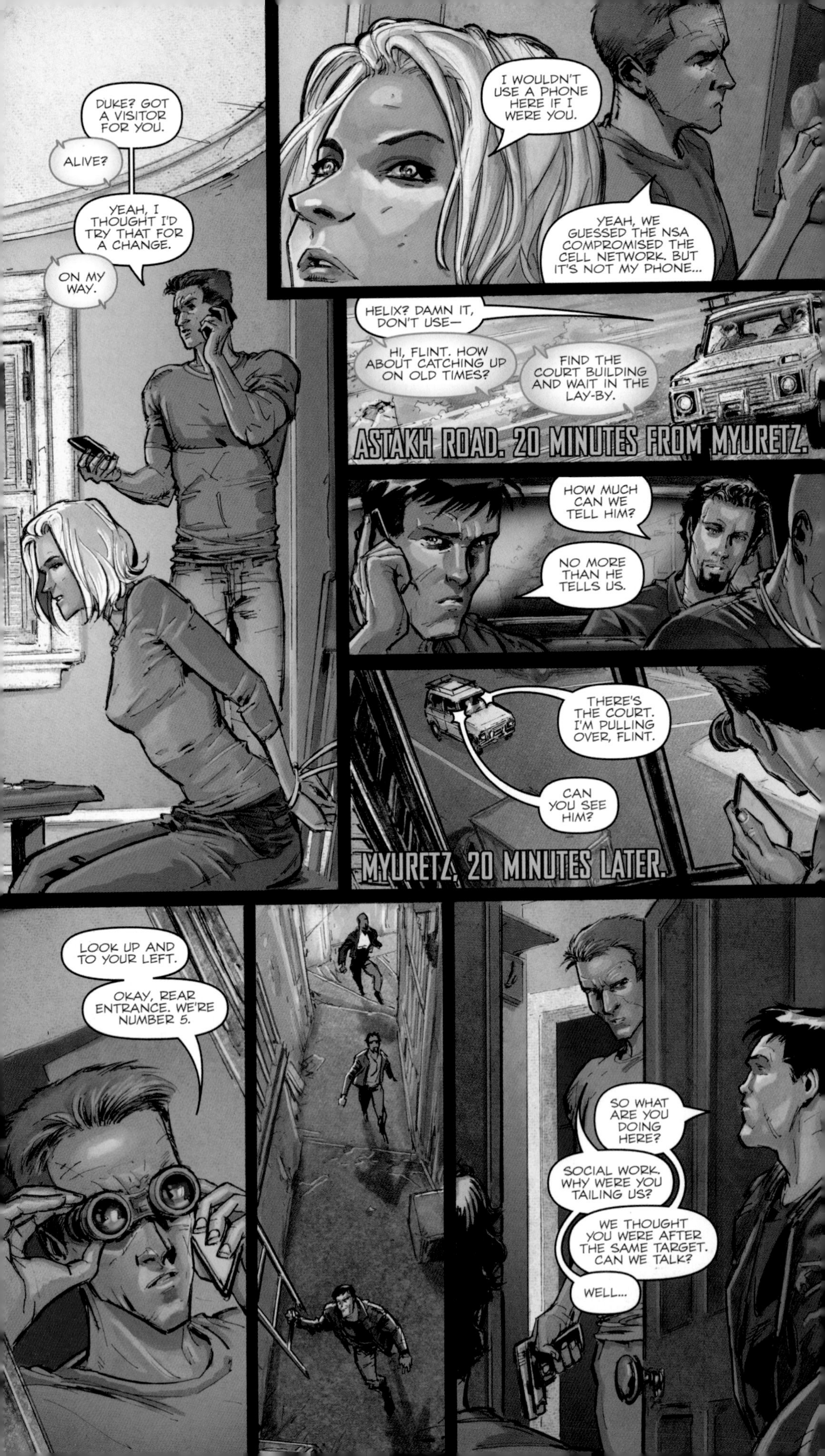
DUKE? GOT A VISITOR FOR YOU.
ALIVE?
YEAH, I THOUGHT I'D TRY THAT FOR A CHANGE.
ON MY WAY.
I WOULDN'T USE A PHONE HERE IF I WERE YOU.
YEAH, WE GUESSED THE NSA COMPROMISED THE CELL NETWORK. BUT IT'S NOT MY PHONE...
HELIX? DAMN IT, DON'T USE—
HI, FLINT. HOW ABOUT CATCHING UP ON OLD TIMES?
FIND THE COURT BUILDING AND WAIT IN THE LAY-BY.
ASTAKH ROAD. 20 MINUTES FROM MYURETZ.
HOW MUCH CAN WE TELL HIM?
NO MORE THAN HE TELLS US.
THERE'S THE COURT. I'M PULLING OVER, FLINT.
CAN YOU SEE HIM?
MYURETZ, 20 MINUTES LATER.
LOOK UP AND TO YOUR LEFT.
OKAY, REAR ENTRANCE. WE'RE NUMBER 5.
SO WHAT ARE YOU DOING HERE?
SOCIAL WORK. WHY WERE YOU TAILING US?
WE THOUGHT YOU WERE AFTER THE SAME TARGET. CAN WE TALK?
WELL...

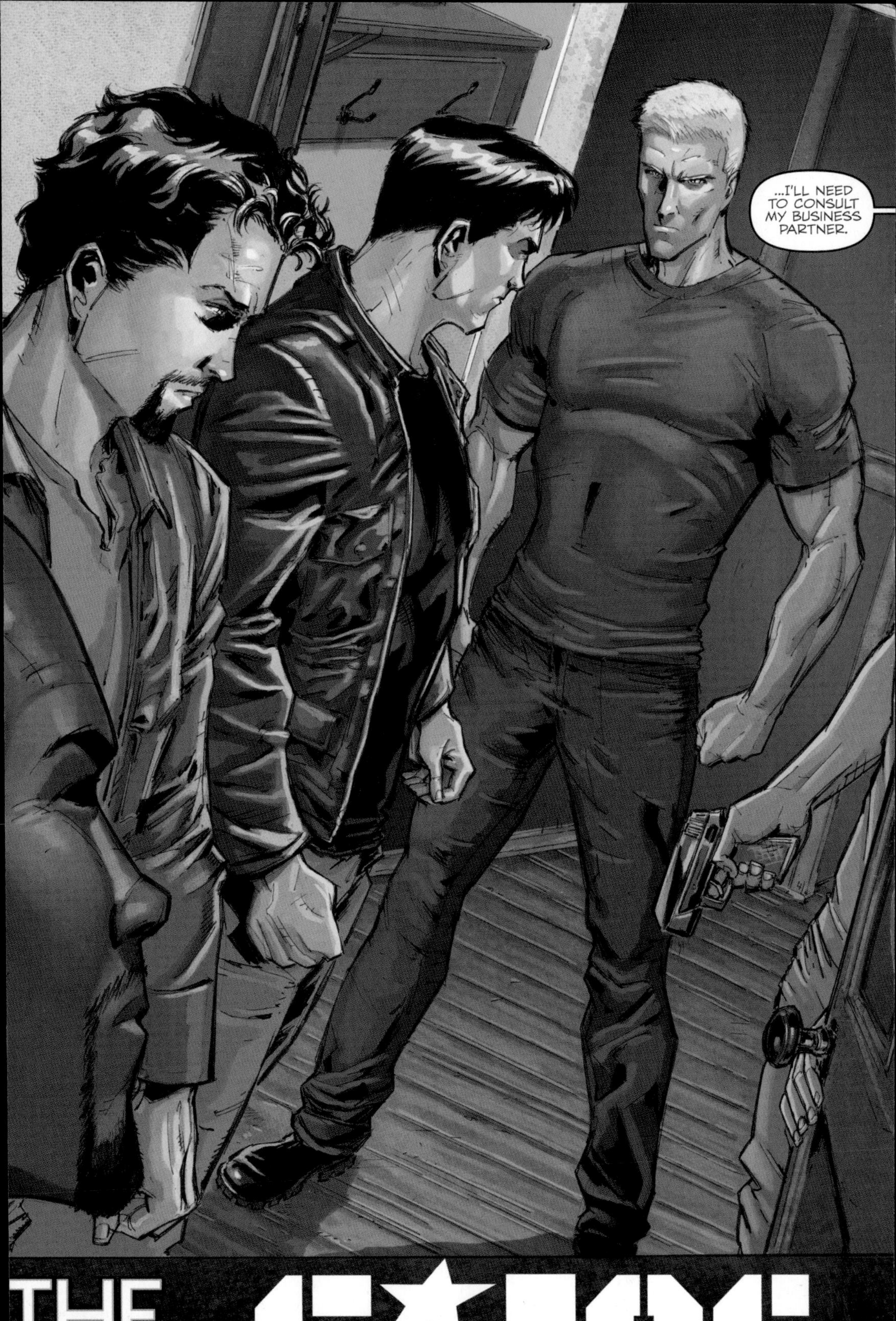
...I'LL NEED TO CONSULT MY BUSINESS PARTNER.

THE FALL OF G.I. JOE

PART FIVE

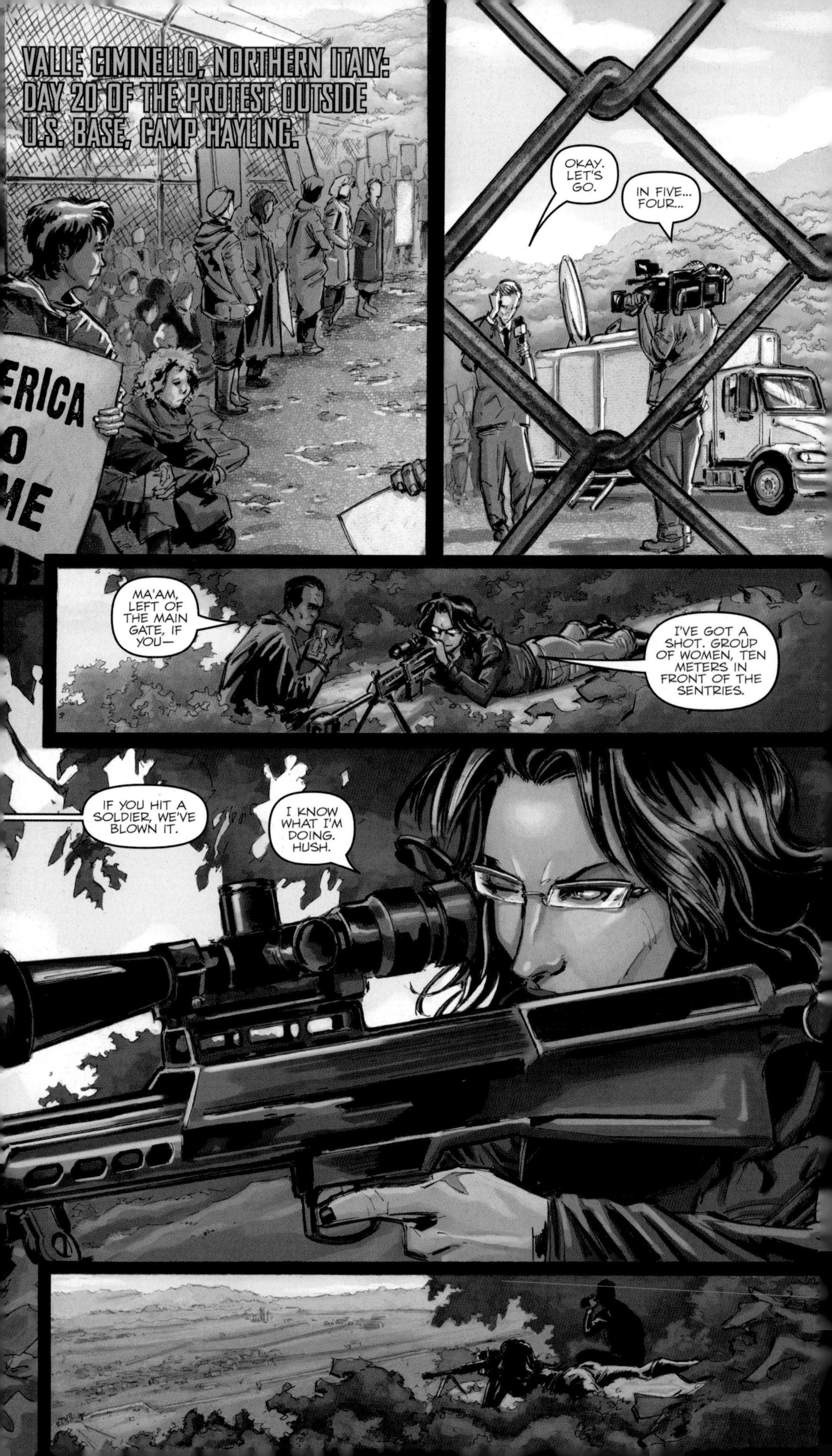
VALLE CIMINELLO, NORTHERN ITALY: DAY 20 OF THE PROTEST OUTSIDE U.S. BASE, CAMP HAYLING.
ERICA
O
ME
OKAY. LET'S GO.
IN FIVE... FOUR...
MA'AM, LEFT OF THE MAIN GATE, IF YOU—
I'VE GOT A SHOT. GROUP OF WOMEN, TEN METERS IN FRONT OF THE SENTRIES.
IF YOU HIT A SOLDIER, WE'VE BLOWN IT.
I KNOW WHAT I'M DOING. HUSH.

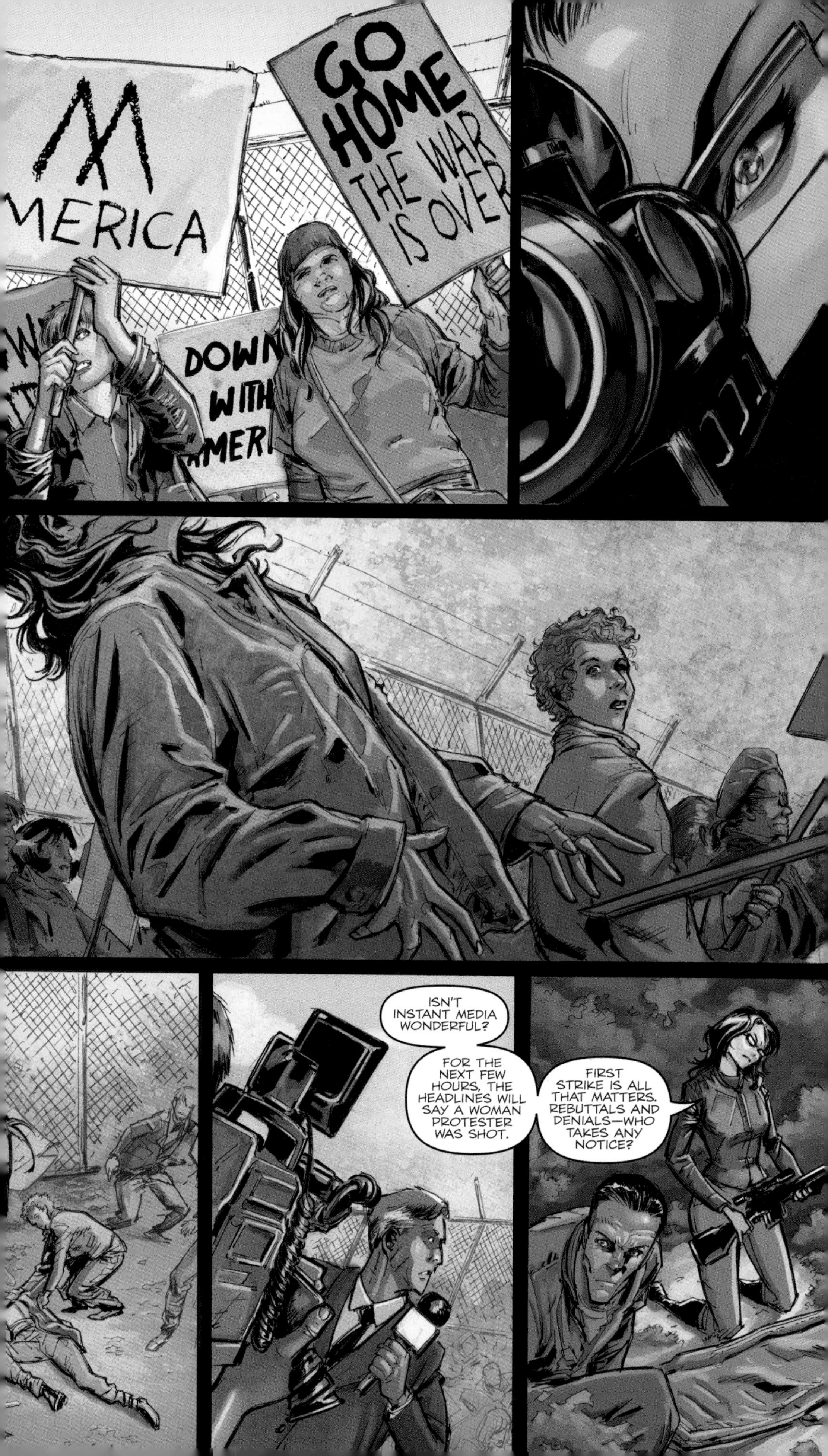

MERICA
GO HOME THE WAR IS OVER
DOWN WITH AMERI
ISN'T INSTANT MEDIA WONDERFUL?
FOR THE NEXT FEW HOURS, THE HEADLINES WILL SAY A WOMAN PROTESTER WAS SHOT.
FIRST STRIKE IS ALL THAT MATTERS. REBUTTALS AND DENIALS—WHO TAKES ANY NOTICE?

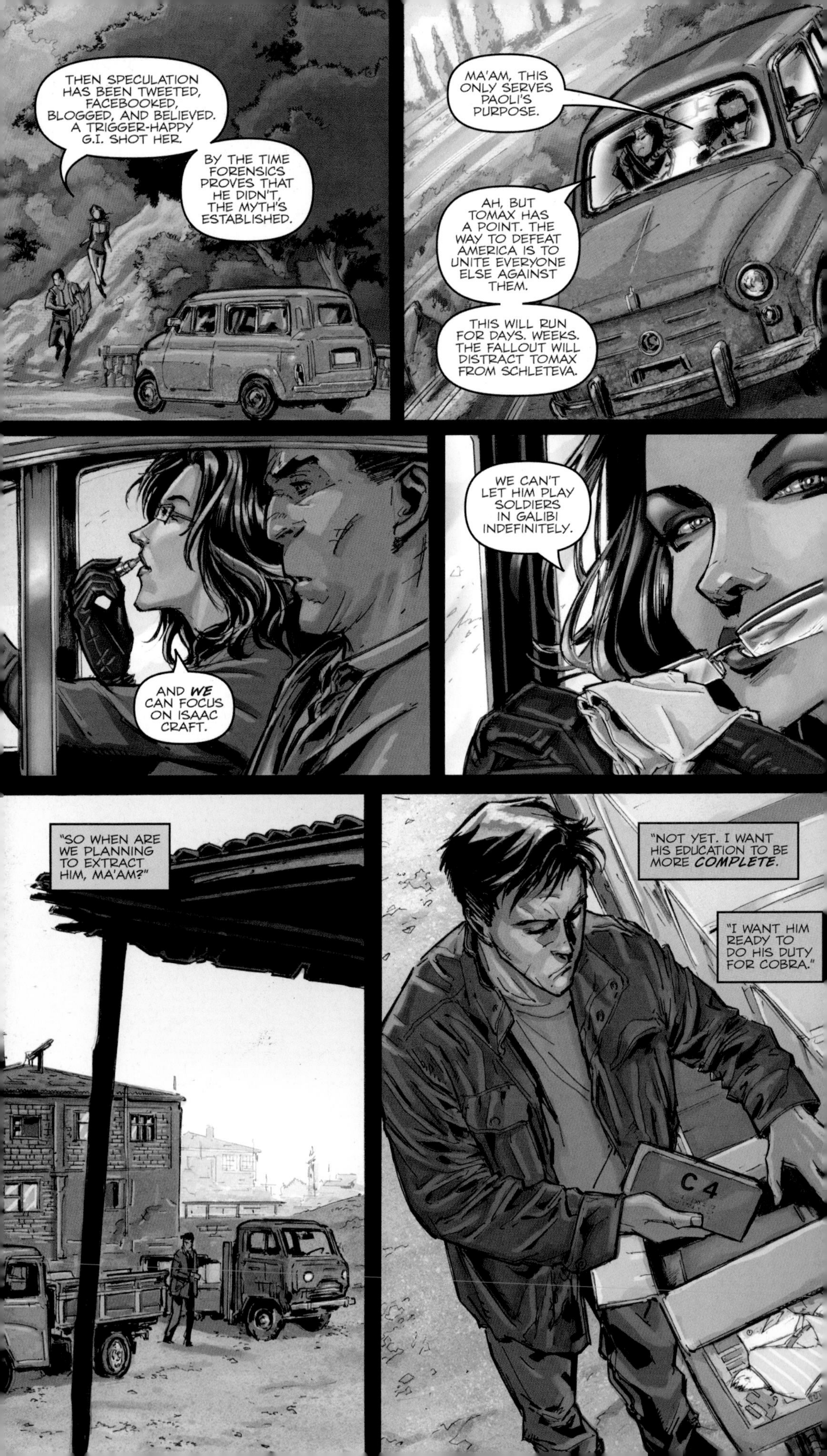

THEN SPECULATION HAS BEEN TWEETED, FACEBOOKED, BLOGGED, AND BELIEVED. A TRIGGER-HAPPY G.I. SHOT HER.
BY THE TIME FORENSICS PROVES THAT HE DIDN'T, THE MYTH'S ESTABLISHED.
MA'AM, THIS ONLY SERVES PAOLI'S PURPOSE.
AH, BUT TOMAX HAS A POINT. THE WAY TO DEFEAT AMERICA IS TO UNITE EVERYONE ELSE AGAINST THEM.
THIS WILL RUN FOR DAYS. WEEKS. THE FALLOUT WILL DISTRACT TOMAX FROM SCHLETEVA.
AND WE CAN FOCUS ON ISAAC CRAFT.
WE CAN'T LET HIM PLAY SOLDIERS IN GALIBI INDEFINITELY.
"SO WHEN ARE WE PLANNING TO EXTRACT HIM, MA'AM?"
"NOT YET. I WANT HIS EDUCATION TO BE MORE COMPLETE.
"I WANT HIM READY TO DO HIS DUTY FOR COBRA."
C4

TOMAX PAOLI'S ON THE NEWS. HE WANTS TO TALK TO US.

THAT'S NICE OF HIM.

MAYBE I SHOULD GIVE HIM MY NUMBER...

HIDOV'S ...PORARY ...QUARTERS, ...HERN GALIBI.

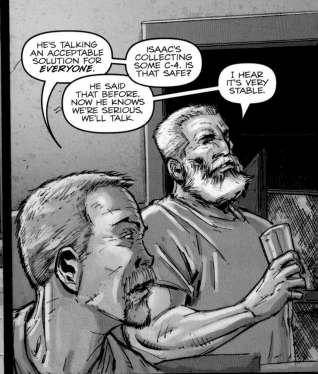

HE'S TALKING AN ACCEPTABLE SOLUTION FOR EVERYONE.

ISAAC'S COLLECTING SOME C-4. IS THAT SAFE?

I HEAR IT'S VERY STABLE.

HE SAID THAT BEFORE. NOW HE KNOWS WE'RE SERIOUS, WE'LL TALK.

I DIDN'T MEAN THE EXPLOSIVES.

HOW DID IT GO, ISAAC?

ALL THE CONSIGNMENT'S ACCOUNTED FOR, SIR.

SIT WITH ME, SON.

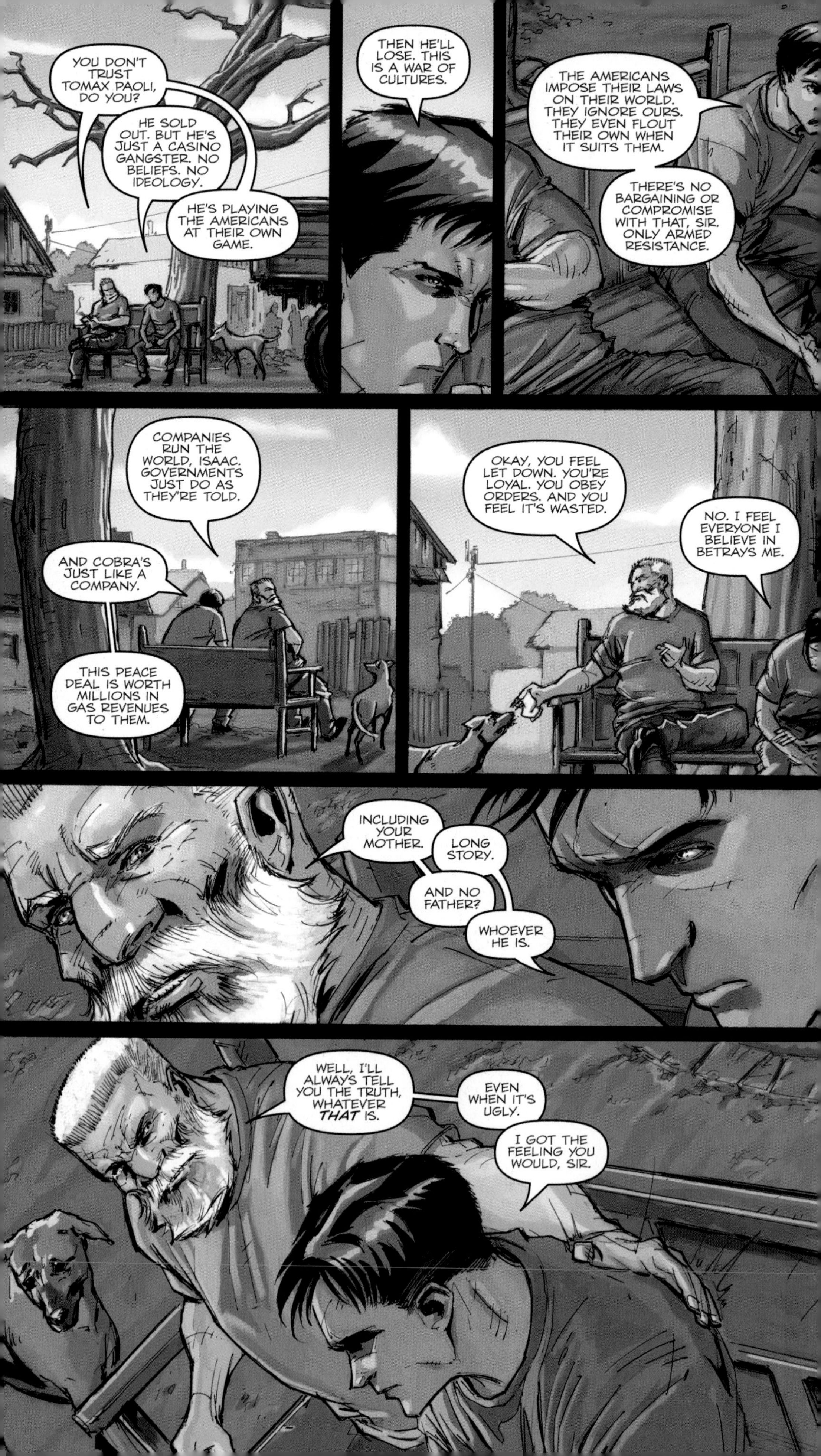
YOU DON'T TRUST TOMAX PAOLI, DO YOU?
HE SOLD OUT. BUT HE'S JUST A CASINO GANGSTER. NO BELIEFS. NO IDEOLOGY.
HE'S PLAYING THE AMERICANS AT THEIR OWN GAME.
THEN HE'LL LOSE. THIS IS A WAR OF CULTURES.
THE AMERICANS IMPOSE THEIR LAWS ON THEIR WORLD. THEY IGNORE OURS. THEY EVEN FLOUT THEIR OWN WHEN IT SUITS THEM.
THERE'S NO BARGAINING OR COMPROMISE WITH THAT, SIR. ONLY ARMED RESISTANCE.
COMPANIES RUN THE WORLD, ISAAC. GOVERNMENTS JUST DO AS THEY'RE TOLD.
AND COBRA'S JUST LIKE A COMPANY.
THIS PEACE DEAL IS WORTH MILLIONS IN GAS REVENUES TO THEM.
OKAY, YOU FEEL LET DOWN. YOU'RE LOYAL. YOU OBEY ORDERS. AND YOU FEEL IT'S WASTED.
NO. I FEEL EVERYONE I BELIEVE IN BETRAYS ME.
INCLUDING YOUR MOTHER.
LONG STORY.
AND NO FATHER?
WHOEVER HE IS.
WELL, I'LL ALWAYS TELL YOU THE TRUTH, WHATEVER *THAT* IS.
EVEN WHEN IT'S UGLY.
I GOT THE FEELING YOU WOULD, SIR.

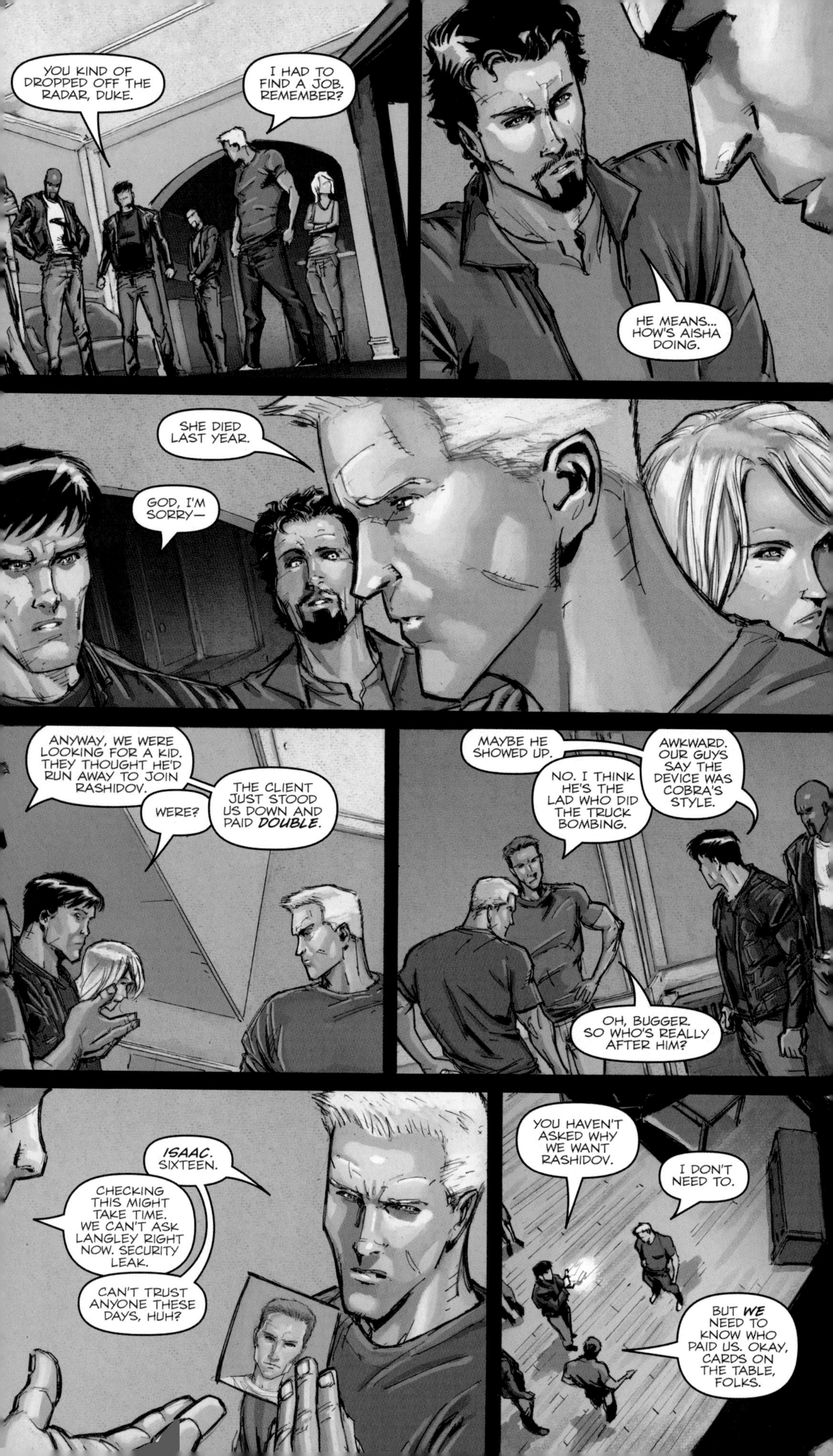
YOU KIND OF DROPPED OFF THE RADAR, DUKE.
I HAD TO FIND A JOB. REMEMBER?
HE MEANS... HOW'S AISHA DOING.
SHE DIED LAST YEAR.
GOD, I'M SORRY—
ANYWAY, WE WERE LOOKING FOR A KID. THEY THOUGHT HE'D RUN AWAY TO JOIN RASHIDOV.
WERE?
THE CLIENT JUST STOOD US DOWN AND PAID *DOUBLE*.
MAYBE HE SHOWED UP.
NO. I THINK HE'S THE LAD WHO DID THE TRUCK BOMBING.
AWKWARD. OUR GUYS SAY THE DEVICE WAS COBRA'S STYLE.
OH, BUGGER. SO WHO'S REALLY AFTER HIM?
ISAAC. SIXTEEN.
CHECKING THIS MIGHT TAKE TIME. WE CAN'T ASK LANGLEY RIGHT NOW. SECURITY LEAK.
CAN'T TRUST ANYONE THESE DAYS, HUH?
YOU HAVEN'T ASKED WHY WE WANT RASHIDOV.
I DON'T NEED TO.
BUT *WE* NEED TO KNOW WHO PAID US. OKAY, CARDS ON THE TABLE, FOLKS.

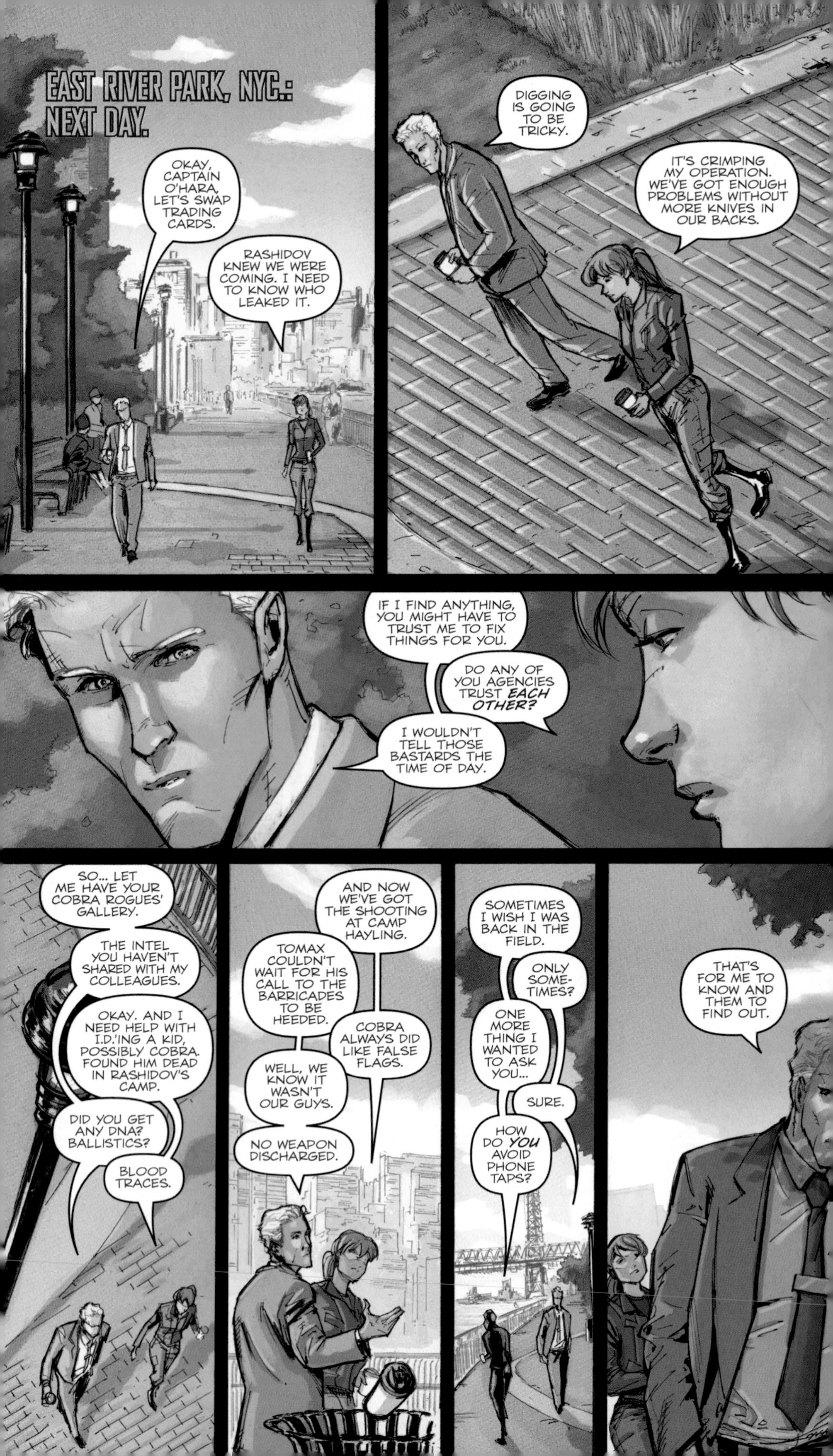
EAST RIVER PARK, NYC.: NEXT DAY.
OKAY, CAPTAIN O'HARA, LET'S SWAP TRADING CARDS.
RASHIDOV KNEW WE WERE COMING. I NEED TO KNOW WHO LEAKED IT.
DIGGING IS GOING TO BE TRICKY.
IT'S CRIMPING MY OPERATION. WE'VE GOT ENOUGH PROBLEMS WITHOUT MORE KNIVES IN OUR BACKS.
IF I FIND ANYTHING, YOU MIGHT HAVE TO TRUST ME TO FIX THINGS FOR YOU.
DO ANY OF YOU AGENCIES TRUST EACH OTHER?
I WOULDN'T TELL THOSE BASTARDS THE TIME OF DAY.
SO... LET ME HAVE YOUR COBRA ROGUES' GALLERY.
THE INTEL YOU HAVEN'T SHARED WITH MY COLLEAGUES.
OKAY. AND I NEED HELP WITH I.D.'ING A KID, POSSIBLY COBRA. FOUND HIM DEAD IN RASHIDOV'S CAMP.
DID YOU GET ANY DNA? BALLISTICS?
BLOOD TRACES.
AND NOW WE'VE GOT THE SHOOTING AT CAMP HAYLING.
TOMAX COULDN'T WAIT FOR HIS CALL TO THE BARRICADES TO BE HEEDED.
COBRA ALWAYS DID LIKE FALSE FLAGS.
WELL, WE KNOW IT WASN'T OUR GUYS.
NO WEAPON DISCHARGED.
SOMETIMES I WISH I WAS BACK IN THE FIELD.
ONLY SOME-TIMES?
ONE MORE THING I WANTED TO ASK YOU...
SURE.
HOW DO YOU AVOID PHONE TAPS?
THAT'S FOR ME TO KNOW AND THEM TO FIND OUT.

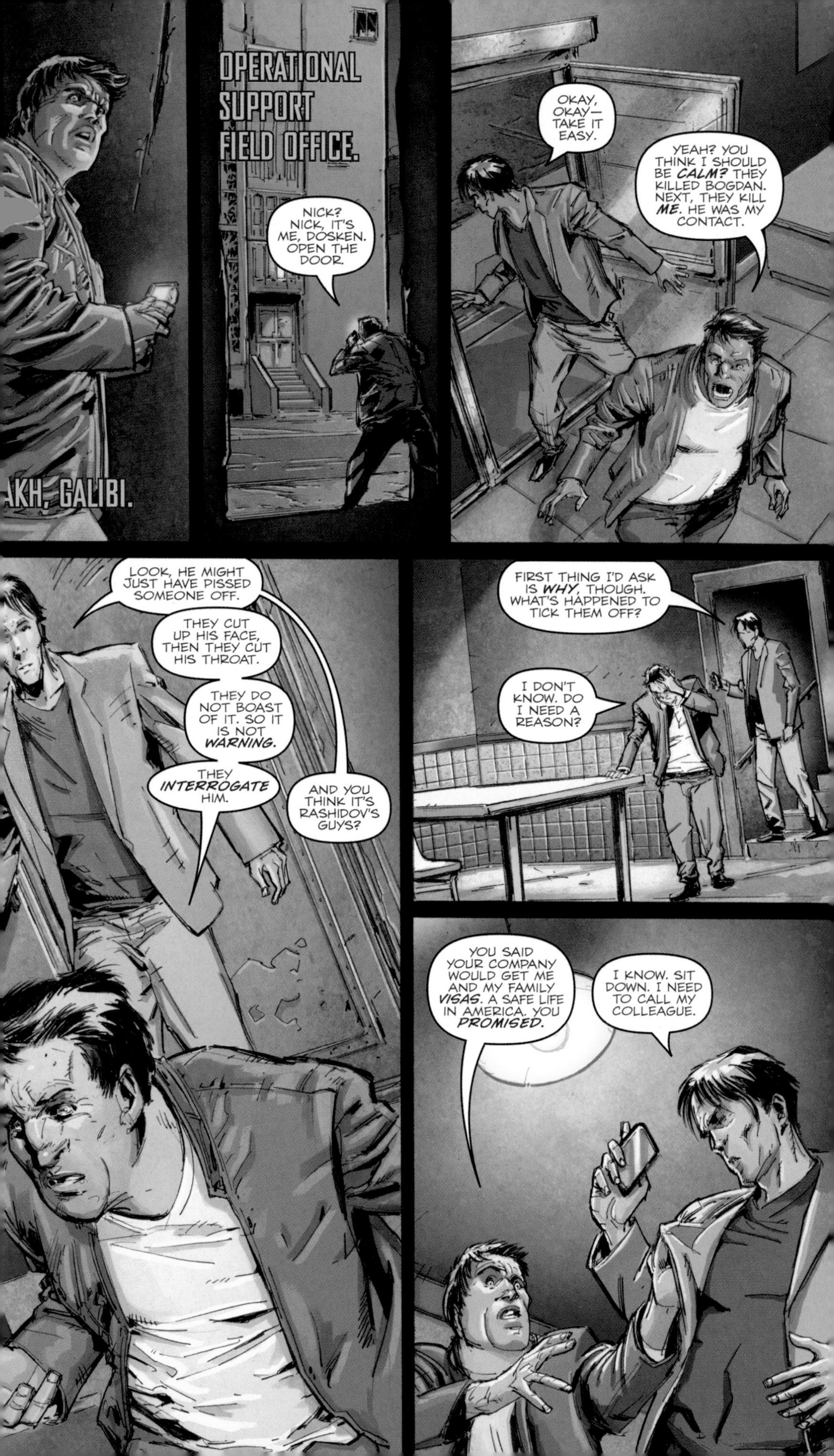
AKH, GALIBI.
OPERATIONAL SUPPORT FIELD OFFICE.
NICK? NICK, IT'S ME, DOSKEN. OPEN THE DOOR.
OKAY, OKAY— TAKE IT EASY.
YEAH? YOU THINK I SHOULD BE CALM? THEY KILLED BOGDAN. NEXT, THEY KILL ME. HE WAS MY CONTACT.
LOOK, HE MIGHT JUST HAVE PISSED SOMEONE OFF.
THEY CUT UP HIS FACE, THEN THEY CUT HIS THROAT.
THEY DO NOT BOAST OF IT. SO IT IS NOT WARNING.
THEY INTERROGATE HIM.
AND YOU THINK IT'S RASHIDOV'S GUYS?
FIRST THING I'D ASK IS WHY, THOUGH. WHAT'S HAPPENED TO TICK THEM OFF?
I DON'T KNOW. DO I NEED A REASON?
YOU SAID YOUR COMPANY WOULD GET ME AND MY FAMILY VISAS. A SAFE LIFE IN AMERICA. YOU PROMISED.
I KNOW. SIT DOWN. I NEED TO CALL MY COLLEAGUE.

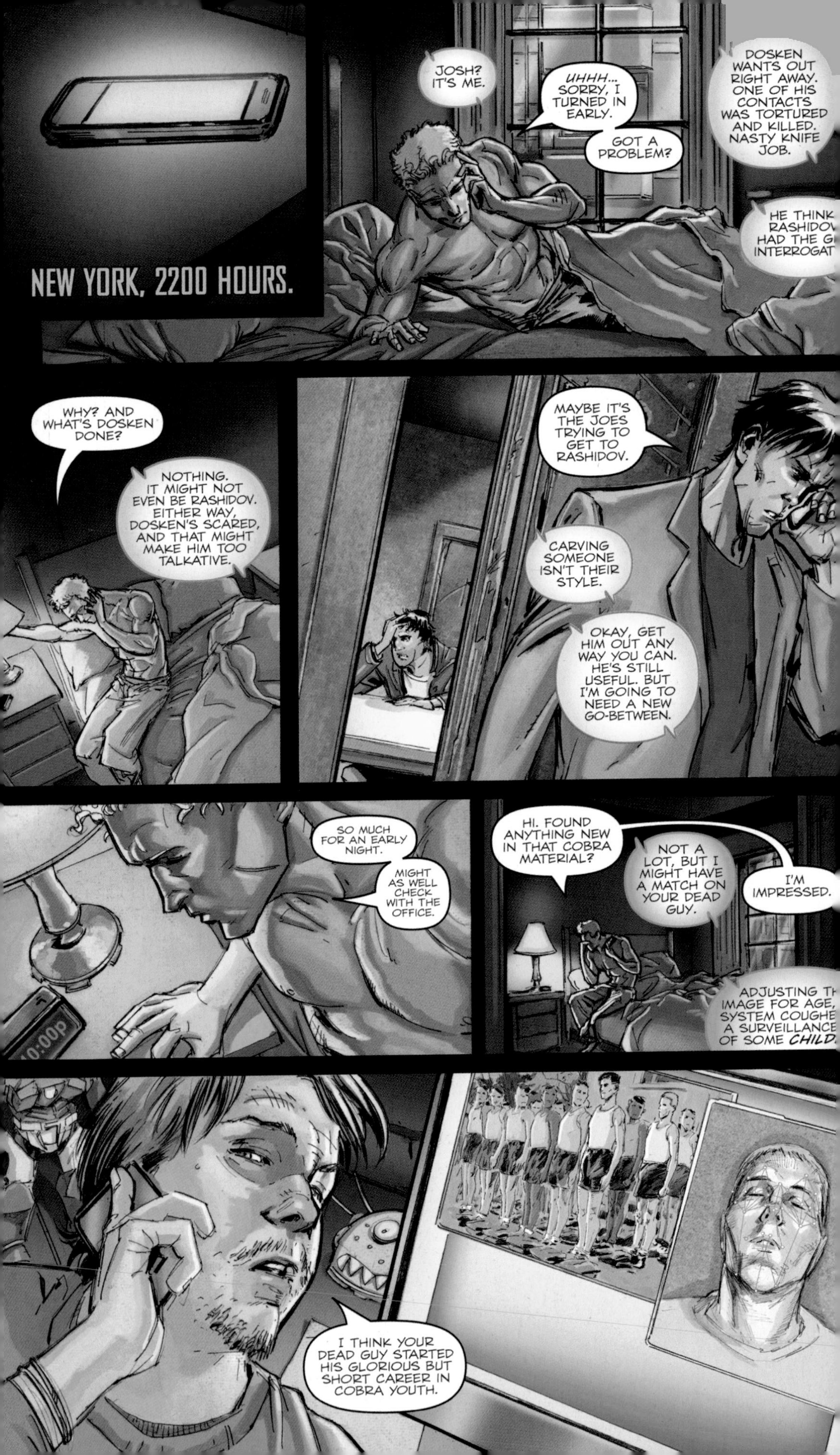
NEW YORK, 2200 HOURS.
JOSH? IT'S ME.
UHHH... SORRY, I TURNED IN EARLY.
GOT A PROBLEM?
DOSKEN WANTS OUT RIGHT AWAY. ONE OF HIS CONTACTS WAS TORTURED AND KILLED. NASTY KNIFE JOB.
HE THINK RASHIDOV HAD THE G INTERROGAT
WHY? AND WHAT'S DOSKEN DONE?
NOTHING. IT MIGHT NOT EVEN BE RASHIDOV. EITHER WAY, DOSKEN'S SCARED, AND THAT MIGHT MAKE HIM TOO TALKATIVE.
MAYBE IT'S THE JOES TRYING TO GET TO RASHIDOV.
CARVING SOMEONE ISN'T THEIR STYLE.
OKAY, GET HIM OUT ANY WAY YOU CAN. HE'S STILL USEFUL. BUT I'M GOING TO NEED A NEW GO-BETWEEN.
SO MUCH FOR AN EARLY NIGHT.
MIGHT AS WELL CHECK WITH THE OFFICE.
10:00P
HI. FOUND ANYTHING NEW IN THAT COBRA MATERIAL?
NOT A LOT, BUT I MIGHT HAVE A MATCH ON YOUR DEAD GUY.
I'M IMPRESSED.
ADJUSTING TH IMAGE FOR AGE, SYSTEM COUGHE A SURVEILLANCE OF SOME CHILD
I THINK YOUR DEAD GUY STARTED HIS GLORIOUS BUT SHORT CAREER IN COBRA YOUTH.

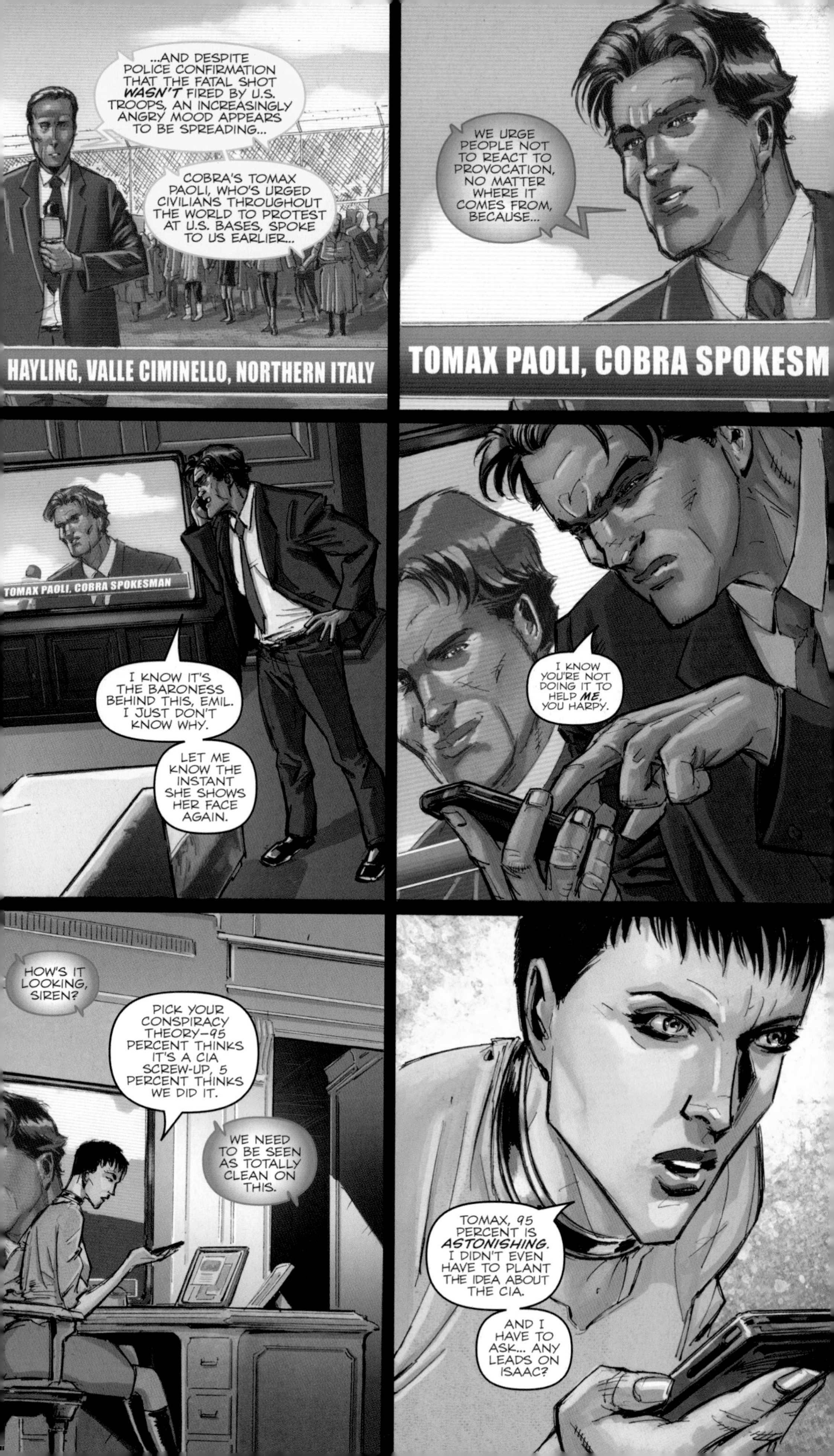
...AND DESPITE POLICE CONFIRMATION THAT THE FATAL SHOT WASN'T FIRED BY U.S. TROOPS, AN INCREASINGLY ANGRY MOOD APPEARS TO BE SPREADING...
COBRA'S TOMAX PAOLI, WHO'S URGED CIVILIANS THROUGHOUT THE WORLD TO PROTEST AT U.S. BASES, SPOKE TO US EARLIER...
HAYLING, VALLE CIMINELLO, NORTHERN ITALY
WE URGE PEOPLE NOT TO REACT TO PROVOCATION, NO MATTER WHERE IT COMES FROM, BECAUSE...
TOMAX PAOLI, COBRA SPOKESM
TOMAX PAOLI, COBRA SPOKESMAN
I KNOW IT'S THE BARONESS BEHIND THIS, EMIL. I JUST DON'T KNOW WHY.
LET ME KNOW THE INSTANT SHE SHOWS HER FACE AGAIN.
I KNOW YOU'RE NOT DOING IT TO HELP ME, YOU HARPY.
HOW'S IT LOOKING, SIREN?
PICK YOUR CONSPIRACY THEORY—95 PERCENT THINKS IT'S A CIA SCREW-UP, 5 PERCENT THINKS WE DID IT.
WE NEED TO BE SEEN AS TOTALLY CLEAN ON THIS.
TOMAX, 95 PERCENT IS ASTONISHING. I DIDN'T EVEN HAVE TO PLANT THE IDEA ABOUT THE CIA.
AND I HAVE TO ASK... ANY LEADS ON ISAAC?

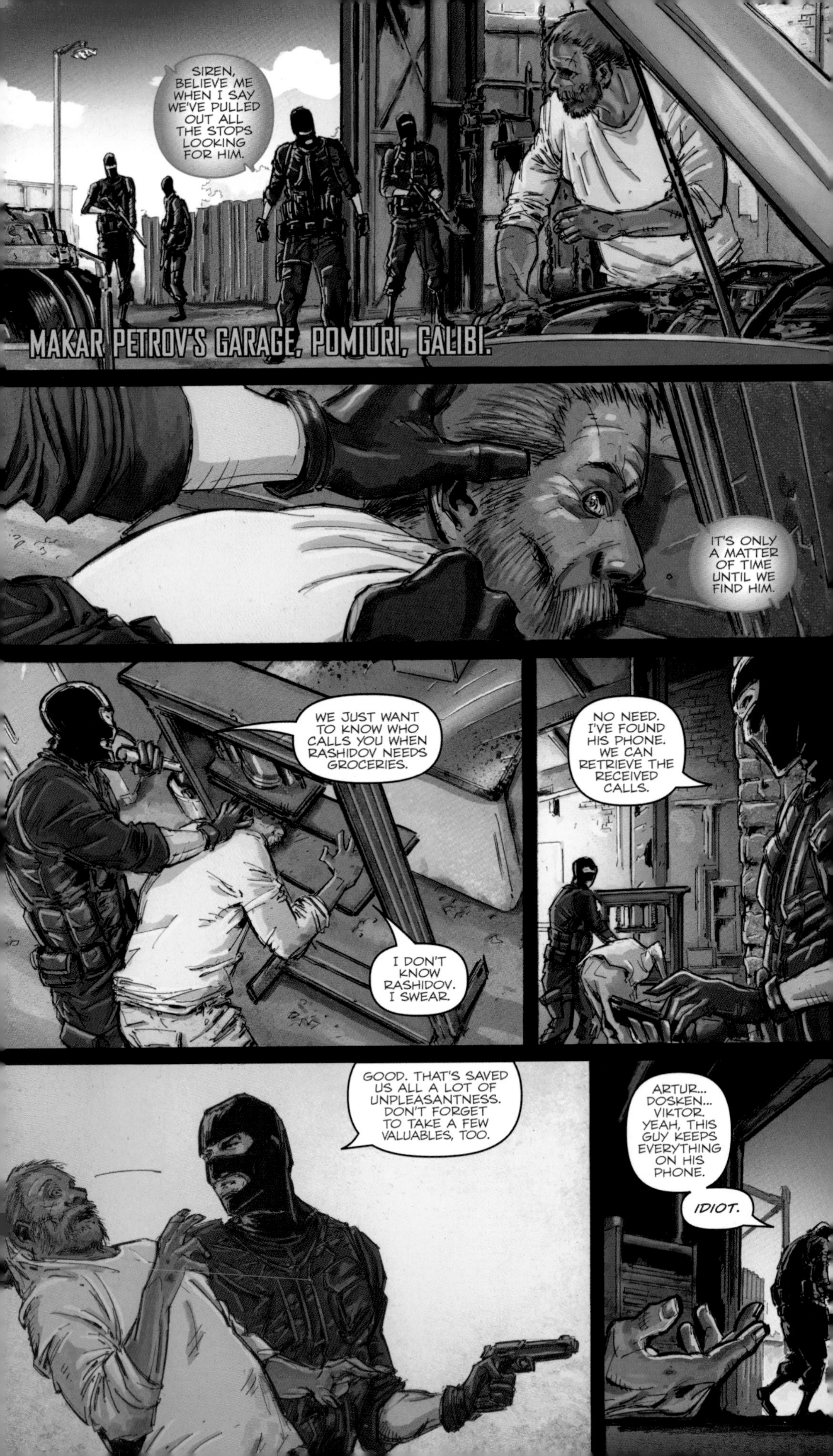
SIREN, BELIEVE ME WHEN I SAY WE'VE PULLED OUT ALL THE STOPS LOOKING FOR HIM.
MAKAR PETROV'S GARAGE, POMIURI, GALIBI.
IT'S ONLY A MATTER OF TIME UNTIL WE FIND HIM.
WE JUST WANT TO KNOW WHO CALLS YOU WHEN RASHIDOV NEEDS GROCERIES.
I DON'T KNOW RASHIDOV. I SWEAR.
NO NEED. I'VE FOUND HIS PHONE. WE CAN RETRIEVE THE RECEIVED CALLS.
GOOD. THAT'S SAVED US ALL A LOT OF UNPLEASANTNESS. DON'T FORGET TO TAKE A FEW VALUABLES, TOO.
ARTUR... DOSKEN... VIKTOR. YEAH, THIS GUY KEEPS EVERYTHING ON HIS PHONE.
IDIOT.

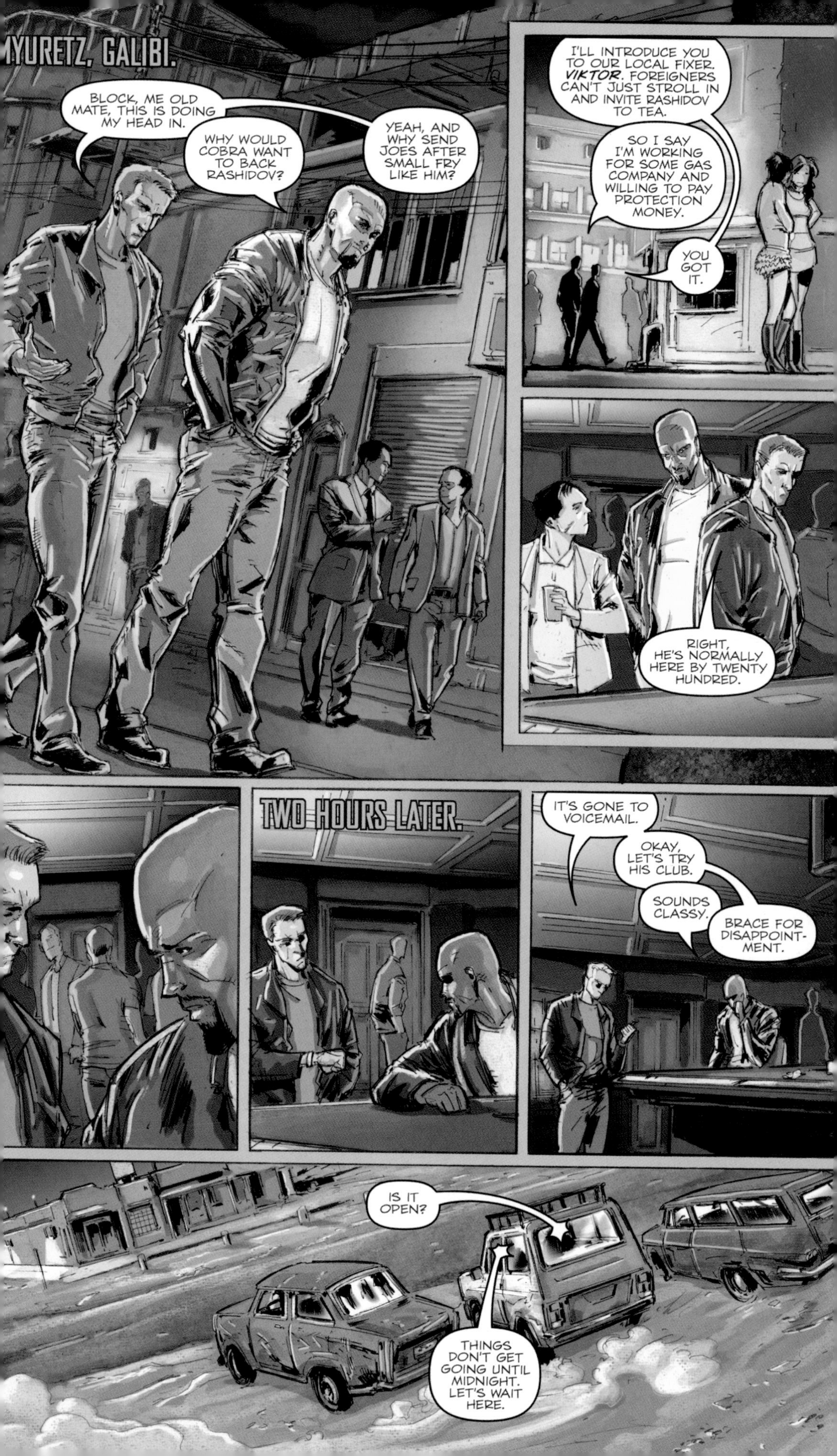

MYURETZ, GALIBI.
BLOCK, ME OLD MATE, THIS IS DOING MY HEAD IN.
WHY WOULD COBRA WANT TO BACK RASHIDOV?
YEAH, AND WHY SEND JOES AFTER SMALL FRY LIKE HIM?
I'LL INTRODUCE YOU TO OUR LOCAL FIXER. VIKTOR. FOREIGNERS CAN'T JUST STROLL IN AND INVITE RASHIDOV TO TEA.
SO I SAY I'M WORKING FOR SOME GAS COMPANY AND WILLING TO PAY PROTECTION MONEY.
YOU GOT IT.
RIGHT, HE'S NORMALLY HERE BY TWENTY HUNDRED.
TWO HOURS LATER.
IT'S GONE TO VOICEMAIL.
OKAY, LET'S TRY HIS CLUB.
SOUNDS CLASSY.
BRACE FOR DISAPPOINT-MENT.
IS IT OPEN?
THINGS DON'T GET GOING UNTIL MIDNIGHT. LET'S WAIT HERE.

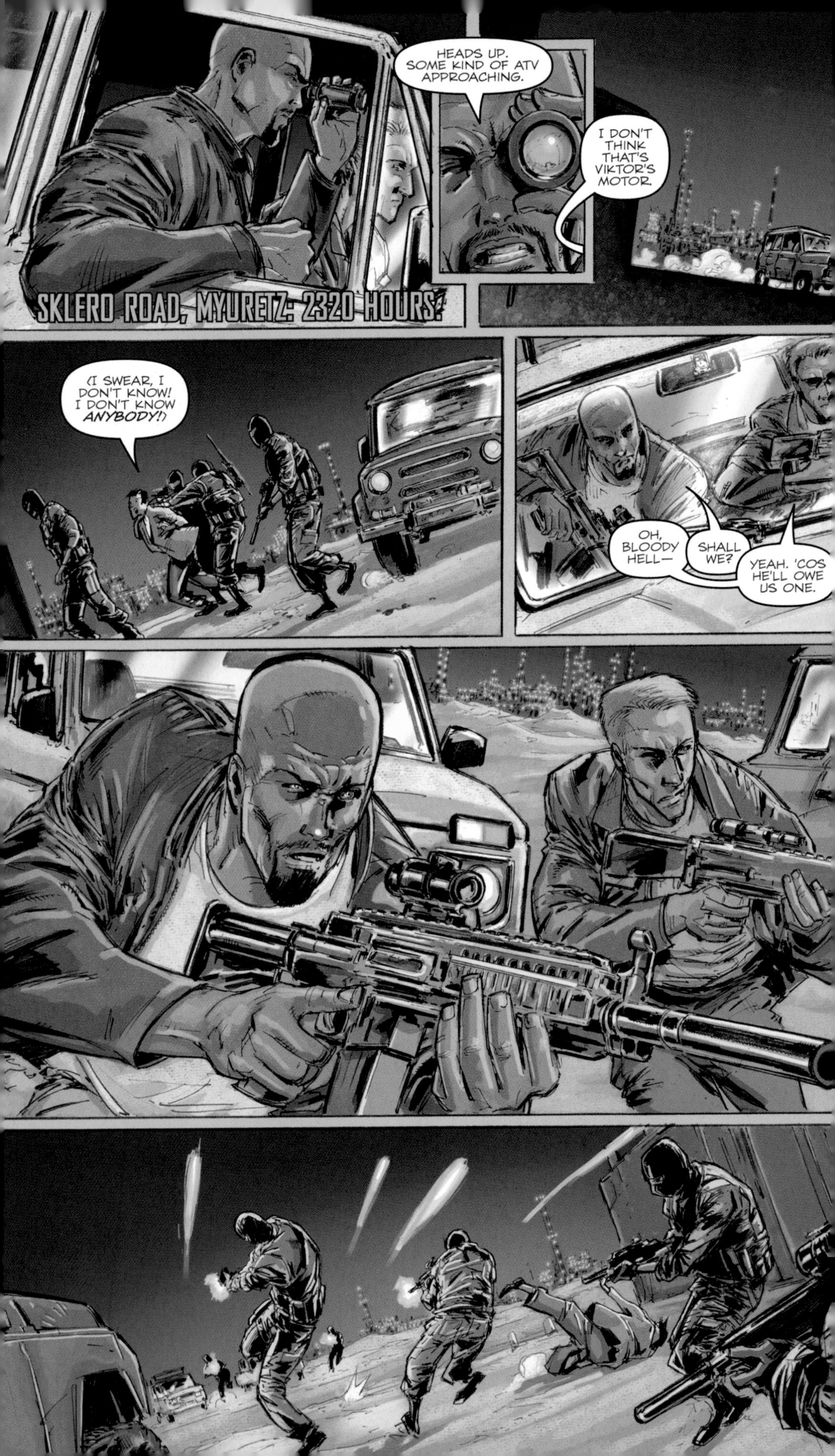
HEADS UP. SOME KIND OF ATV APPROACHING.
I DON'T THINK THAT'S VIKTOR'S MOTOR.
SKLERO ROAD, MYURETZ: 2320 HOURS.
(I SWEAR, I DON'T KNOW! I DON'T KNOW ANYBODY!)
OH, BLOODY HELL—
SHALL WE?
YEAH. 'COS HE'LL OWE US ONE.

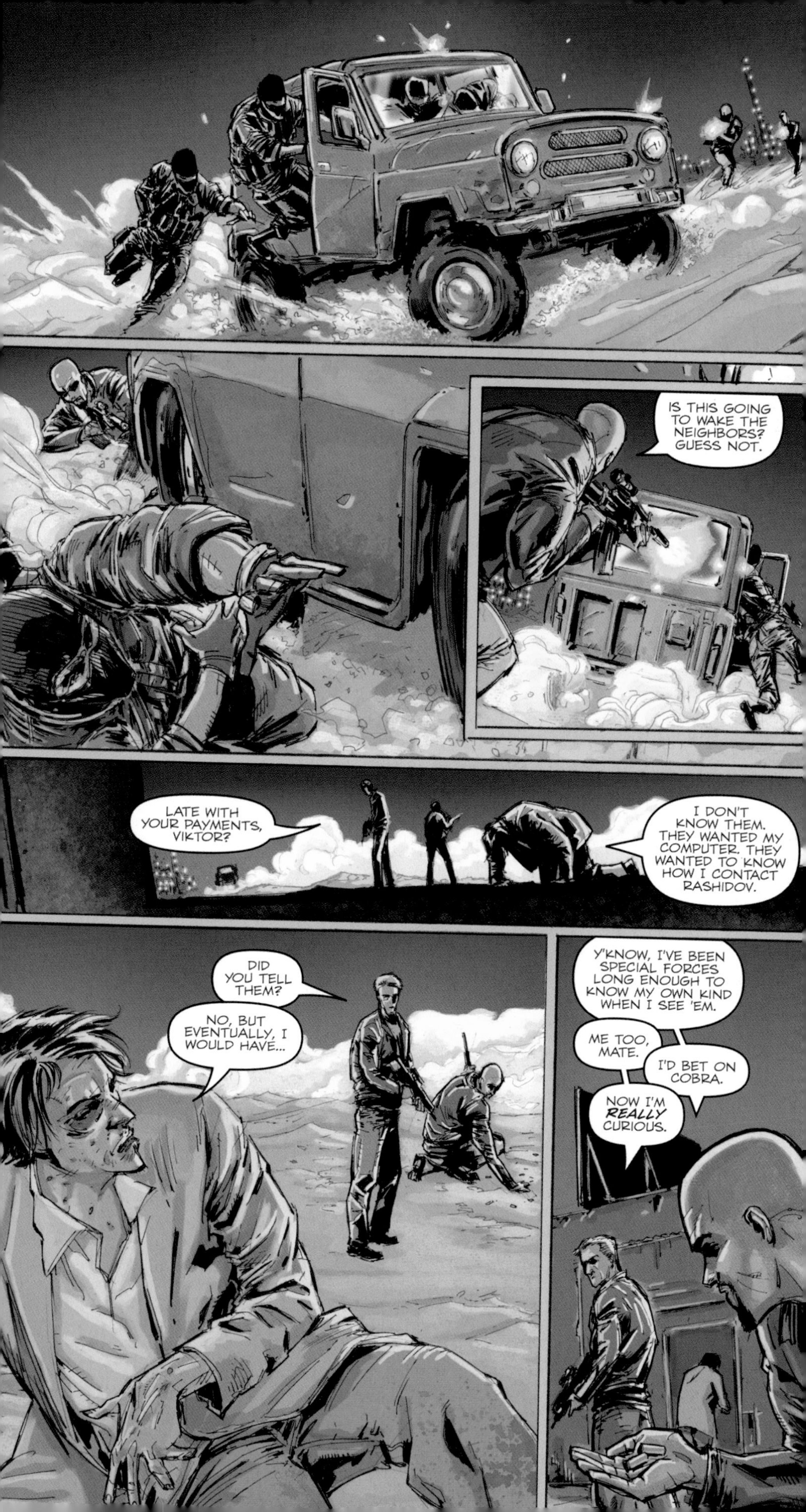
IS THIS GOING TO WAKE THE NEIGHBORS? GUESS NOT.
LATE WITH YOUR PAYMENTS, VIKTOR?
I DON'T KNOW THEM. THEY WANTED MY COMPUTER. THEY WANTED TO KNOW HOW I CONTACT RASHIDOV.
DID YOU TELL THEM?
NO, BUT EVENTUALLY, I WOULD HAVE...
Y'KNOW, I'VE BEEN SPECIAL FORCES LONG ENOUGH TO KNOW MY OWN KIND WHEN I SEE 'EM.
ME TOO, MATE.
I'D BET ON COBRA.
NOW I'M *REALLY* CURIOUS.

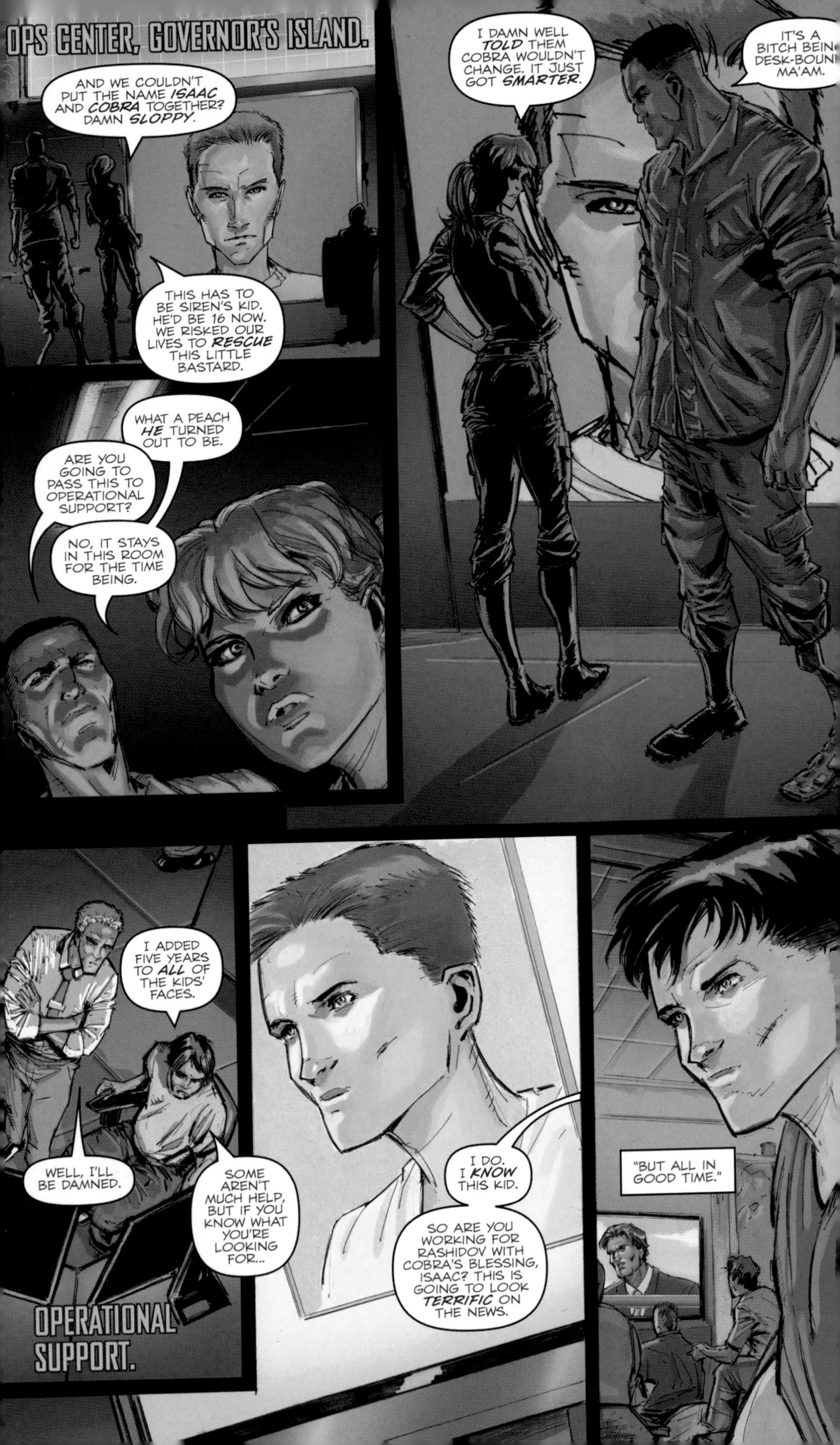
OPS CENTER, GOVERNOR'S ISLAND.
AND WE COULDN'T PUT THE NAME ISAAC AND COBRA TOGETHER? DAMN SLOPPY.
THIS HAS TO BE SIREN'S KID. HE'D BE 16 NOW. WE RISKED OUR LIVES TO RESCUE THIS LITTLE BASTARD.
WHAT A PEACH HE TURNED OUT TO BE.
ARE YOU GOING TO PASS THIS TO OPERATIONAL SUPPORT?
NO, IT STAYS IN THIS ROOM FOR THE TIME BEING.
I DAMN WELL TOLD THEM COBRA WOULDN'T CHANGE. IT JUST GOT SMARTER.
IT'S A BITCH BEIN DESK-BOUN MA'AM.
I ADDED FIVE YEARS TO ALL OF THE KIDS' FACES.
WELL, I'LL BE DAMNED.
SOME AREN'T MUCH HELP, BUT IF YOU KNOW WHAT YOU'RE LOOKING FOR...
OPERATIONAL SUPPORT.
I DO. I KNOW THIS KID.
SO ARE YOU WORKING FOR RASHIDOV WITH COBRA'S BLESSING, ISAAC? THIS IS GOING TO LOOK TERRIFIC ON THE NEWS.
"BUT ALL IN GOOD TIME."

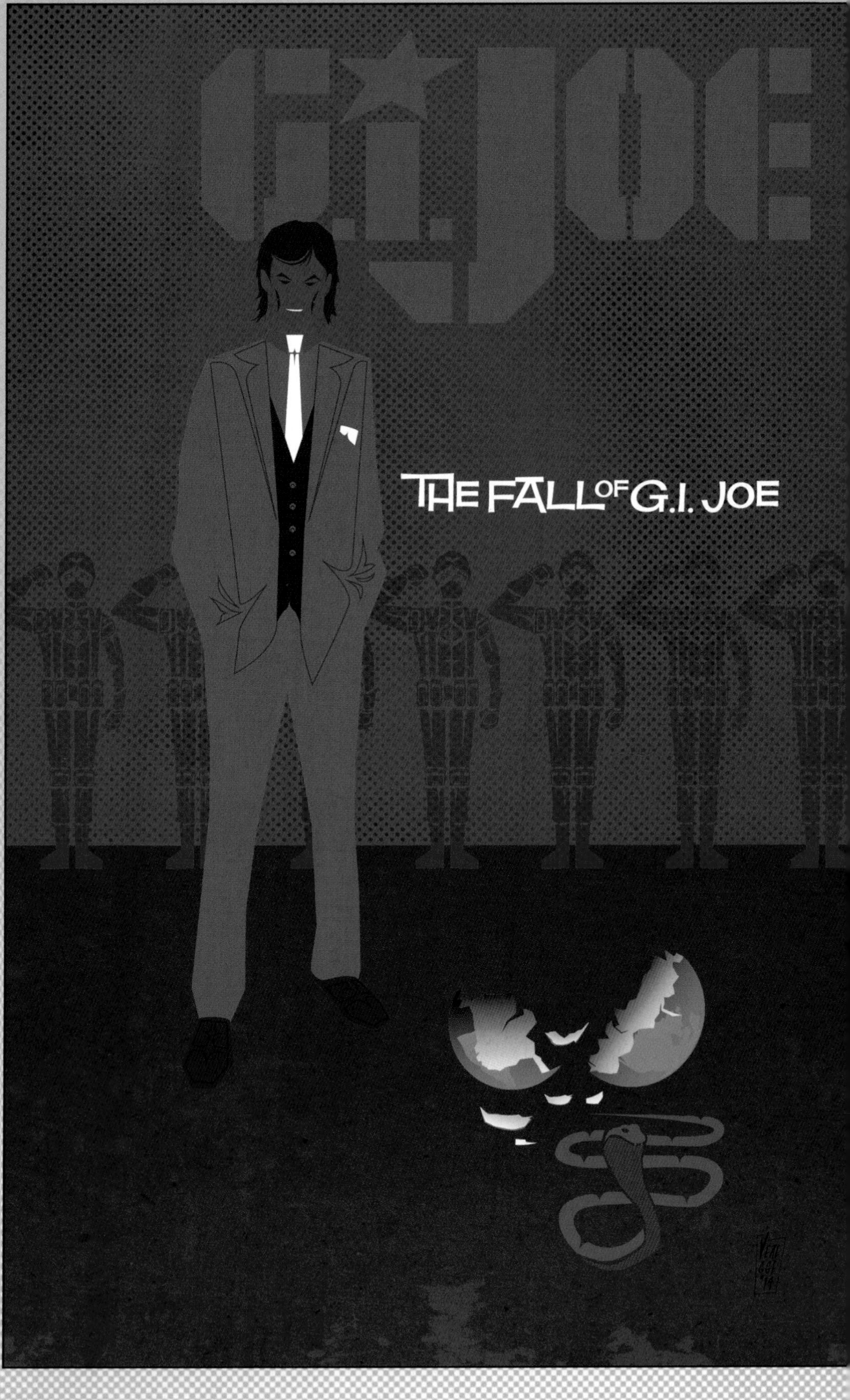
G.I. JOE
THE FALL OF G.I. JOE

ARTWORK BY
JEFFREY VEREGGE

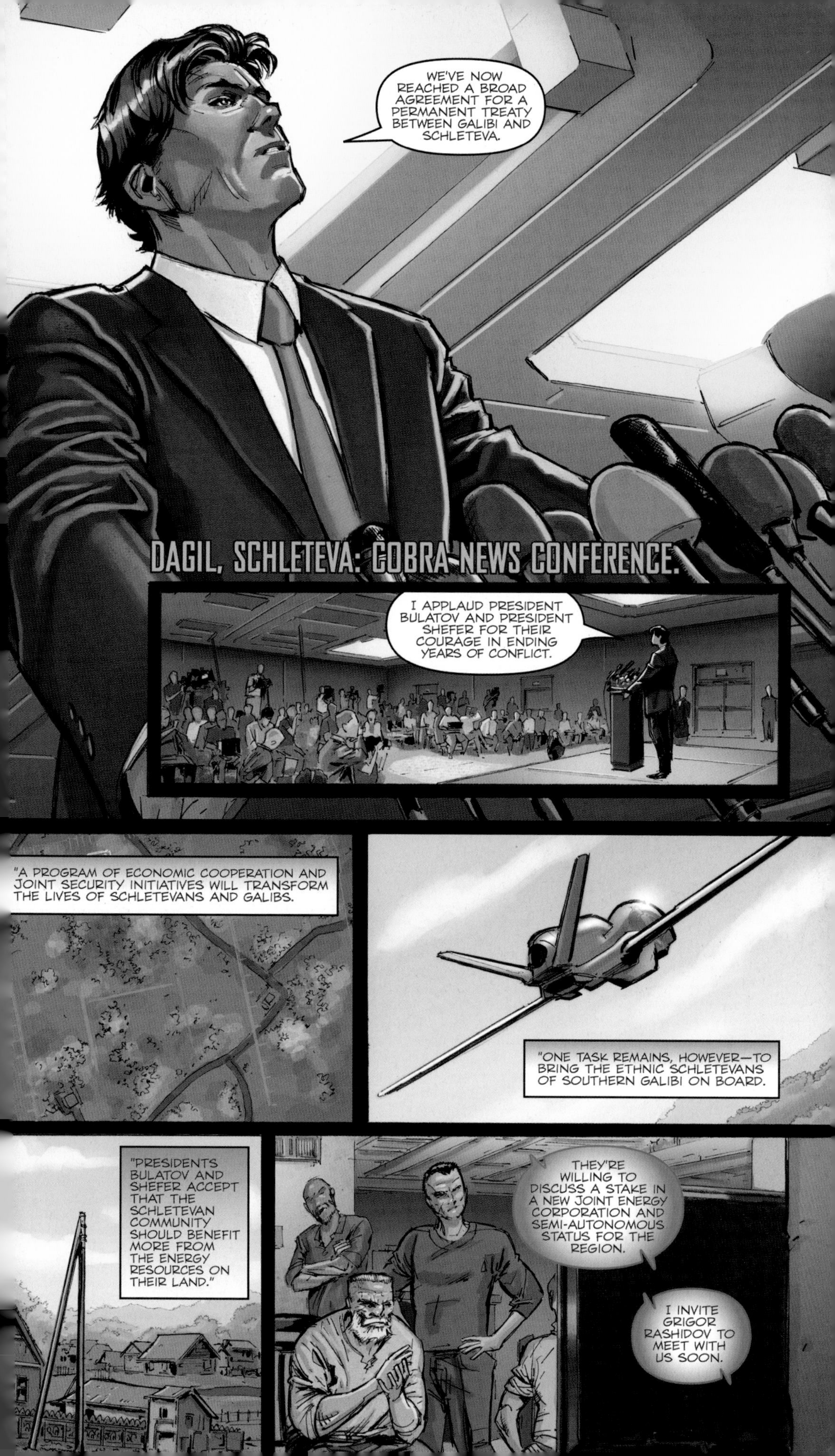
WE'VE NOW REACHED A BROAD AGREEMENT FOR A PERMANENT TREATY BETWEEN GALIBI AND SCHLETEVA.
DAGIL, SCHLETEVA: COBRA NEWS CONFERENCE.
I APPLAUD PRESIDENT BULATOV AND PRESIDENT SHEFER FOR THEIR COURAGE IN ENDING YEARS OF CONFLICT.
"A PROGRAM OF ECONOMIC COOPERATION AND JOINT SECURITY INITIATIVES WILL TRANSFORM THE LIVES OF SCHLETEVANS AND GALIBS.
"ONE TASK REMAINS, HOWEVER—TO BRING THE ETHNIC SCHLETEVANS OF SOUTHERN GALIBI ON BOARD.
"PRESIDENTS BULATOV AND SHEFER ACCEPT THAT THE SCHLETEVAN COMMUNITY SHOULD BENEFIT MORE FROM THE ENERGY RESOURCES ON THEIR LAND."
THEY'RE WILLING TO DISCUSS A STAKE IN A NEW JOINT ENERGY CORPORATION AND SEMI-AUTONOMOUS STATUS FOR THE REGION.
I INVITE GRIGOR RASHIDOV TO MEET WITH US SOON.

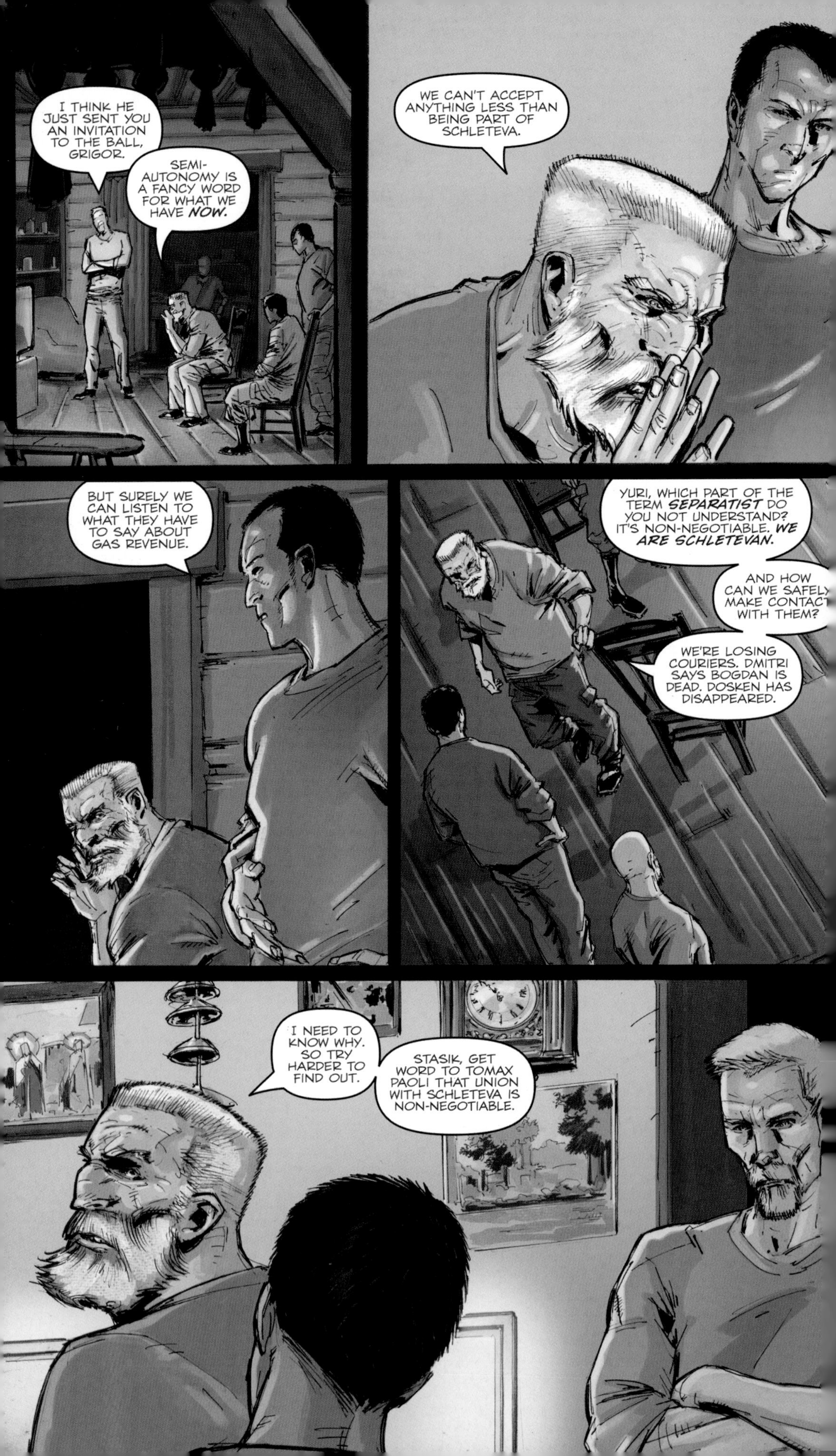
I THINK HE JUST SENT YOU AN INVITATION TO THE BALL, GRIGOR.
SEMI-AUTONOMY IS A FANCY WORD FOR WHAT WE HAVE NOW.
WE CAN'T ACCEPT ANYTHING LESS THAN BEING PART OF SCHLETEVA.
BUT SURELY WE CAN LISTEN TO WHAT THEY HAVE TO SAY ABOUT GAS REVENUE.
YURI, WHICH PART OF THE TERM SEPARATIST DO YOU NOT UNDERSTAND? IT'S NON-NEGOTIABLE. WE ARE SCHLETEVAN.
AND HOW CAN WE SAFELY MAKE CONTACT WITH THEM?
WE'RE LOSING COURIERS. DMITRI SAYS BOGDAN IS DEAD. DOSKEN HAS DISAPPEARED.
I NEED TO KNOW WHY. SO TRY HARDER TO FIND OUT.
STASIK, GET WORD TO TOMAX PAOLI THAT UNION WITH SCHLETEVA IS NON-NEGOTIABLE.

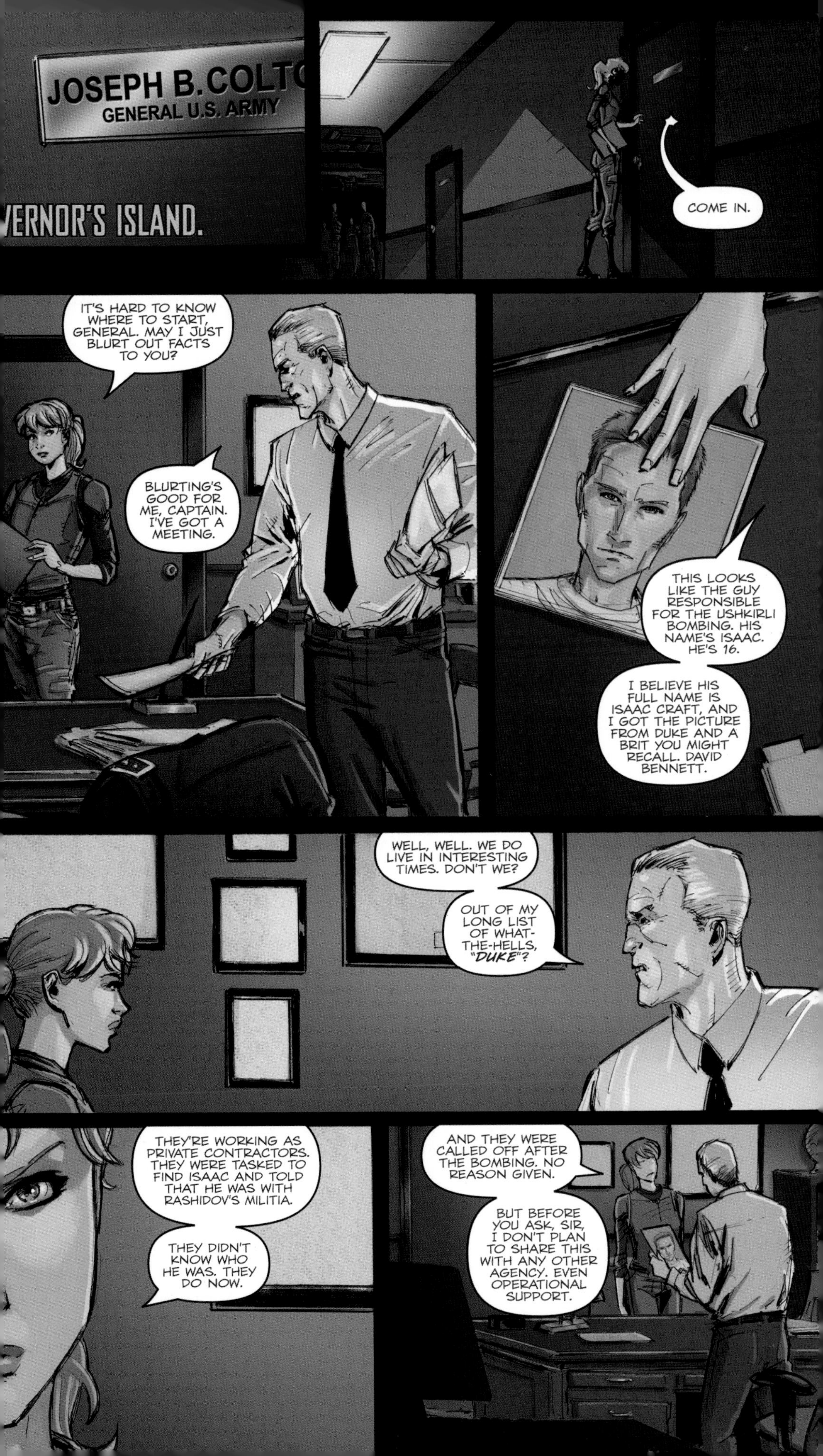
JOSEPH B. COLTO
GENERAL U.S. ARMY
VERNOR'S ISLAND.
COME IN.
IT'S HARD TO KNOW WHERE TO START, GENERAL. MAY I JUST BLURT OUT FACTS TO YOU?
BLURTING'S GOOD FOR ME, CAPTAIN. I'VE GOT A MEETING.
THIS LOOKS LIKE THE GUY RESPONSIBLE FOR THE USHKIRLI BOMBING. HIS NAME'S ISAAC. HE'S 16.
I BELIEVE HIS FULL NAME IS ISAAC CRAFT, AND I GOT THE PICTURE FROM DUKE AND A BRIT YOU MIGHT RECALL. DAVID BENNETT.
WELL, WELL. WE DO LIVE IN INTERESTING TIMES. DON'T WE?
OUT OF MY LONG LIST OF WHAT-THE-HELLS, "DUKE"?
THEY'RE WORKING AS PRIVATE CONTRACTORS. THEY WERE TASKED TO FIND ISAAC AND TOLD THAT HE WAS WITH RASHIDOV'S MILITIA.
THEY DIDN'T KNOW WHO HE WAS. THEY DO NOW.
AND THEY WERE CALLED OFF AFTER THE BOMBING. NO REASON GIVEN.
BUT BEFORE YOU ASK, SIR, I DON'T PLAN TO SHARE THIS WITH ANY OTHER AGENCY. EVEN OPERATIONAL SUPPORT.

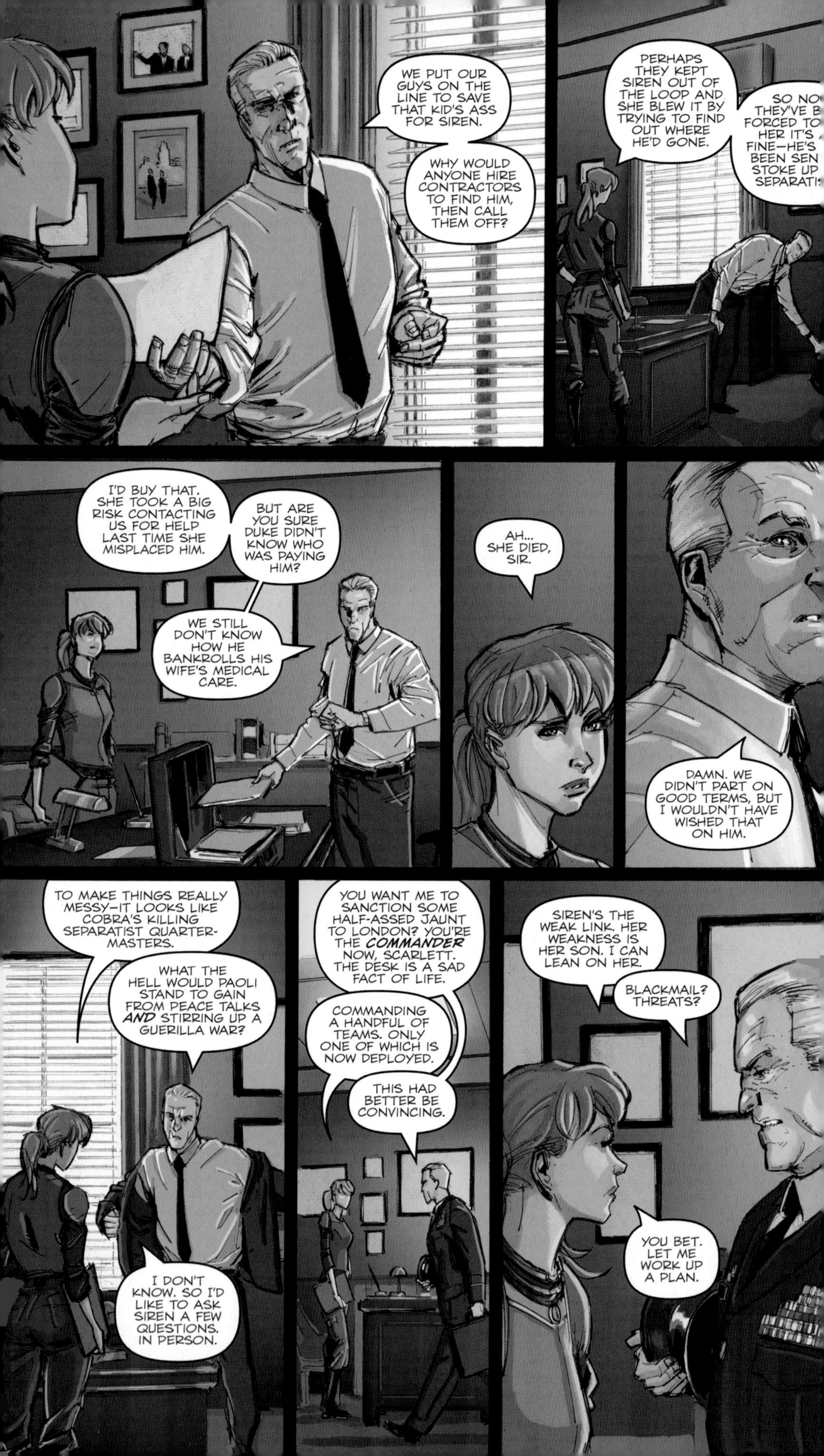

WE PUT OUR GUYS ON THE LINE TO SAVE THAT KID'S ASS FOR SIREN.
WHY WOULD ANYONE HIRE CONTRACTORS TO FIND HIM, THEN CALL THEM OFF?
PERHAPS THEY KEPT SIREN OUT OF THE LOOP AND SHE BLEW IT BY TRYING TO FIND OUT WHERE HE'D GONE.
SO NO THEY'VE B FORCED TO HER IT'S FINE—HE'S BEEN SEN STOKE UP SEPARATI
I'D BUY THAT. SHE TOOK A BIG RISK CONTACTING US FOR HELP LAST TIME SHE MISPLACED HIM.
BUT ARE YOU SURE DUKE DIDN'T KNOW WHO WAS PAYING HIM?
WE STILL DON'T KNOW HOW HE BANKROLLS HIS WIFE'S MEDICAL CARE.
AH... SHE DIED, SIR.
DAMN. WE DIDN'T PART ON GOOD TERMS, BUT I WOULDN'T HAVE WISHED THAT ON HIM.
TO MAKE THINGS REALLY MESSY—IT LOOKS LIKE COBRA'S KILLING SEPARATIST QUARTER-MASTERS.
WHAT THE HELL WOULD PAOLI STAND TO GAIN FROM PEACE TALKS ***AND*** STIRRING UP A GUERILLA WAR?
I DON'T KNOW. SO I'D LIKE TO ASK SIREN A FEW QUESTIONS. IN PERSON.
YOU WANT ME TO SANCTION SOME HALF-ASSED JAUNT TO LONDON? YOU'RE THE ***COMMANDER*** NOW, SCARLETT. THE DESK IS A SAD FACT OF LIFE.
COMMANDING A HANDFUL OF TEAMS. ONLY ONE OF WHICH IS NOW DEPLOYED.
THIS HAD BETTER BE CONVINCING.
SIREN'S THE WEAK LINK. HER WEAKNESS IS HER SON. I CAN LEAN ON HER.
BLACKMAIL? THREATS?
YOU BET. LET ME WORK UP A PLAN.

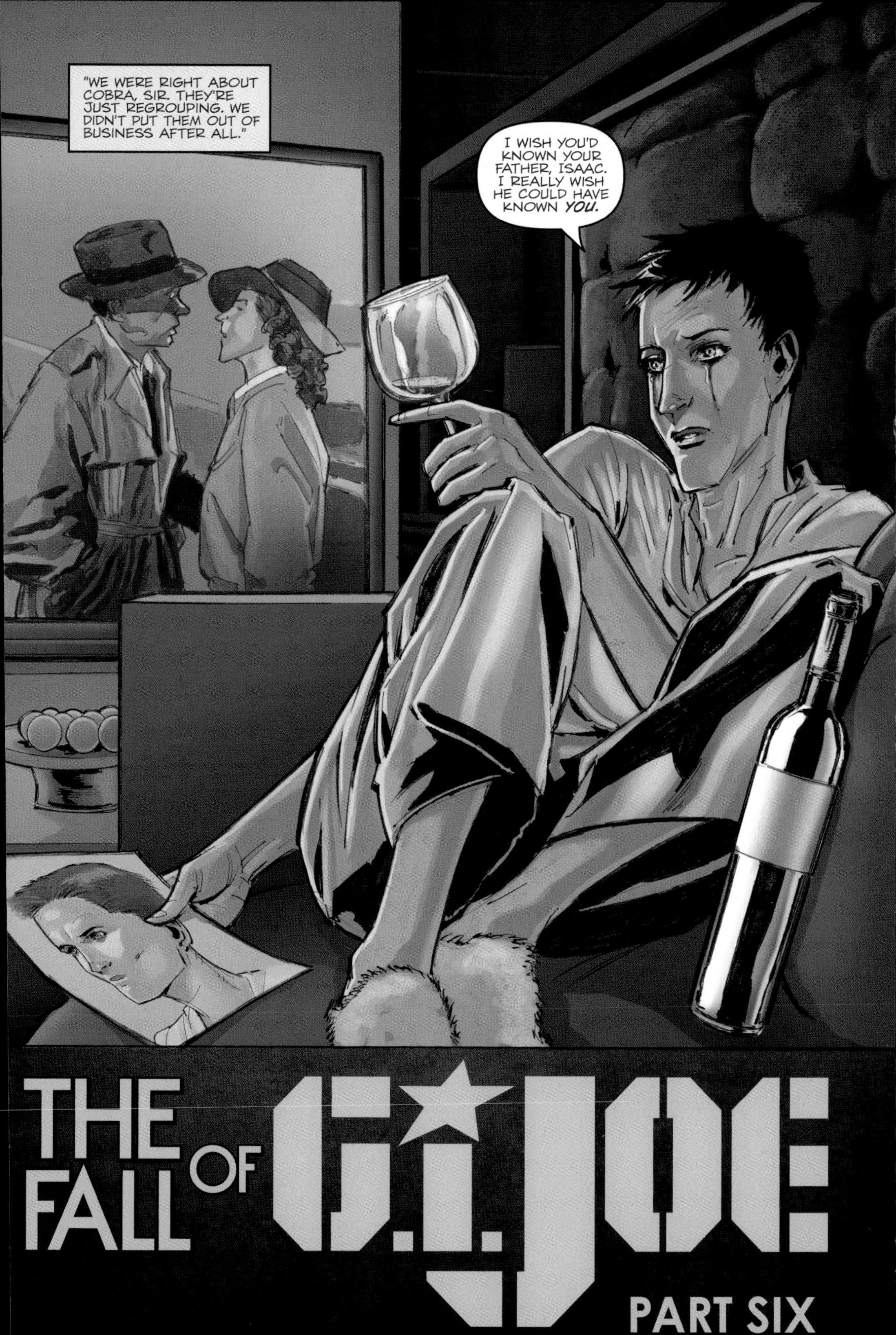

"WE WERE RIGHT ABOUT COBRA, SIR. THEY'RE JUST REGROUPING. WE DIDN'T PUT THEM OUT OF BUSINESS AFTER ALL."
I WISH YOU'D KNOWN YOUR FATHER, ISAAC. I REALLY WISH HE COULD HAVE KNOWN *YOU.*
THE FALL OF G.I. JOE
PART SIX

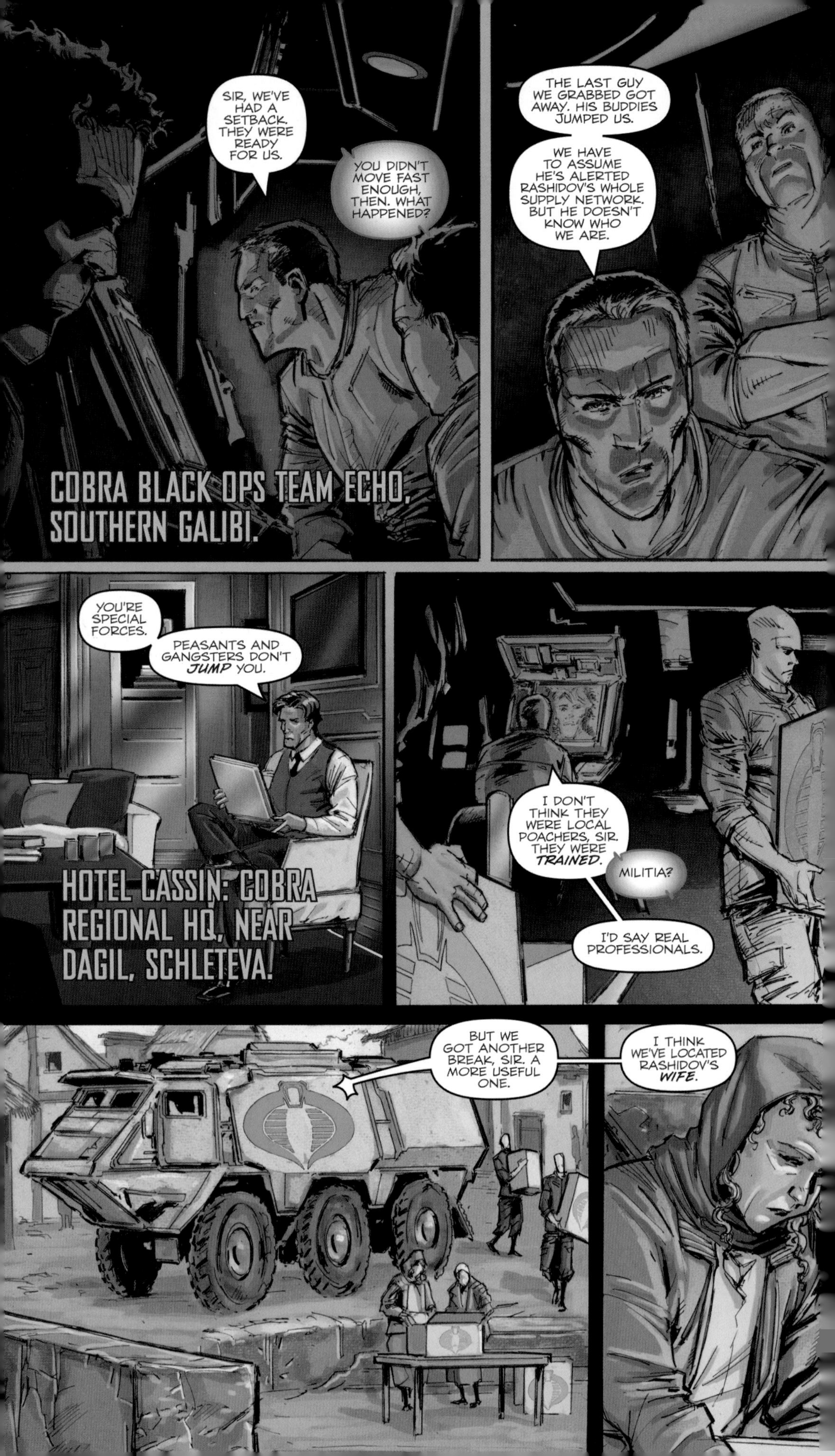
SIR, WE'VE HAD A SETBACK. THEY WERE READY FOR US.
YOU DIDN'T MOVE FAST ENOUGH, THEN. WHAT HAPPENED?
COBRA BLACK OPS TEAM ECHO, SOUTHERN GALIBI.
THE LAST GUY WE GRABBED GOT AWAY. HIS BUDDIES JUMPED US.
WE HAVE TO ASSUME HE'S ALERTED RASHIDOV'S WHOLE SUPPLY NETWORK. BUT HE DOESN'T KNOW WHO WE ARE.
YOU'RE SPECIAL FORCES.
PEASANTS AND GANGSTERS DON'T *JUMP* YOU.
HOTEL CASSIN: COBRA REGIONAL HQ, NEAR DAGIL, SCHLETEVA.
I DON'T THINK THEY WERE LOCAL POACHERS, SIR. THEY WERE *TRAINED*.
MILITIA?
I'D SAY REAL PROFESSIONALS.
BUT WE GOT ANOTHER BREAK, SIR. A MORE USEFUL ONE.
I THINK WE'VE LOCATED RASHIDOV'S *WIFE*.

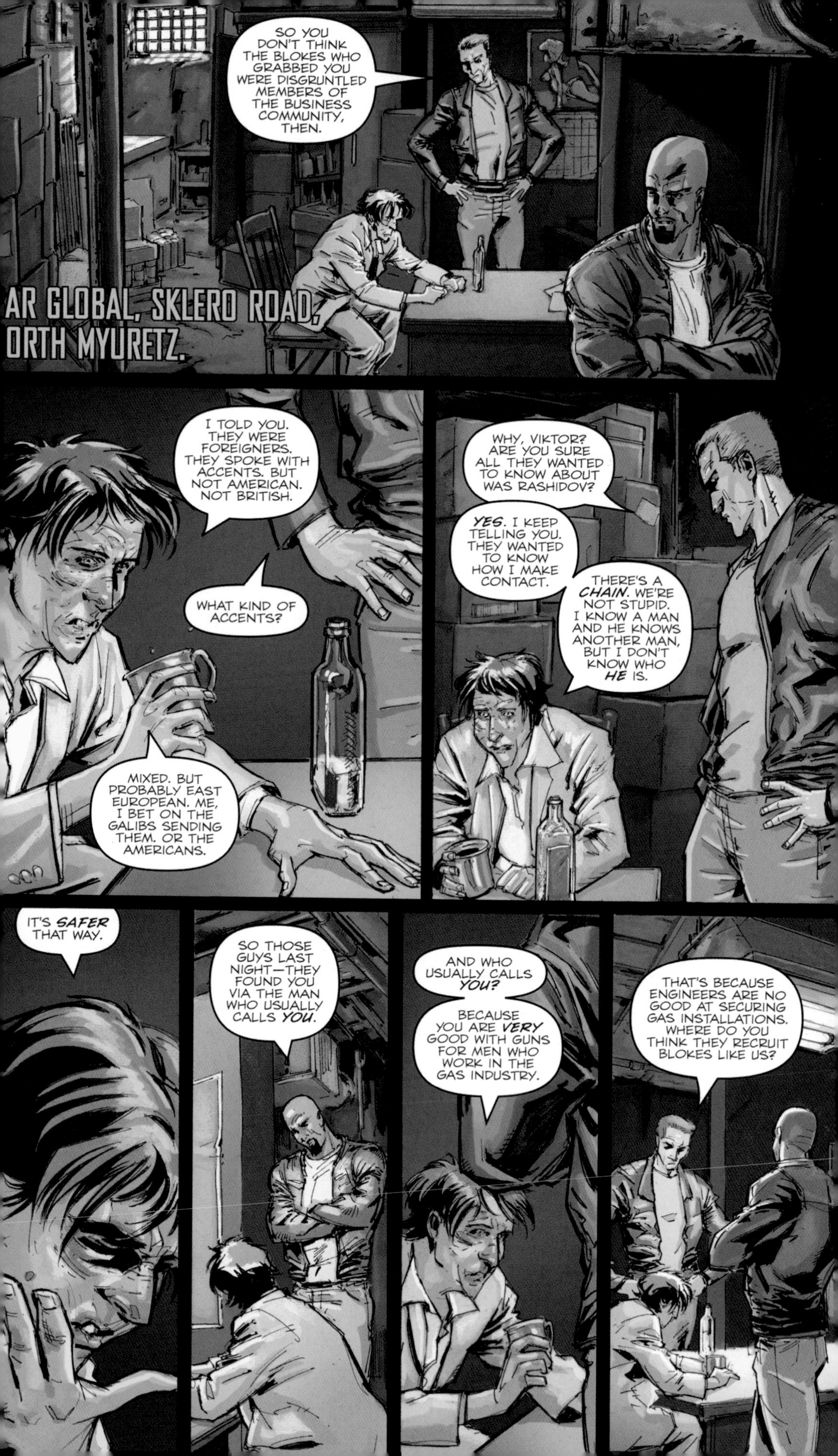
SO YOU DON'T THINK THE BLOKES WHO GRABBED YOU WERE DISGRUNTLED MEMBERS OF THE BUSINESS COMMUNITY, THEN.
AR GLOBAL, SKLERO ROAD, ORTH MYURETZ.
I TOLD YOU. THEY WERE FOREIGNERS. THEY SPOKE WITH ACCENTS. BUT NOT AMERICAN. NOT BRITISH.
WHAT KIND OF ACCENTS?
MIXED. BUT PROBABLY EAST EUROPEAN. ME, I BET ON THE GALIBS SENDING THEM. OR THE AMERICANS.
WHY, VIKTOR? ARE YOU SURE ALL THEY WANTED TO KNOW ABOUT WAS RASHIDOV?
YES. I KEEP TELLING YOU. THEY WANTED TO KNOW HOW I MAKE CONTACT.
THERE'S A CHAIN. WE'RE NOT STUPID. I KNOW A MAN AND HE KNOWS ANOTHER MAN, BUT I DON'T KNOW WHO HE IS.
IT'S SAFER THAT WAY.
SO THOSE GUYS LAST NIGHT—THEY FOUND YOU VIA THE MAN WHO USUALLY CALLS YOU.
AND WHO USUALLY CALLS YOU?
BECAUSE YOU ARE VERY GOOD WITH GUNS FOR MEN WHO WORK IN THE GAS INDUSTRY.
THAT'S BECAUSE ENGINEERS ARE NO GOOD AT SECURING GAS INSTALLATIONS. WHERE DO YOU THINK THEY RECRUIT BLOKES LIKE US?

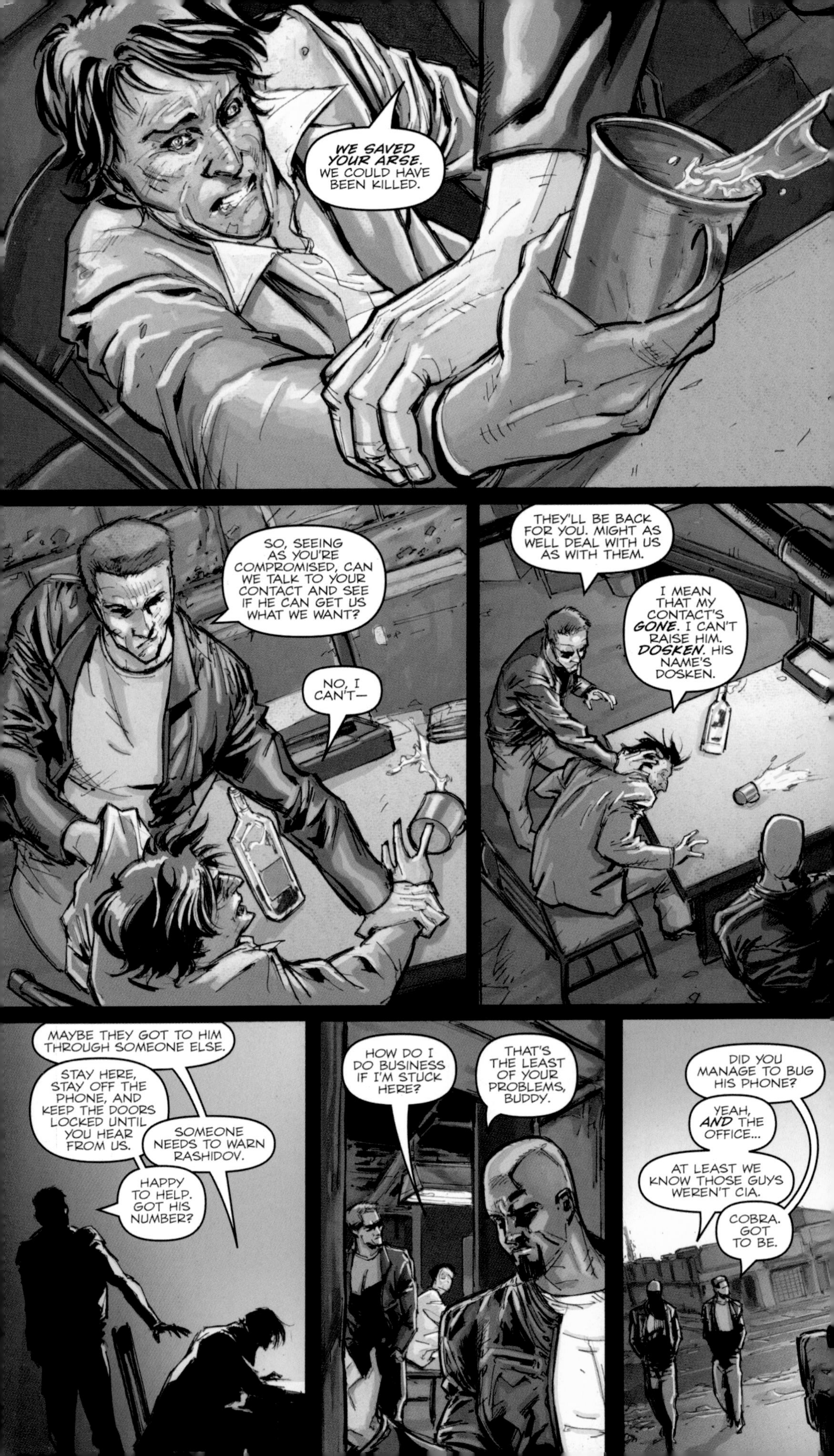
WE SAVED YOUR ARSE. WE COULD HAVE BEEN KILLED.
SO, SEEING AS YOU'RE COMPROMISED, CAN WE TALK TO YOUR CONTACT AND SEE IF HE CAN GET US WHAT WE WANT?
NO, I CAN'T—
THEY'LL BE BACK FOR YOU. MIGHT AS WELL DEAL WITH US AS WITH THEM.
I MEAN THAT MY CONTACT'S GONE. I CAN'T RAISE HIM. DOSKEN. HIS NAME'S DOSKEN.
MAYBE THEY GOT TO HIM THROUGH SOMEONE ELSE.
STAY HERE, STAY OFF THE PHONE, AND KEEP THE DOORS LOCKED UNTIL YOU HEAR FROM US.
SOMEONE NEEDS TO WARN RASHIDOV.
HAPPY TO HELP. GOT HIS NUMBER?
HOW DO I DO BUSINESS IF I'M STUCK HERE?
THAT'S THE LEAST OF YOUR PROBLEMS, BUDDY.
DID YOU MANAGE TO BUG HIS PHONE?
YEAH, AND THE OFFICE...
AT LEAST WE KNOW THOSE GUYS WEREN'T CIA.
COBRA. GOT TO BE.

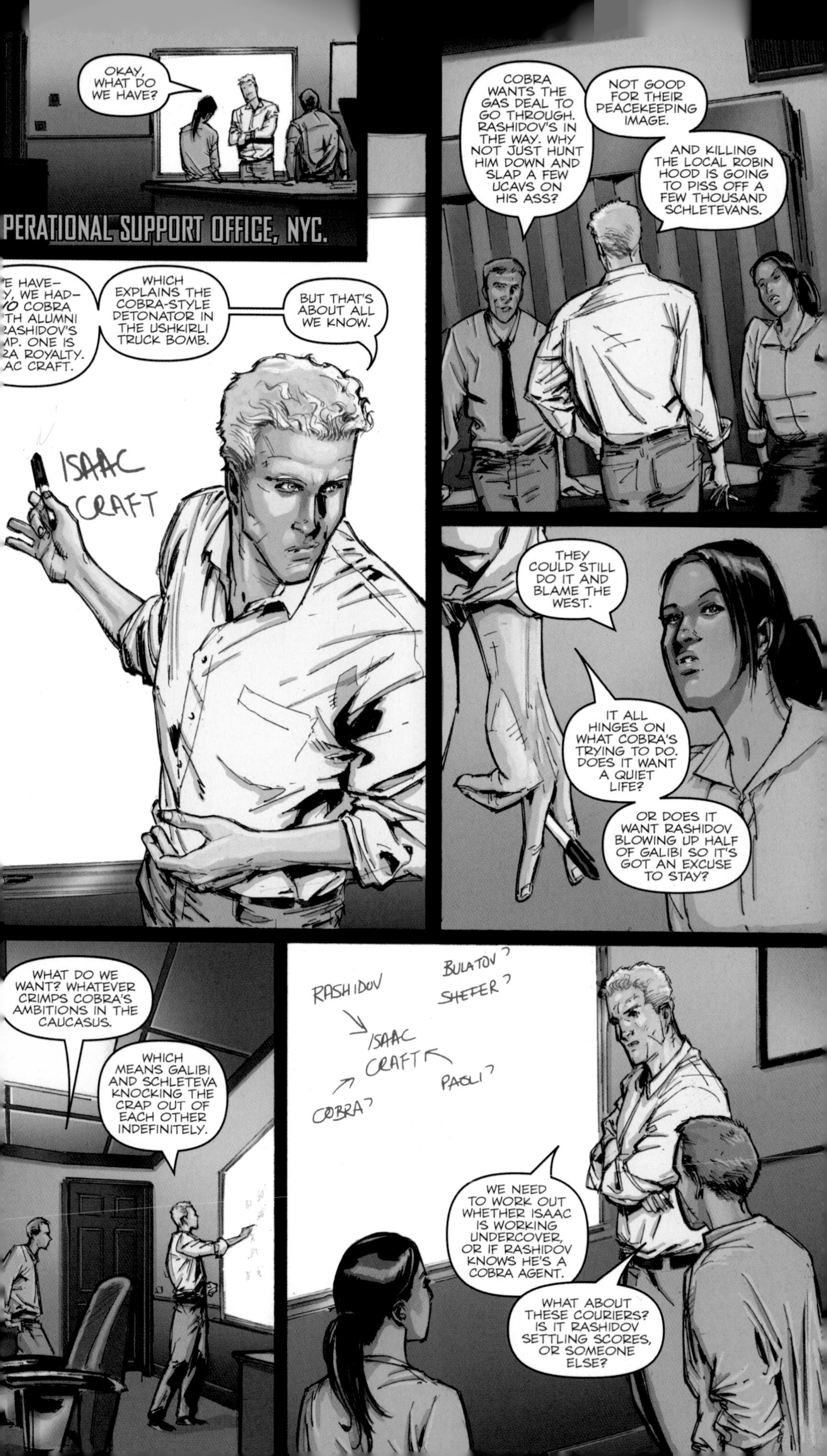
OKAY, WHAT DO WE HAVE?
PERATIONAL SUPPORT OFFICE, NYC.
COBRA WANTS THE GAS DEAL TO GO THROUGH. RASHIDOV'S IN THE WAY. WHY NOT JUST HUNT HIM DOWN AND SLAP A FEW UCAVS ON HIS ASS?
NOT GOOD FOR THEIR PEACEKEEPING IMAGE.
AND KILLING THE LOCAL ROBIN HOOD IS GOING TO PISS OFF A FEW THOUSAND SCHLETEVANS.
E HAVE– Y, WE HAD– O COBRA TH ALUMNI RASHIDOV'S MP. ONE IS RA ROYALTY. AC CRAFT.
WHICH EXPLAINS THE COBRA-STYLE DETONATOR IN THE USHKIRLI TRUCK BOMB.
BUT THAT'S ABOUT ALL WE KNOW.
ISAAC CRAFT
THEY COULD STILL DO IT AND BLAME THE WEST.
IT ALL HINGES ON WHAT COBRA'S TRYING TO DO. DOES IT WANT A QUIET LIFE?
OR DOES IT WANT RASHIDOV BLOWING UP HALF OF GALIBI SO IT'S GOT AN EXCUSE TO STAY?
WHAT DO WE WANT? WHATEVER CRIMPS COBRA'S AMBITIONS IN THE CAUCASUS.
WHICH MEANS GALIBI AND SCHLETEVA KNOCKING THE CRAP OUT OF EACH OTHER INDEFINITELY.
RASHIDOV
BULATOV?
SHEFER?
ISAAC CRAFT
PAOLI?
COBRA?
WE NEED TO WORK OUT WHETHER ISAAC IS WORKING UNDERCOVER, OR IF RASHIDOV KNOWS HE'S A COBRA AGENT.
WHAT ABOUT THESE COURIERS? IS IT RASHIDOV SETTLING SCORES, OR SOMEONE ELSE?

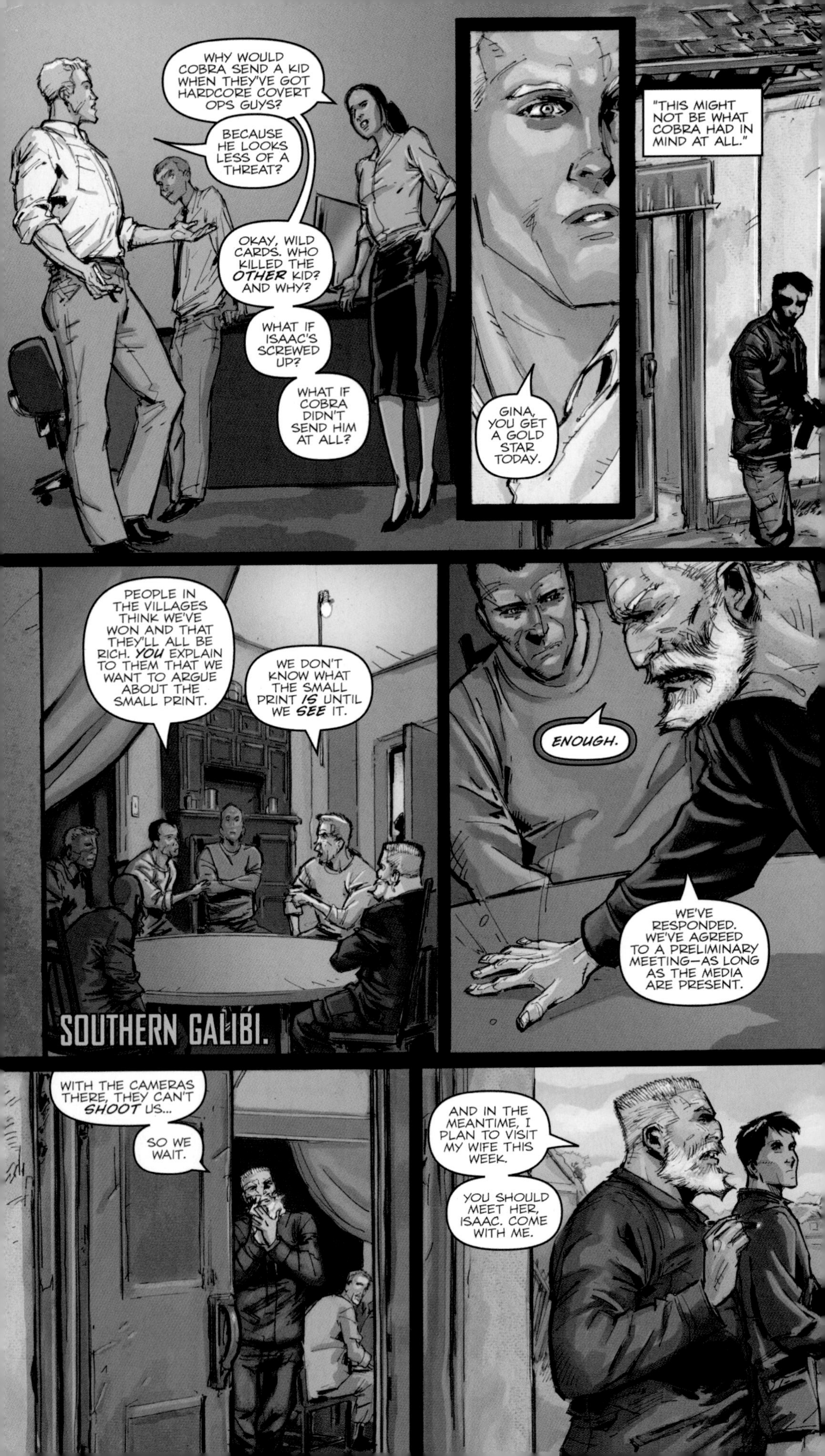

WHY WOULD COBRA SEND A KID WHEN THEY'VE GOT HARDCORE COVERT OPS GUYS?
BECAUSE HE LOOKS LESS OF A THREAT?
OKAY, WILD CARDS. WHO KILLED THE OTHER KID? AND WHY?
WHAT IF ISAAC'S SCREWED UP?
WHAT IF COBRA DIDN'T SEND HIM AT ALL?
GINA, YOU GET A GOLD STAR TODAY.
"THIS MIGHT NOT BE WHAT COBRA HAD IN MIND AT ALL."
PEOPLE IN THE VILLAGES THINK WE'VE WON AND THAT THEY'LL ALL BE RICH. YOU EXPLAIN TO THEM THAT WE WANT TO ARGUE ABOUT THE SMALL PRINT.
WE DON'T KNOW WHAT THE SMALL PRINT IS UNTIL WE SEE IT.
SOUTHERN GALIBI.
ENOUGH.
WE'VE RESPONDED. WE'VE AGREED TO A PRELIMINARY MEETING—AS LONG AS THE MEDIA ARE PRESENT.
WITH THE CAMERAS THERE, THEY CAN'T SHOOT US...
SO WE WAIT.
AND IN THE MEANTIME, I PLAN TO VISIT MY WIFE THIS WEEK.
YOU SHOULD MEET HER, ISAAC. COME WITH ME.

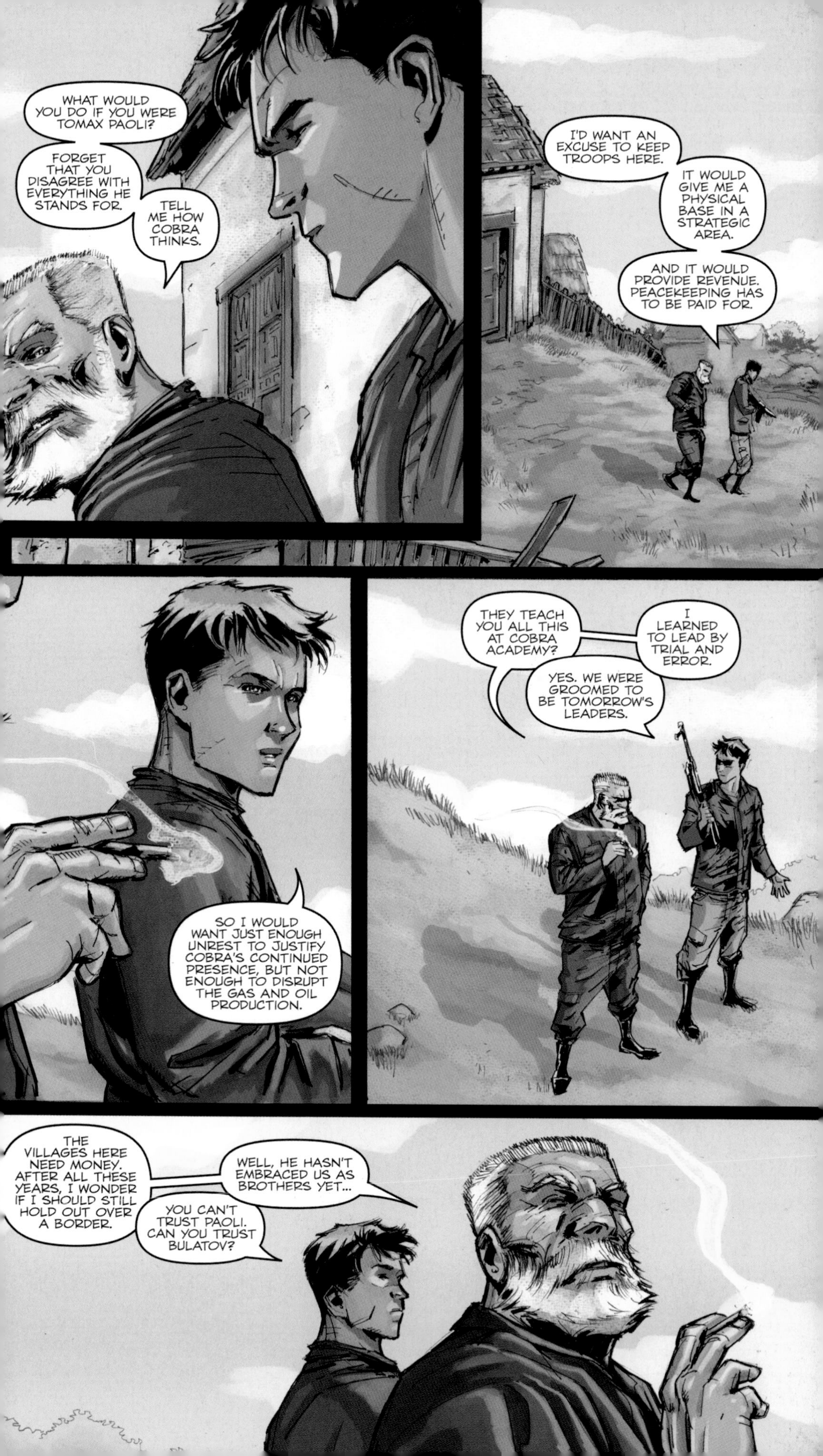
WHAT WOULD YOU DO IF YOU WERE TOMAX PAOLI?
FORGET THAT YOU DISAGREE WITH EVERYTHING HE STANDS FOR.
TELL ME HOW COBRA THINKS.
I'D WANT AN EXCUSE TO KEEP TROOPS HERE.
IT WOULD GIVE ME A PHYSICAL BASE IN A STRATEGIC AREA.
AND IT WOULD PROVIDE REVENUE. PEACEKEEPING HAS TO BE PAID FOR.
SO I WOULD WANT JUST ENOUGH UNREST TO JUSTIFY COBRA'S CONTINUED PRESENCE, BUT NOT ENOUGH TO DISRUPT THE GAS AND OIL PRODUCTION.
THEY TEACH YOU ALL THIS AT COBRA ACADEMY?
YES. WE WERE GROOMED TO BE TOMORROW'S LEADERS.
I LEARNED TO LEAD BY TRIAL AND ERROR.
THE VILLAGES HERE NEED MONEY. AFTER ALL THESE YEARS, I WONDER IF I SHOULD STILL HOLD OUT OVER A BORDER.
WELL, HE HASN'T EMBRACED US AS BROTHERS YET...
YOU CAN'T TRUST PAOLI. CAN YOU TRUST BULATOV?

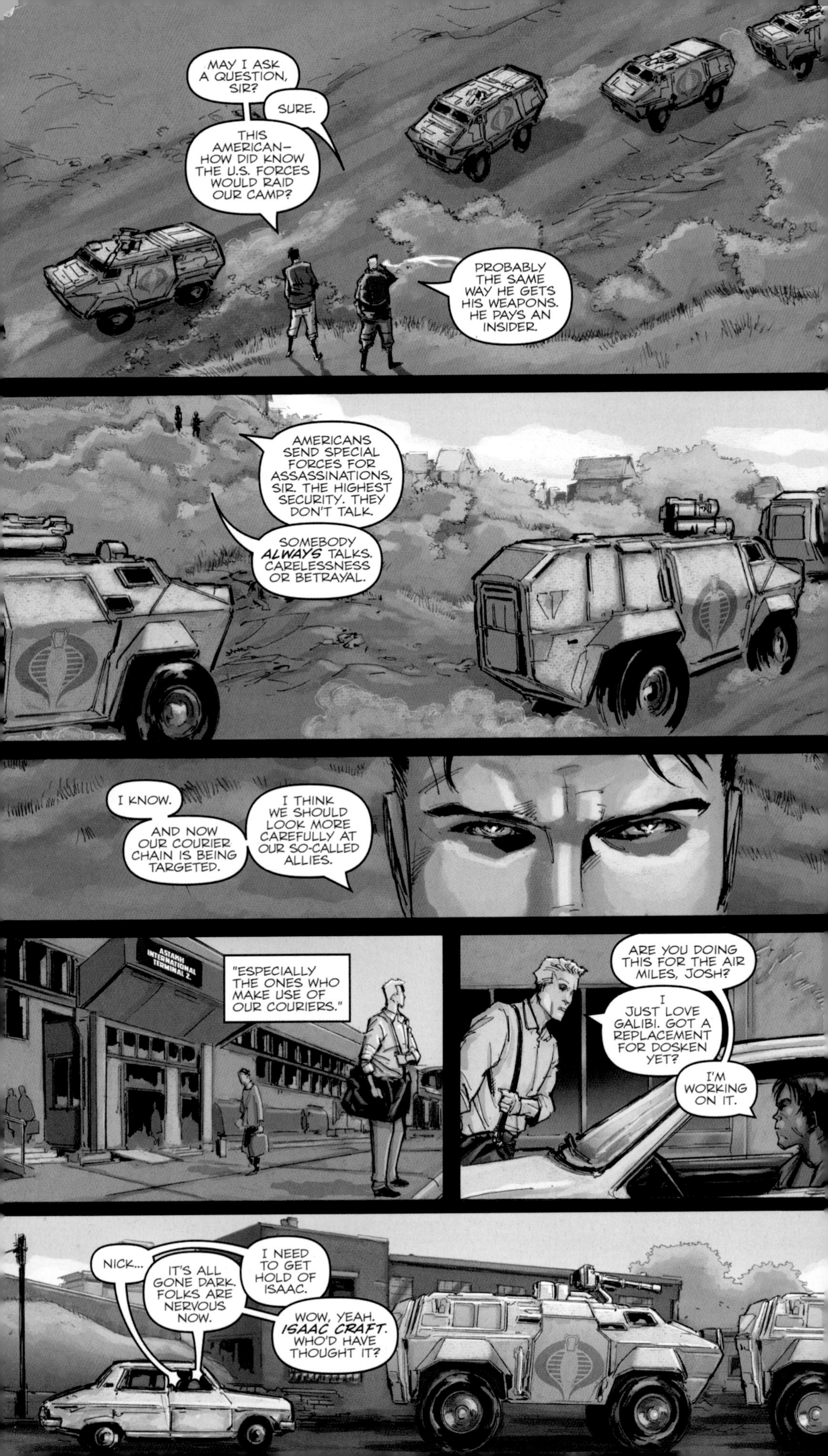
MAY I ASK A QUESTION, SIR?
SURE.
THIS AMERICAN— HOW DID KNOW THE U.S. FORCES WOULD RAID OUR CAMP?
PROBABLY THE SAME WAY HE GETS HIS WEAPONS. HE PAYS AN INSIDER.
AMERICANS SEND SPECIAL FORCES FOR ASSASSINATIONS, SIR. THE HIGHEST SECURITY. THEY DON'T TALK.
SOMEBODY *ALWAYS* TALKS. CARELESSNESS OR BETRAYAL.
I KNOW.
AND NOW OUR COURIER CHAIN IS BEING TARGETED.
I THINK WE SHOULD LOOK MORE CAREFULLY AT OUR SO-CALLED ALLIES.
ASTANH INTERNATIONAL TERMINAL 2.
"ESPECIALLY THE ONES WHO MAKE USE OF OUR COURIERS."
ARE YOU DOING THIS FOR THE AIR MILES, JOSH?
I JUST LOVE GALIBI. GOT A REPLACEMENT FOR DOSKEN YET?
I'M WORKING ON IT.
NICK...
IT'S ALL GONE DARK. FOLKS ARE NERVOUS NOW.
I NEED TO GET HOLD OF ISAAC.
WOW, YEAH. *ISAAC CRAFT*. WHO'D HAVE THOUGHT IT?

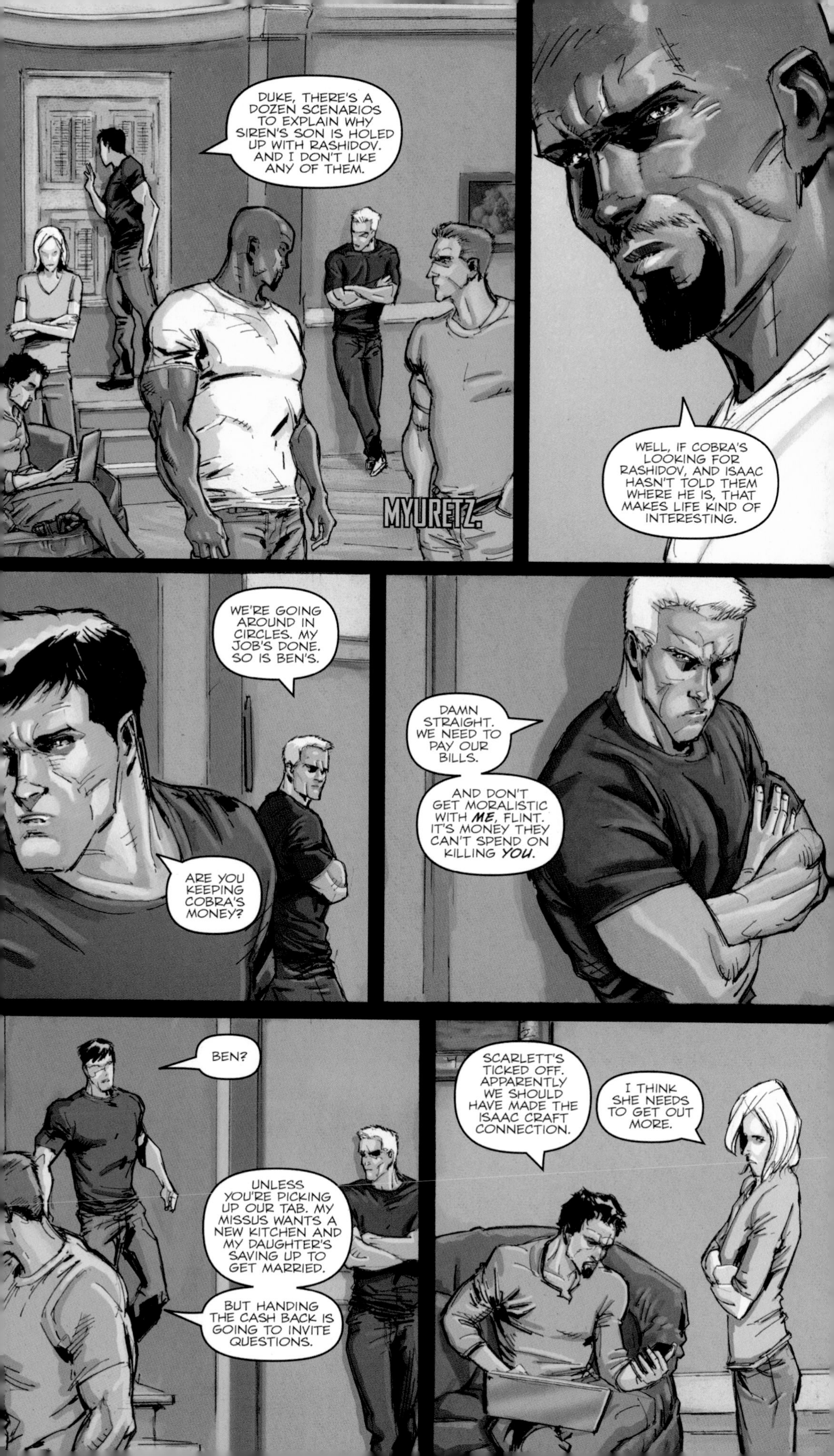
DUKE, THERE'S A DOZEN SCENARIOS TO EXPLAIN WHY SIREN'S SON IS HOLED UP WITH RASHIDOV. AND I DON'T LIKE ANY OF THEM.
MYURETZ.
WELL, IF COBRA'S LOOKING FOR RASHIDOV, AND ISAAC HASN'T TOLD THEM WHERE HE IS, THAT MAKES LIFE KIND OF INTERESTING.
WE'RE GOING AROUND IN CIRCLES. MY JOB'S DONE. SO IS BEN'S.
ARE YOU KEEPING COBRA'S MONEY?
DAMN STRAIGHT. WE NEED TO PAY OUR BILLS.
AND DON'T GET MORALISTIC WITH ME, FLINT. IT'S MONEY THEY CAN'T SPEND ON KILLING YOU.
BEN?
UNLESS YOU'RE PICKING UP OUR TAB. MY MISSUS WANTS A NEW KITCHEN AND MY DAUGHTER'S SAVING UP TO GET MARRIED.
BUT HANDING THE CASH BACK IS GOING TO INVITE QUESTIONS.
SCARLETT'S TICKED OFF. APPARENTLY WE SHOULD HAVE MADE THE ISAAC CRAFT CONNECTION.
I THINK SHE NEEDS TO GET OUT MORE.

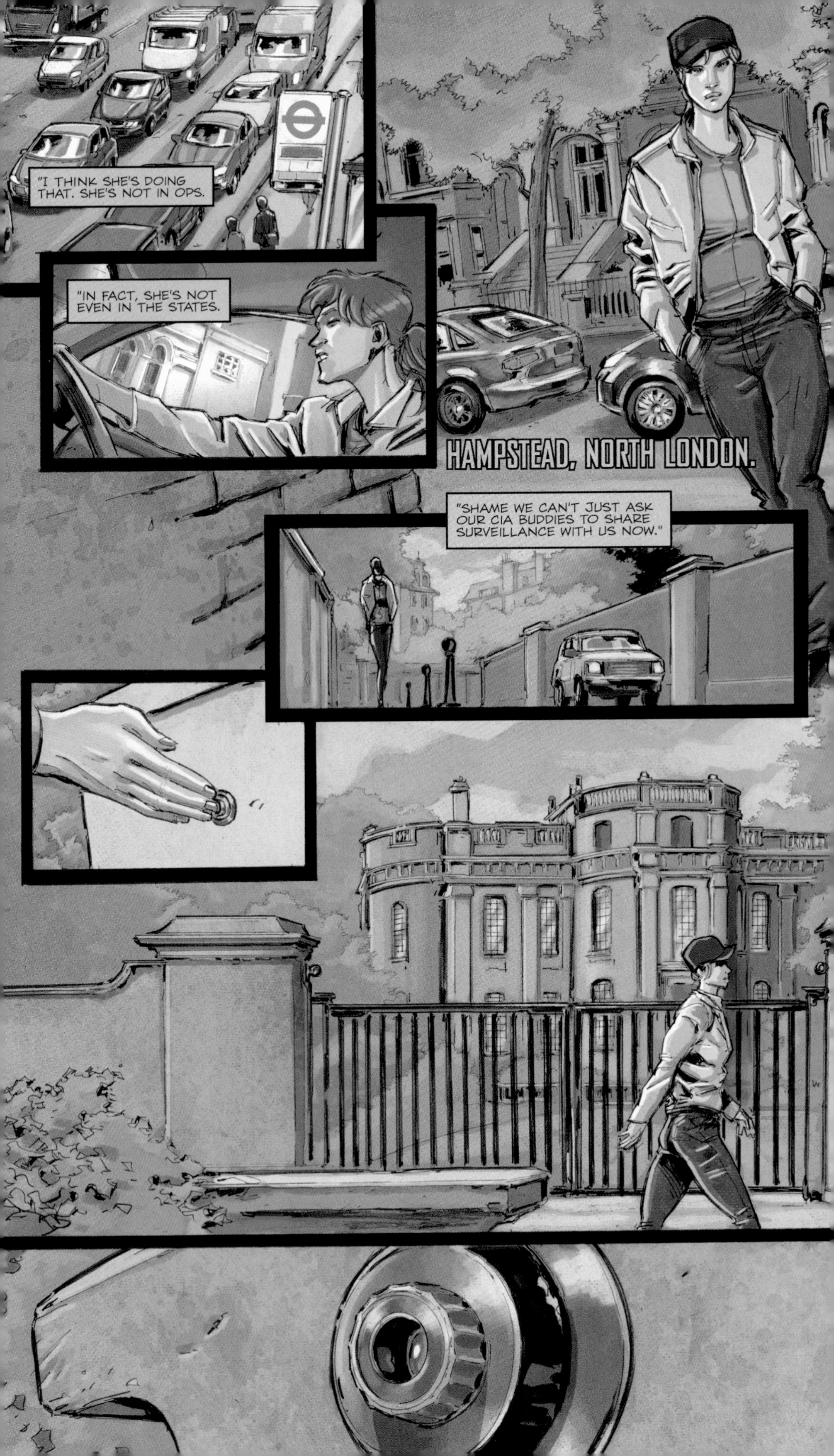
"I THINK SHE'S DOING THAT. SHE'S NOT IN OPS.
"IN FACT, SHE'S NOT EVEN IN THE STATES.
HAMPSTEAD, NORTH LONDON.
"SHAME WE CAN'T JUST ASK OUR CIA BUDDIES TO SHARE SURVEILLANCE WITH US NOW."

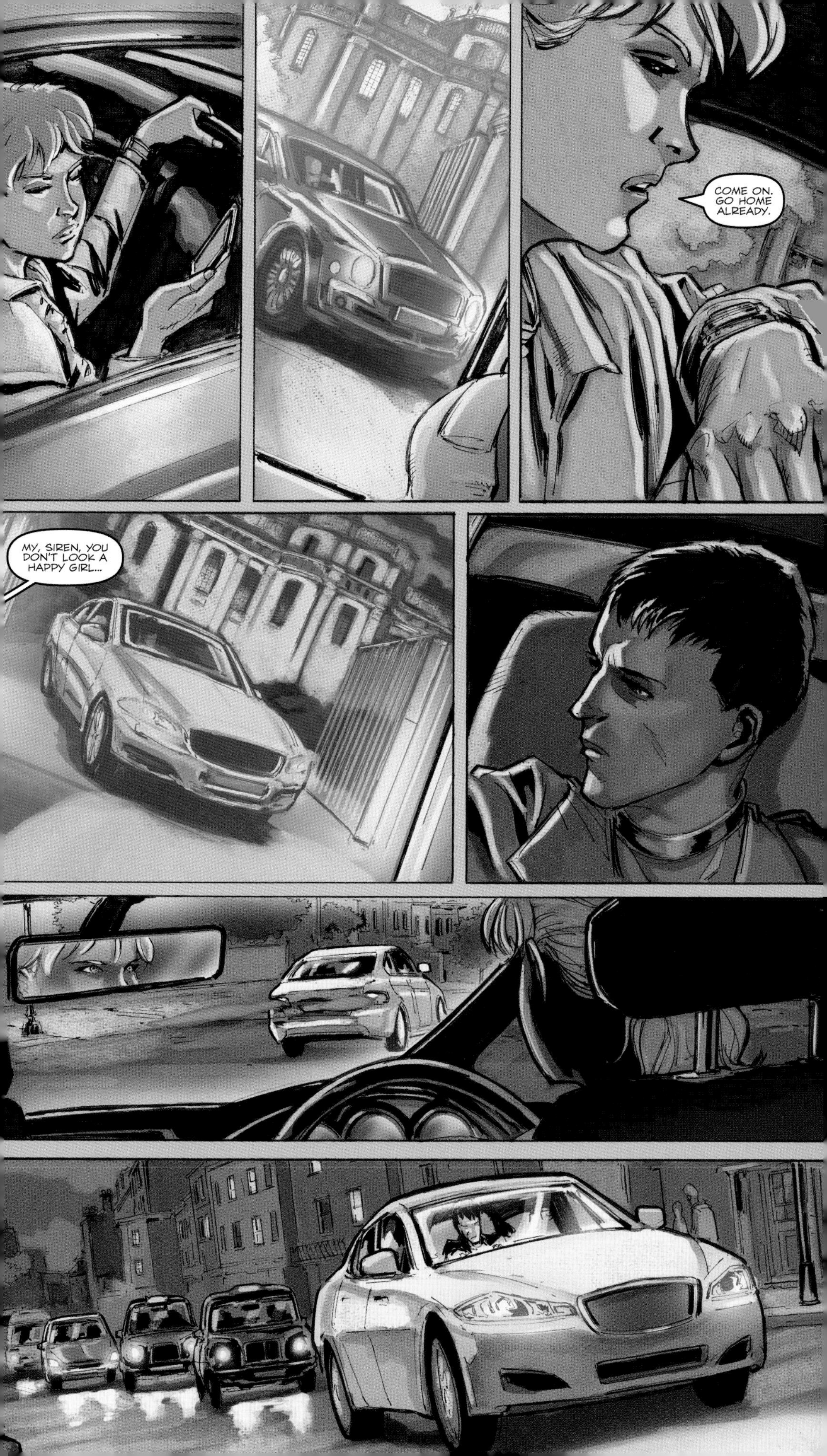
COME ON. GO HOME ALREADY.
MY, SIREN, YOU DON'T LOOK A HAPPY GIRL...

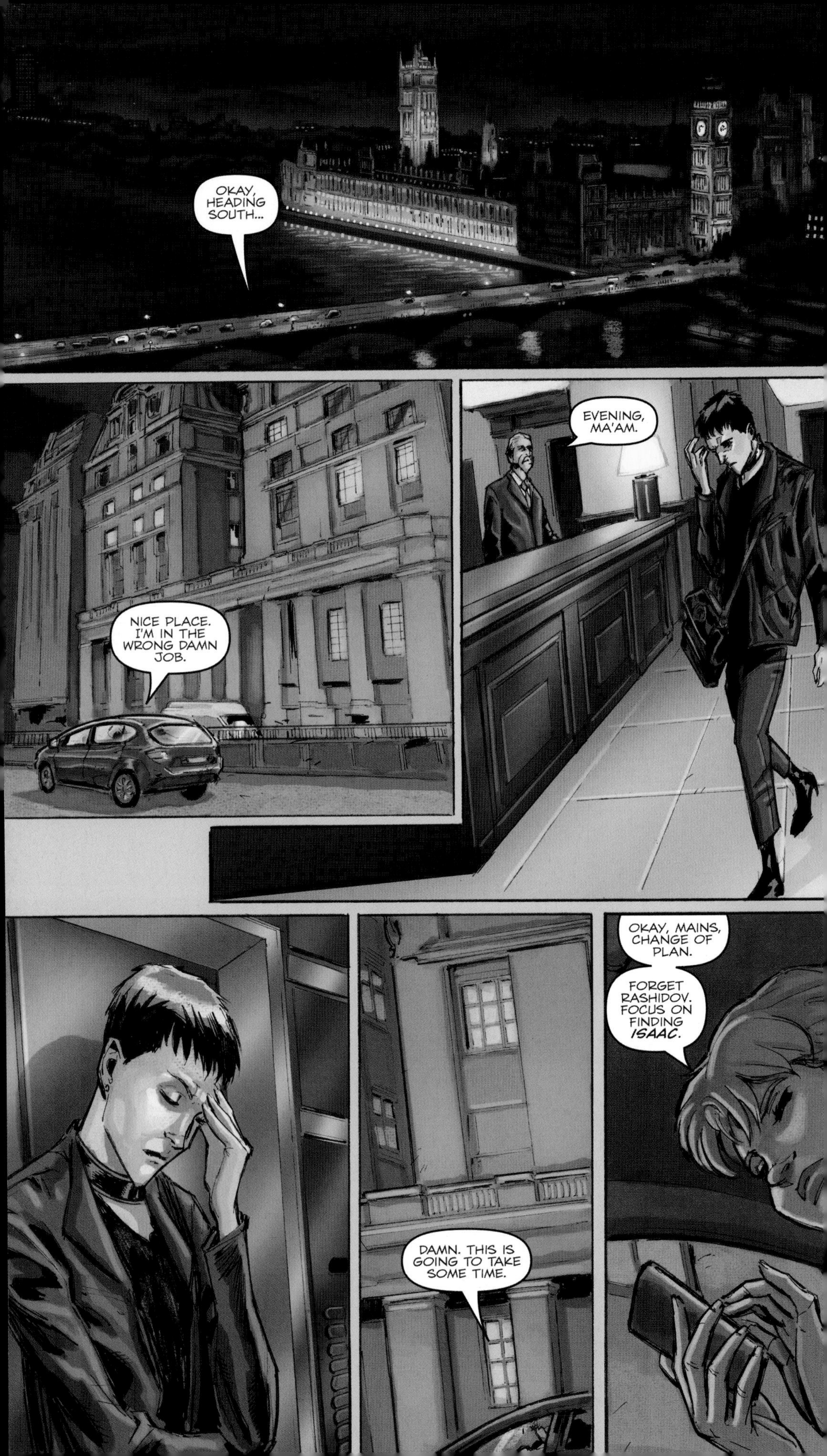
OKAY, HEADING SOUTH...
NICE PLACE. I'M IN THE WRONG DAMN JOB.
EVENING, MA'AM.
DAMN. THIS IS GOING TO TAKE SOME TIME.
OKAY, MAINS, CHANGE OF PLAN.
FORGET RASHIDOV. FOCUS ON FINDING ISAAC.

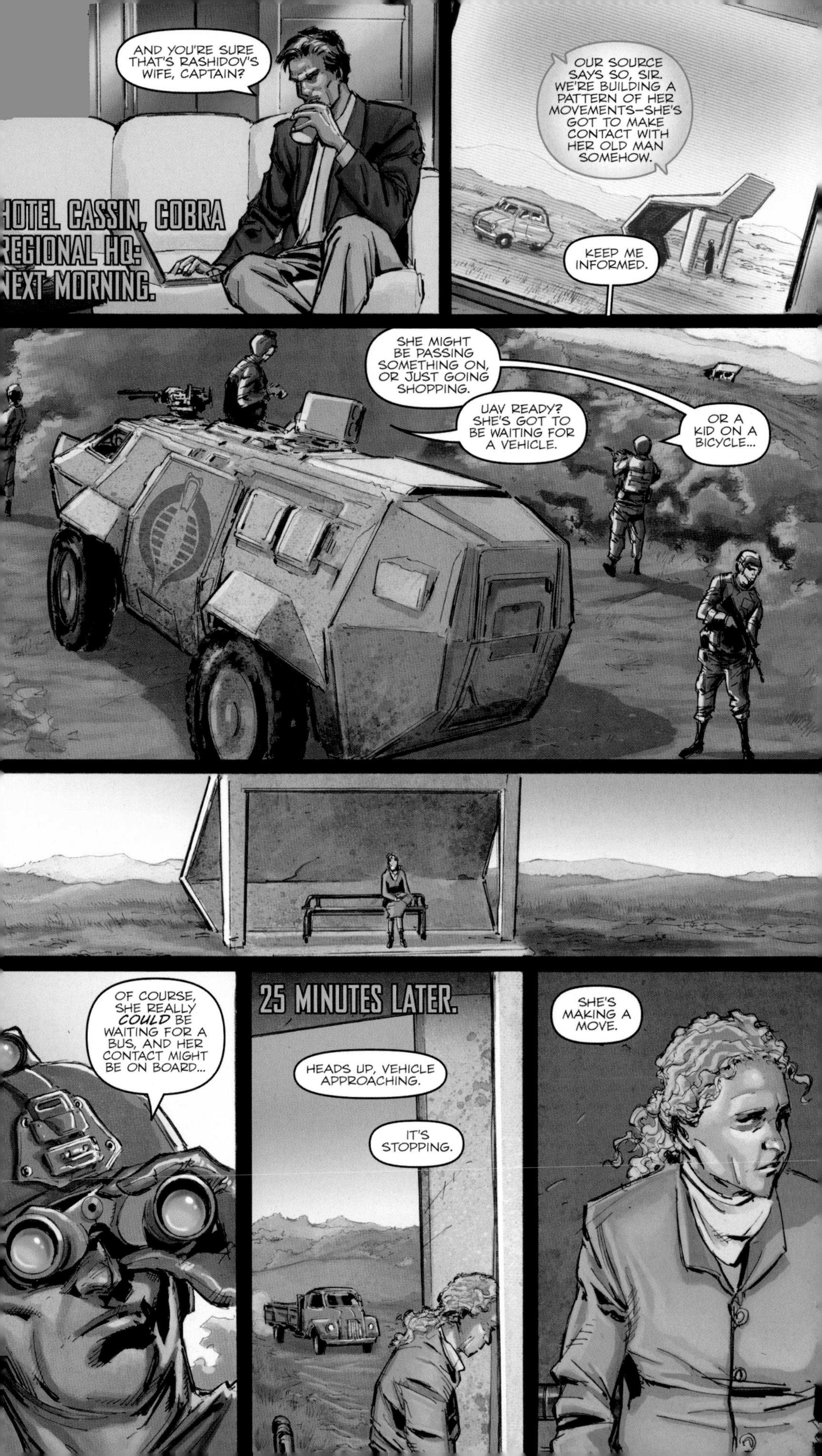
AND YOU'RE SURE THAT'S RASHIDOV'S WIFE, CAPTAIN?
HOTEL CASSIN, COBRA REGIONAL HQ: NEXT MORNING.
OUR SOURCE SAYS SO, SIR. WE'RE BUILDING A PATTERN OF HER MOVEMENTS—SHE'S GOT TO MAKE CONTACT WITH HER OLD MAN SOMEHOW.
KEEP ME INFORMED.
SHE MIGHT BE PASSING SOMETHING ON, OR JUST GOING SHOPPING.
UAV READY? SHE'S GOT TO BE WAITING FOR A VEHICLE.
OR A KID ON A BICYCLE...
OF COURSE, SHE REALLY COULD BE WAITING FOR A BUS, AND HER CONTACT MIGHT BE ON BOARD...
25 MINUTES LATER.
HEADS UP, VEHICLE APPROACHING.
IT'S STOPPING.
SHE'S MAKING A MOVE.

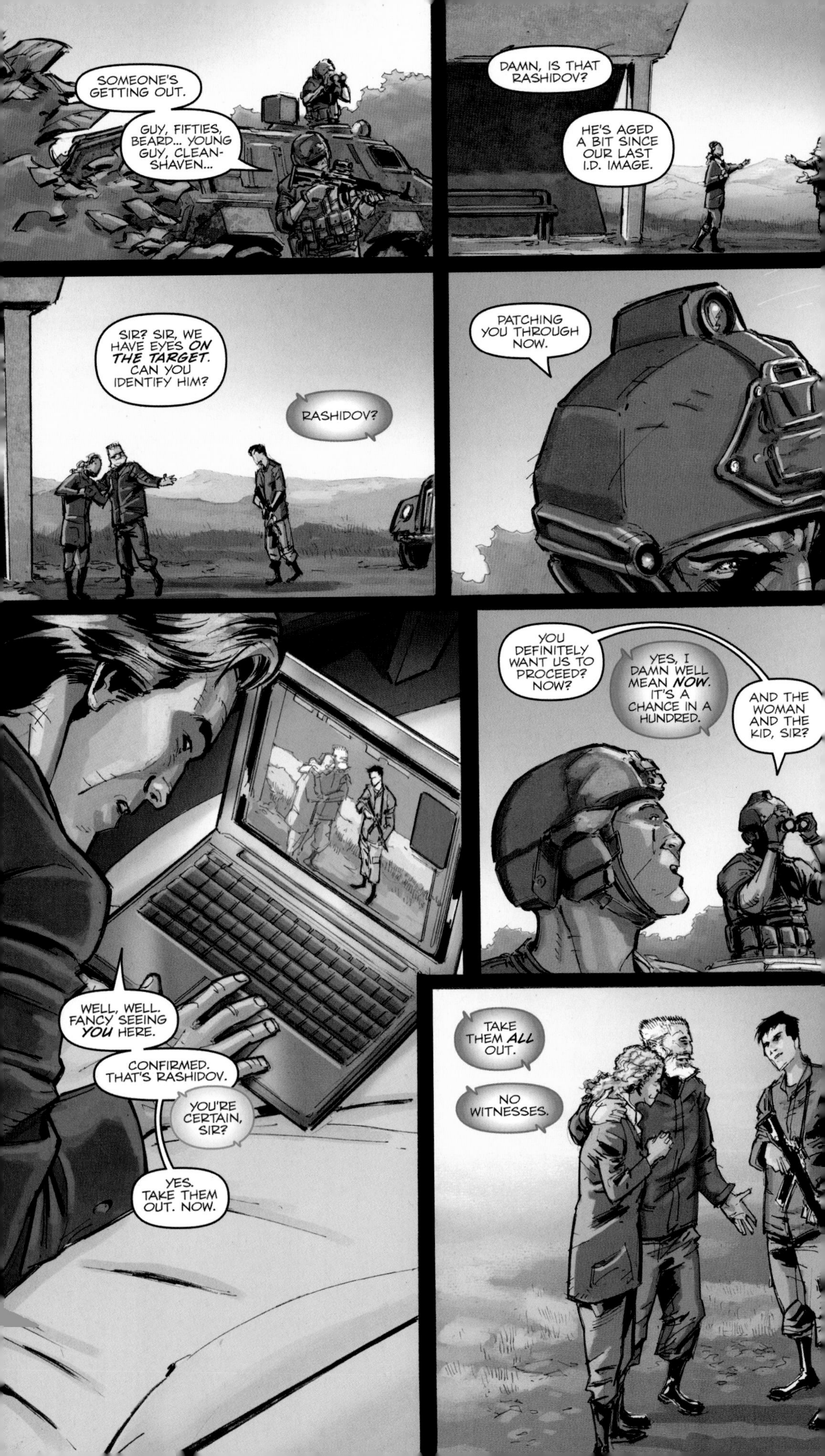
SOMEONE'S GETTING OUT.
GUY, FIFTIES, BEARD... YOUNG GUY, CLEAN-SHAVEN...
DAMN, IS THAT RASHIDOV?
HE'S AGED A BIT SINCE OUR LAST I.D. IMAGE.
SIR? SIR, WE HAVE EYES ON THE TARGET. CAN YOU IDENTIFY HIM?
RASHIDOV?
PATCHING YOU THROUGH NOW.
WELL, WELL. FANCY SEEING YOU HERE.
CONFIRMED. THAT'S RASHIDOV.
YOU'RE CERTAIN, SIR?
YES. TAKE THEM OUT. NOW.
YOU DEFINITELY WANT US TO PROCEED? NOW?
YES, I DAMN WELL MEAN NOW. IT'S A CHANCE IN A HUNDRED.
AND THE WOMAN AND THE KID, SIR?
TAKE THEM ALL OUT.
NO WITNESSES.

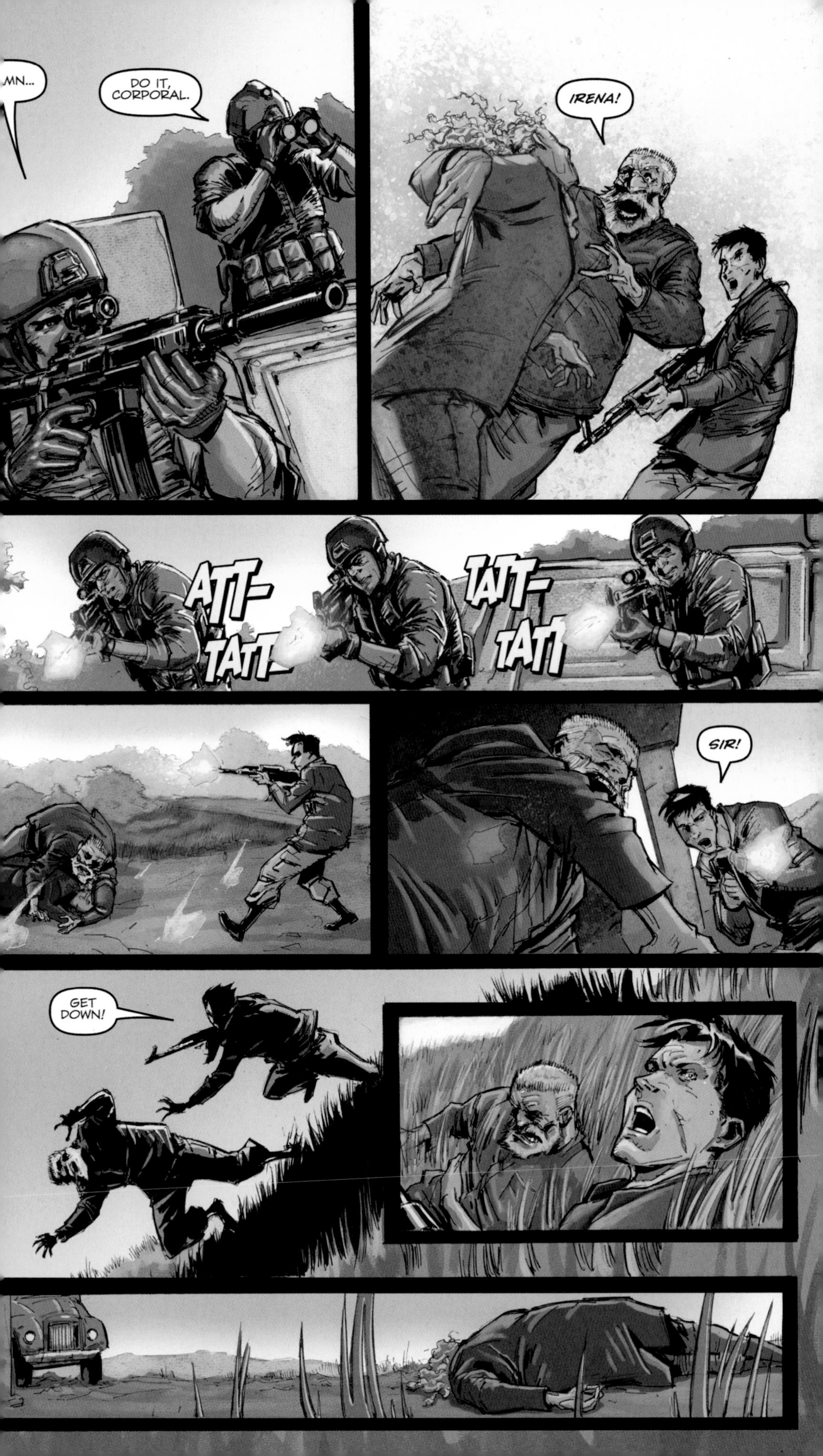

MN...
DO IT, CORPORAL.
IRENA!
ATT-TATT
TATT-TATT
SIR!
GET DOWN!

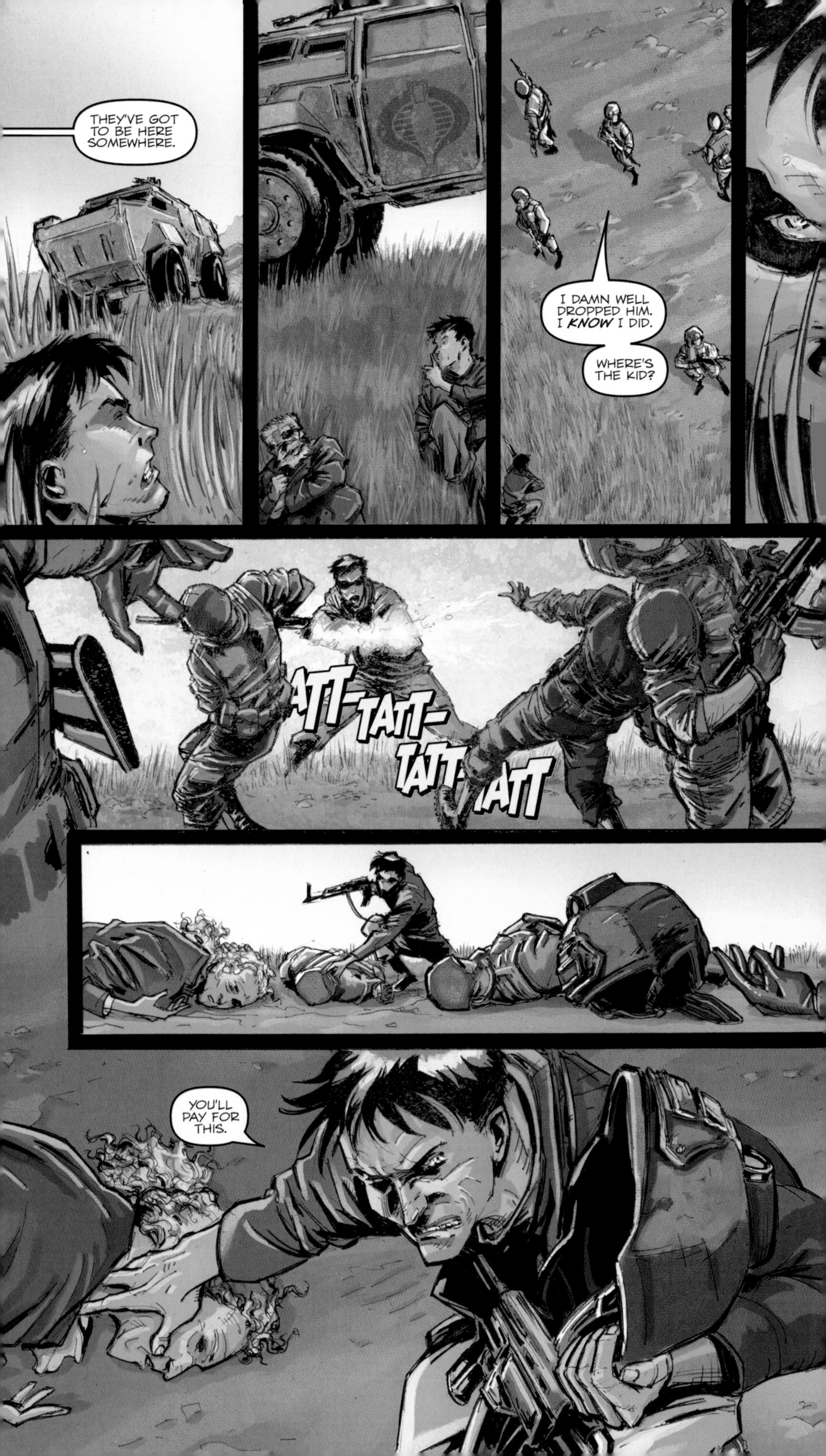
THEY'VE GOT TO BE HERE SOMEWHERE.
I DAMN WELL DROPPED HIM. I *KNOW* I DID.
WHERE'S THE KID?
TATT-TATT-TATT-TATT
YOU'LL PAY FOR THIS.

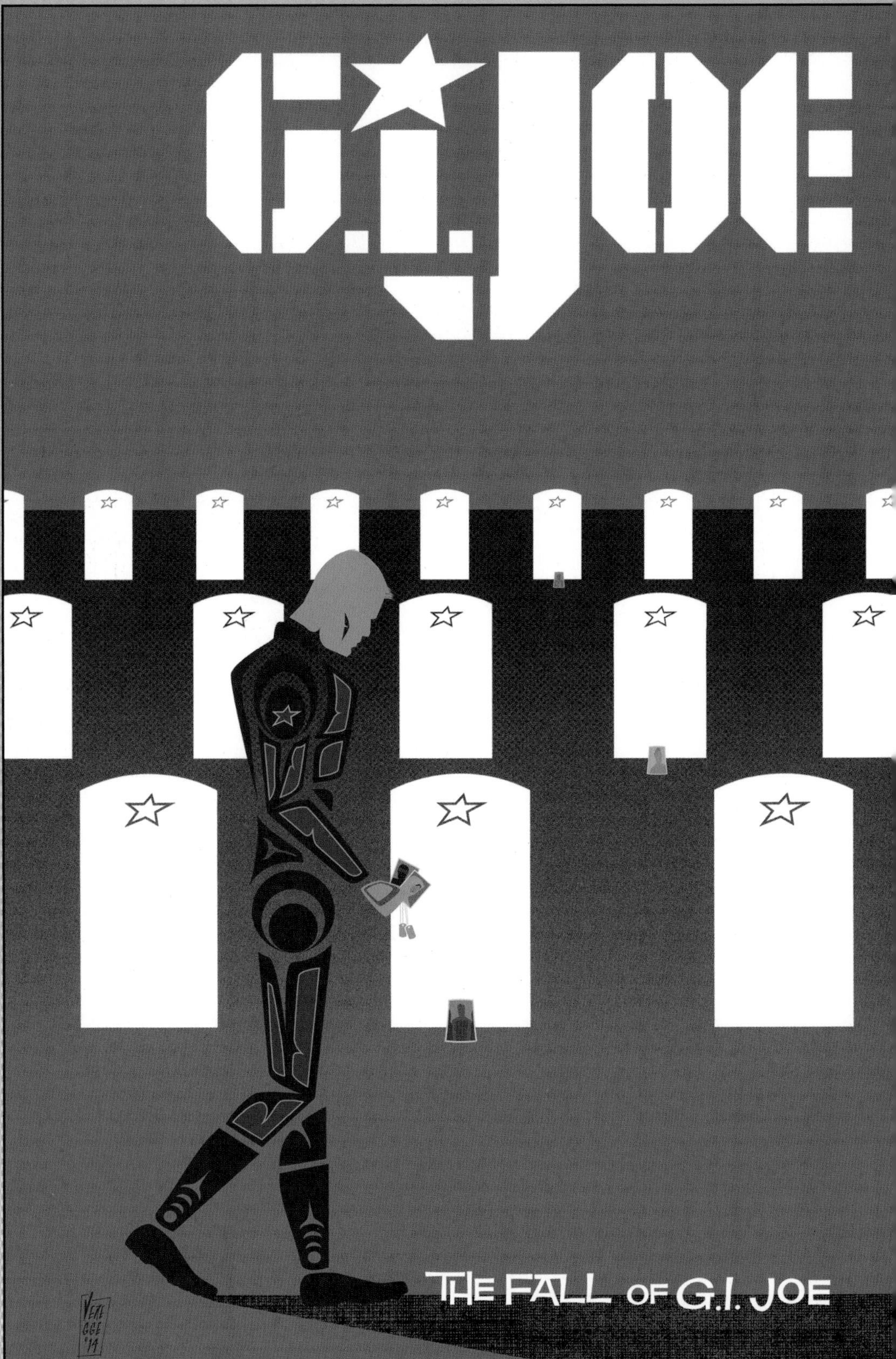
G.I. JOE
THE FALL OF G.I. JOE
VEREGGE '14

ARTWORK BY
JEFFREY VEREGGE

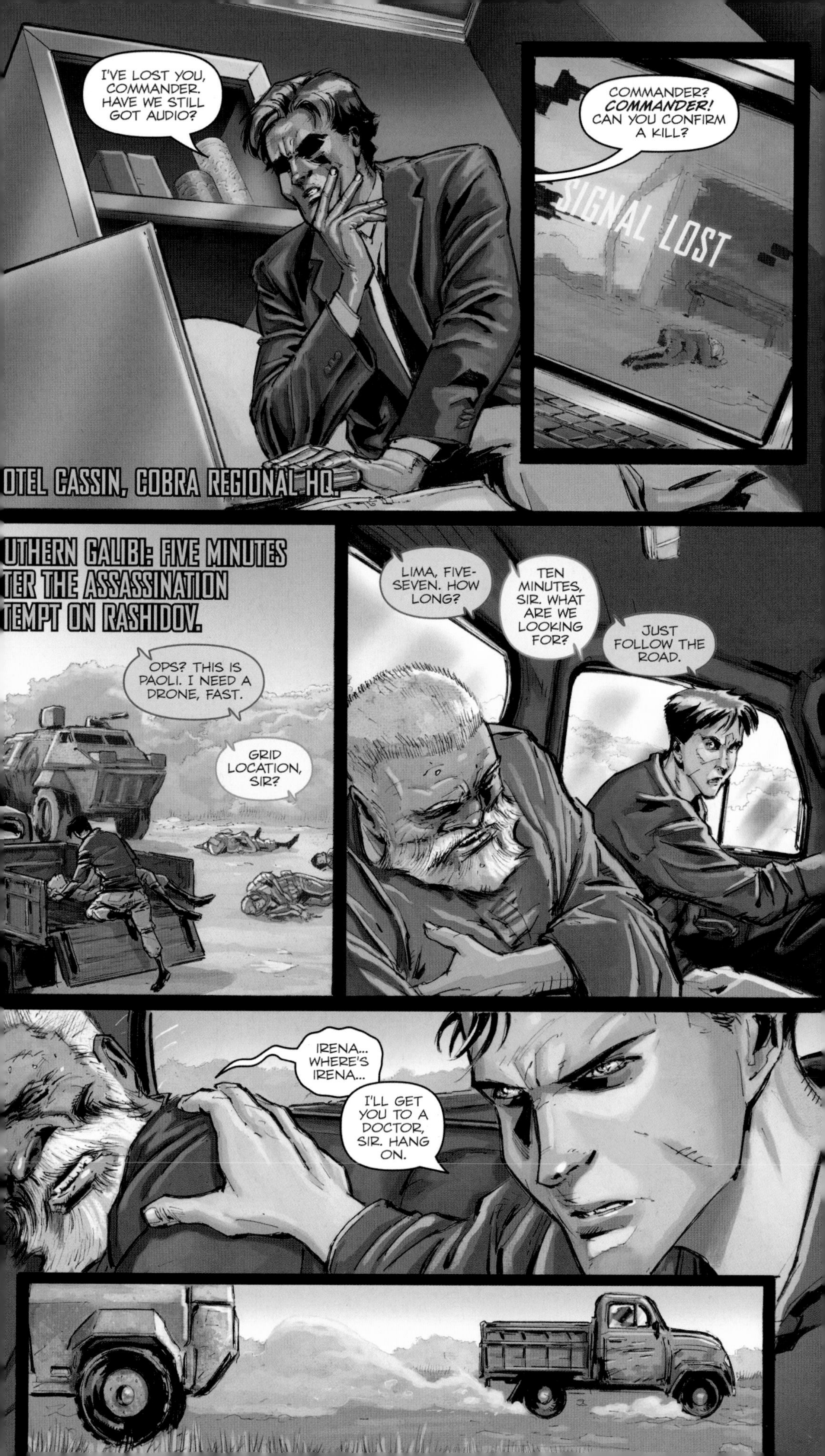

OTEL CASSIN, COBRA REGIONAL HQ.
I'VE LOST YOU, COMMANDER. HAVE WE STILL GOT AUDIO?
COMMANDER? COMMANDER! CAN YOU CONFIRM A KILL?
SIGNAL LOST
UTHERN GALIBI: FIVE MINUTES TER THE ASSASSINATION TEMPT ON RASHIDOV.
OPS? THIS IS PAOLI. I NEED A DRONE, FAST.
GRID LOCATION, SIR?
LIMA, FIVE-SEVEN. HOW LONG?
TEN MINUTES, SIR. WHAT ARE WE LOOKING FOR?
JUST FOLLOW THE ROAD.
IRENA... WHERE'S IRENA...
I'LL GET YOU TO A DOCTOR, SIR. HANG ON.

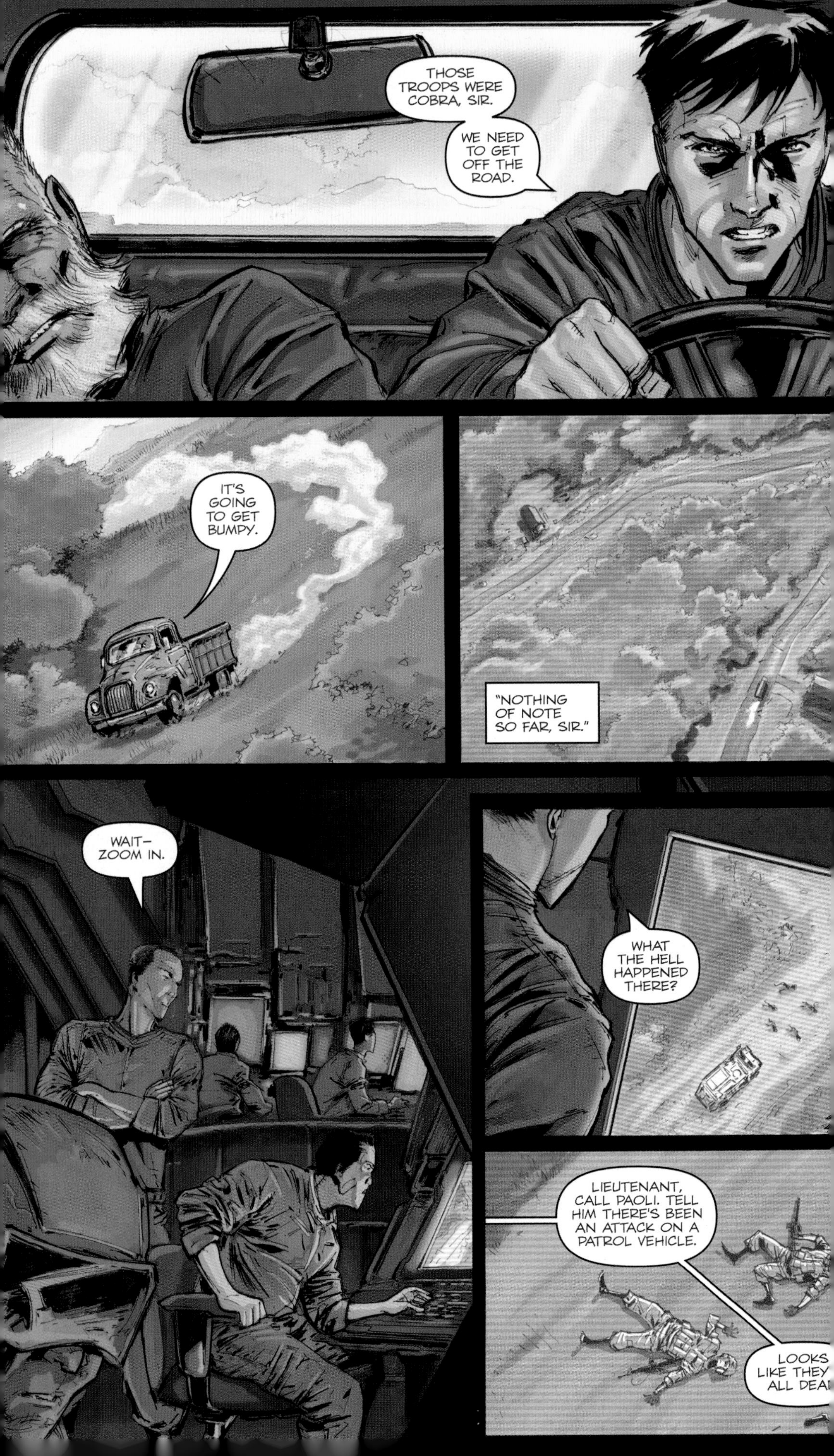
THOSE TROOPS WERE COBRA, SIR.
WE NEED TO GET OFF THE ROAD.
IT'S GOING TO GET BUMPY.
"NOTHING OF NOTE SO FAR, SIR."
WAIT— ZOOM IN.
WHAT THE HELL HAPPENED THERE?
LIEUTENANT, CALL PAOLI. TELL HIM THERE'S BEEN AN ATTACK ON A PATROL VEHICLE.
LOOKS LIKE THEY ALL DEA

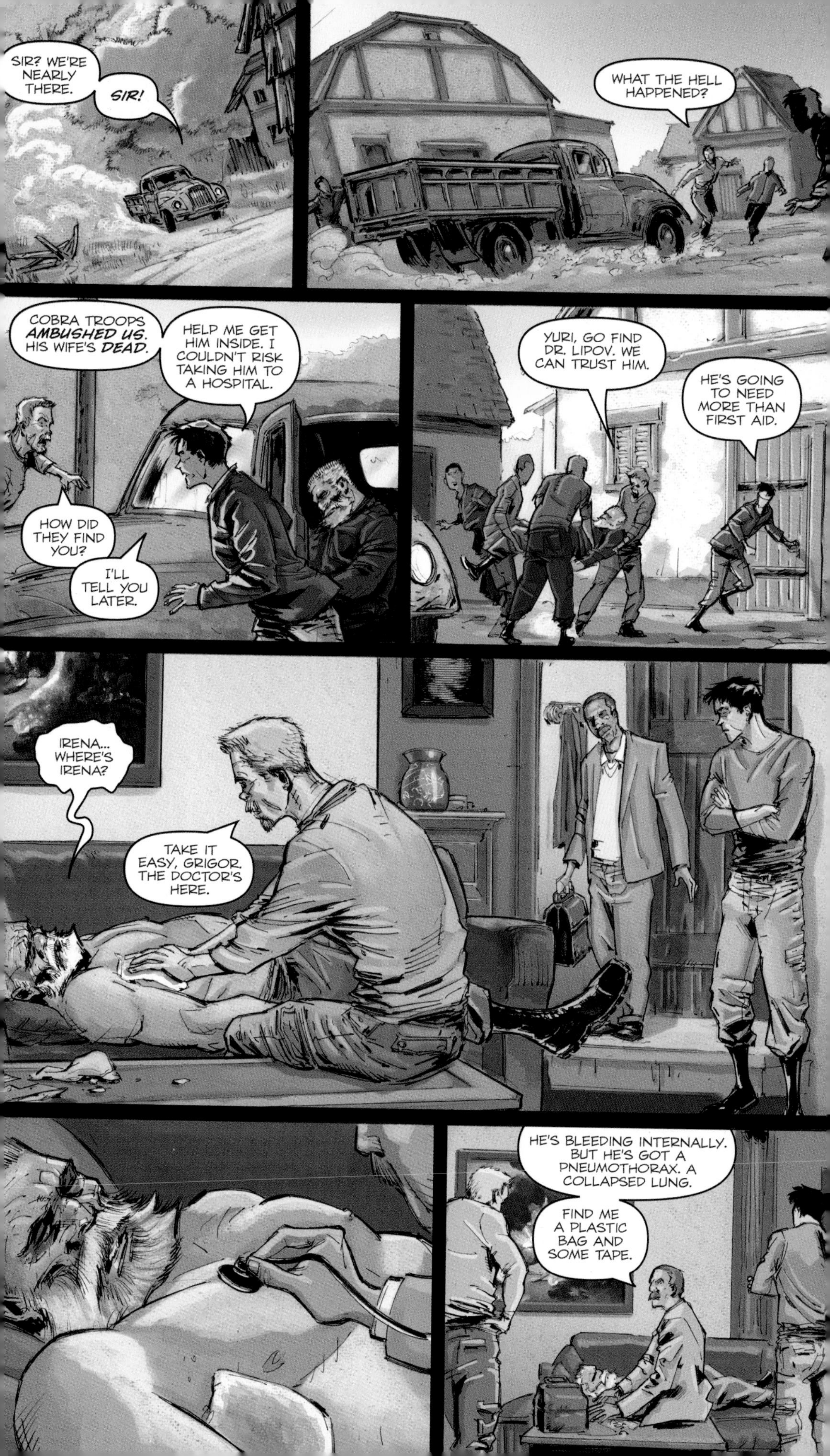
SIR? WE'RE NEARLY THERE.
SIR!
WHAT THE HELL HAPPENED?
COBRA TROOPS AMBUSHED US. HIS WIFE'S DEAD.
HELP ME GET HIM INSIDE. I COULDN'T RISK TAKING HIM TO A HOSPITAL.
HOW DID THEY FIND YOU?
I'LL TELL YOU LATER.
YURI, GO FIND DR. LIPOV. WE CAN TRUST HIM.
HE'S GOING TO NEED MORE THAN FIRST AID.
IRENA... WHERE'S IRENA?
TAKE IT EASY, GRIGOR. THE DOCTOR'S HERE.
HE'S BLEEDING INTERNALLY. BUT HE'S GOT A PNEUMOTHORAX. A COLLAPSED LUNG.
FIND ME A PLASTIC BAG AND SOME TAPE.

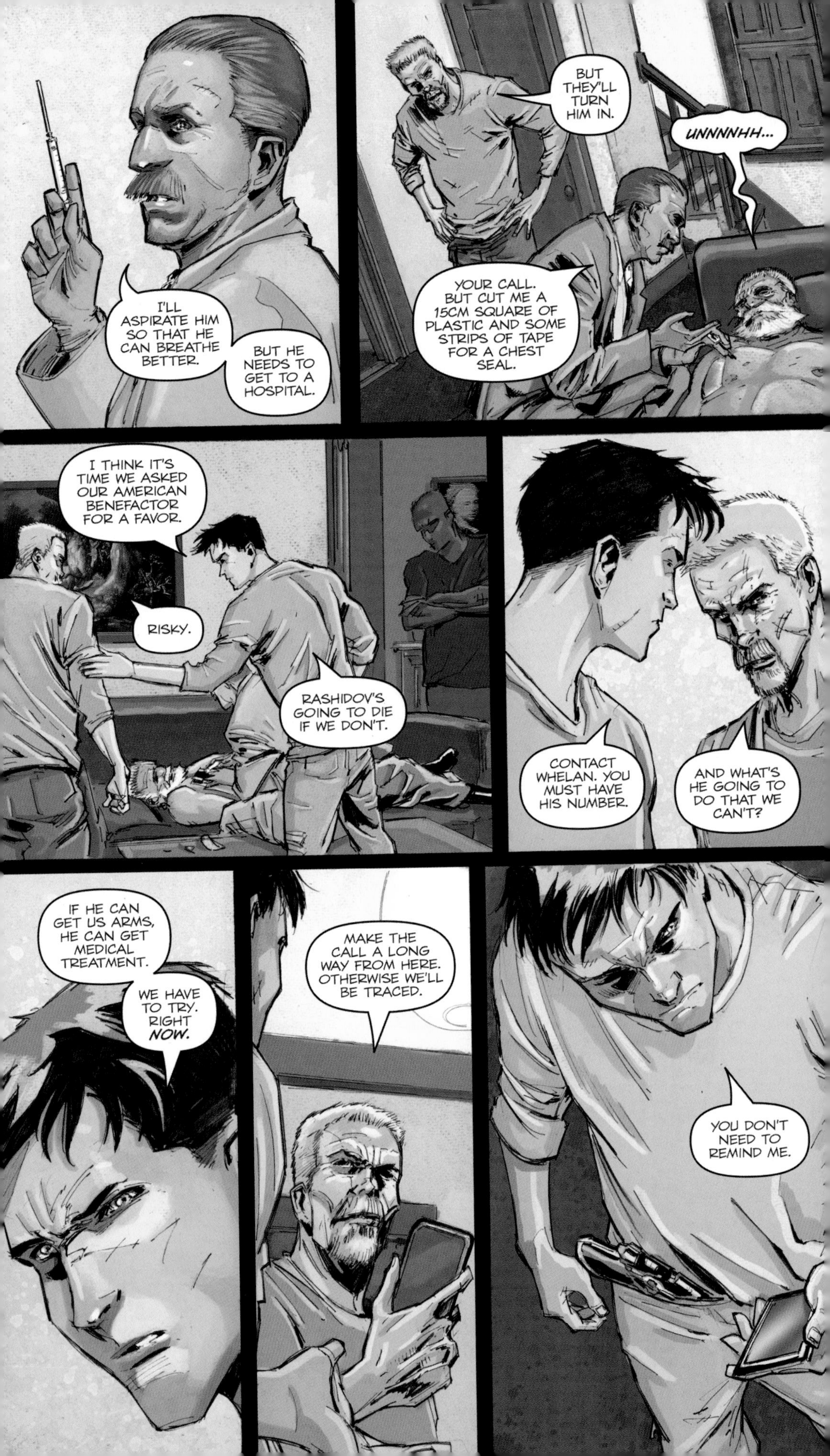
I'LL ASPIRATE HIM SO THAT HE CAN BREATHE BETTER.
BUT HE NEEDS TO GET TO A HOSPITAL.
BUT THEY'LL TURN HIM IN.
UNNNNHH...
YOUR CALL. BUT CUT ME A 15CM SQUARE OF PLASTIC AND SOME STRIPS OF TAPE FOR A CHEST SEAL.
I THINK IT'S TIME WE ASKED OUR AMERICAN BENEFACTOR FOR A FAVOR.
RISKY.
RASHIDOV'S GOING TO DIE IF WE DON'T.
CONTACT WHELAN. YOU MUST HAVE HIS NUMBER.
AND WHAT'S HE GOING TO DO THAT WE CAN'T?
IF HE CAN GET US ARMS, HE CAN GET MEDICAL TREATMENT.
WE HAVE TO TRY. RIGHT *NOW.*
MAKE THE CALL A LONG WAY FROM HERE. OTHERWISE WE'LL BE TRACED.
YOU DON'T NEED TO REMIND ME.

FIVE KILOMETERS NORTH OF ASTAKH, GALIBI.
WE BOTH NEED RASHIDOV ALIVE, MR. WHELAN. I'M ASKING FOR YOUR HELP.
YOU SEEM TO HAVE ACCESS TO CONSIDERABLE RESOURCES.
AND THERE'S SOMETHING ELSE I'D LIKE TO DISCUSS WITH YOU.
THE FALL OF G.I. JOE
PART SEVEN

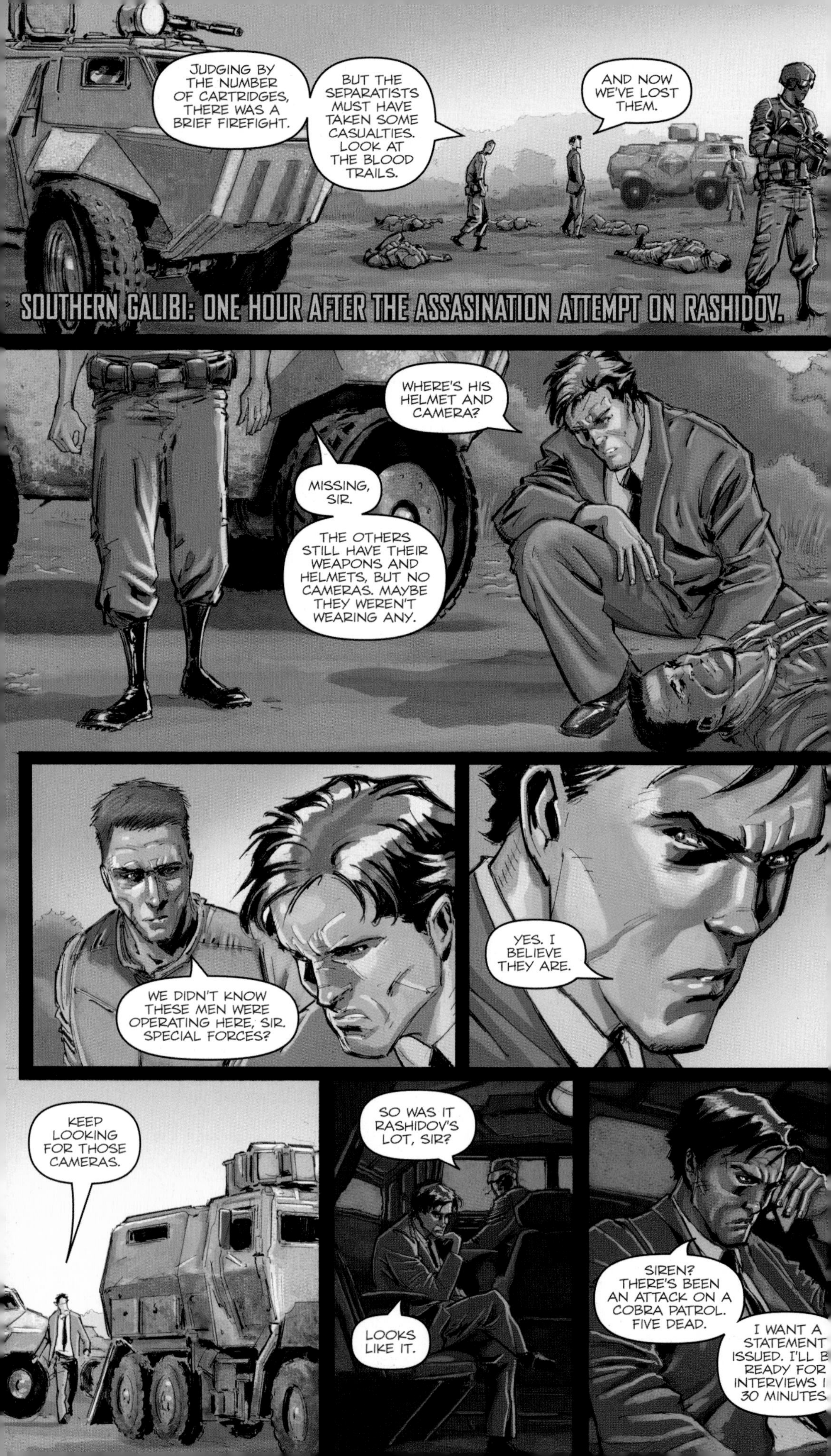
JUDGING BY THE NUMBER OF CARTRIDGES, THERE WAS A BRIEF FIREFIGHT.
BUT THE SEPARATISTS MUST HAVE TAKEN SOME CASUALTIES. LOOK AT THE BLOOD TRAILS.
AND NOW WE'VE LOST THEM.
SOUTHERN GALIBI: ONE HOUR AFTER THE ASSASINATION ATTEMPT ON RASHIDOV.
WHERE'S HIS HELMET AND CAMERA?
MISSING, SIR.
THE OTHERS STILL HAVE THEIR WEAPONS AND HELMETS, BUT NO CAMERAS. MAYBE THEY WEREN'T WEARING ANY.
WE DIDN'T KNOW THESE MEN WERE OPERATING HERE, SIR. SPECIAL FORCES?
YES. I BELIEVE THEY ARE.
KEEP LOOKING FOR THOSE CAMERAS.
SO WAS IT RASHIDOV'S LOT, SIR?
LOOKS LIKE IT.
SIREN? THERE'S BEEN AN ATTACK ON A COBRA PATROL. FIVE DEAD.
I WANT A STATEMENT ISSUED. I'LL B READY FOR INTERVIEWS I 30 MINUTES

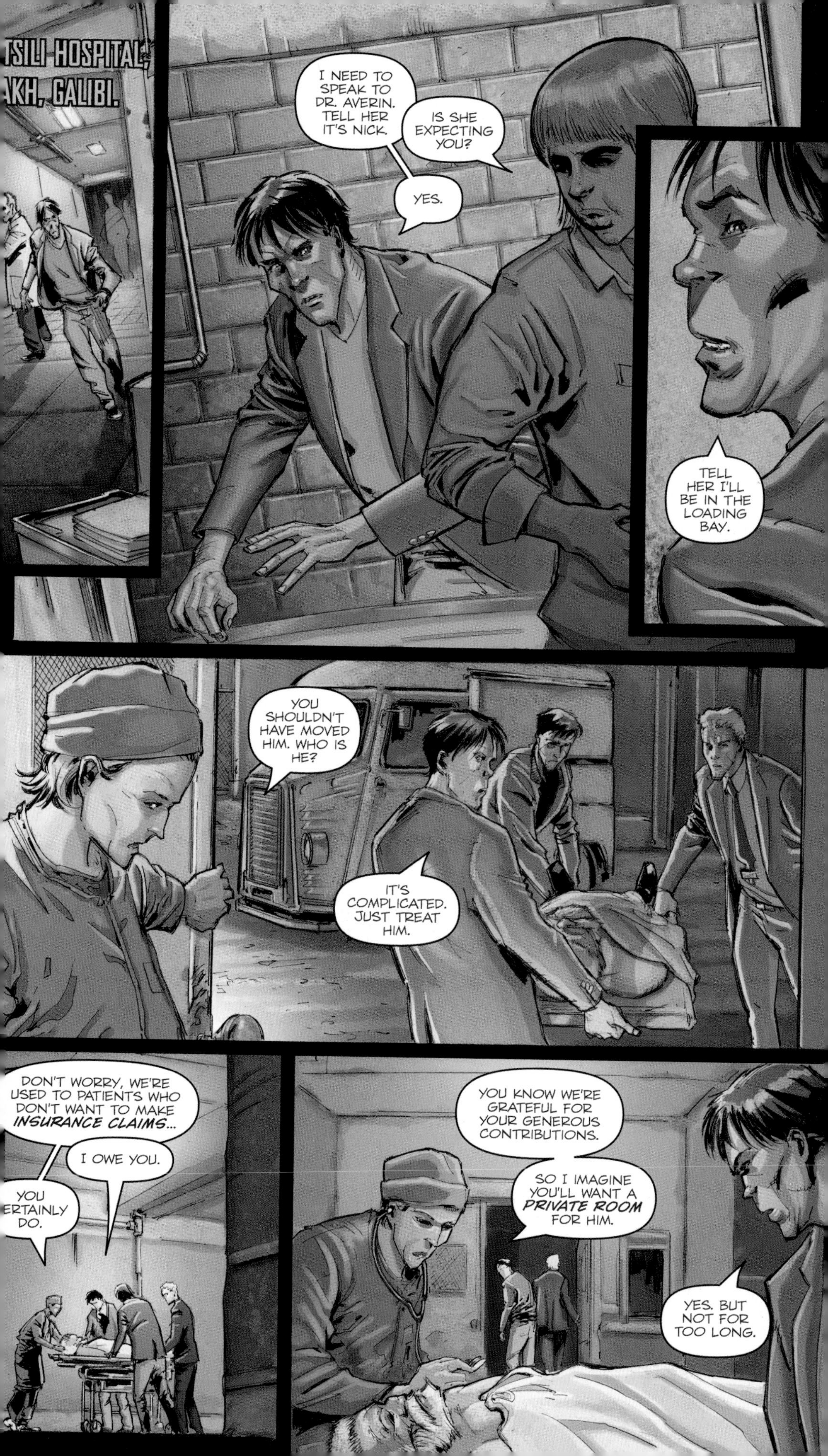
TSILI HOSPITAL, AKH, GALIBI.
I NEED TO SPEAK TO DR. AVERIN. TELL HER IT'S NICK.
IS SHE EXPECTING YOU?
YES.
TELL HER I'LL BE IN THE LOADING BAY.
YOU SHOULDN'T HAVE MOVED HIM. WHO IS HE?
IT'S COMPLICATED. JUST TREAT HIM.
DON'T WORRY, WE'RE USED TO PATIENTS WHO DON'T WANT TO MAKE *INSURANCE CLAIMS*...
I OWE YOU.
YOU ERTAINLY DO.
YOU KNOW WE'RE GRATEFUL FOR YOUR GENEROUS CONTRIBUTIONS.
SO I IMAGINE YOU'LL WANT A *PRIVATE ROOM* FOR HIM.
YES. BUT NOT FOR TOO LONG.

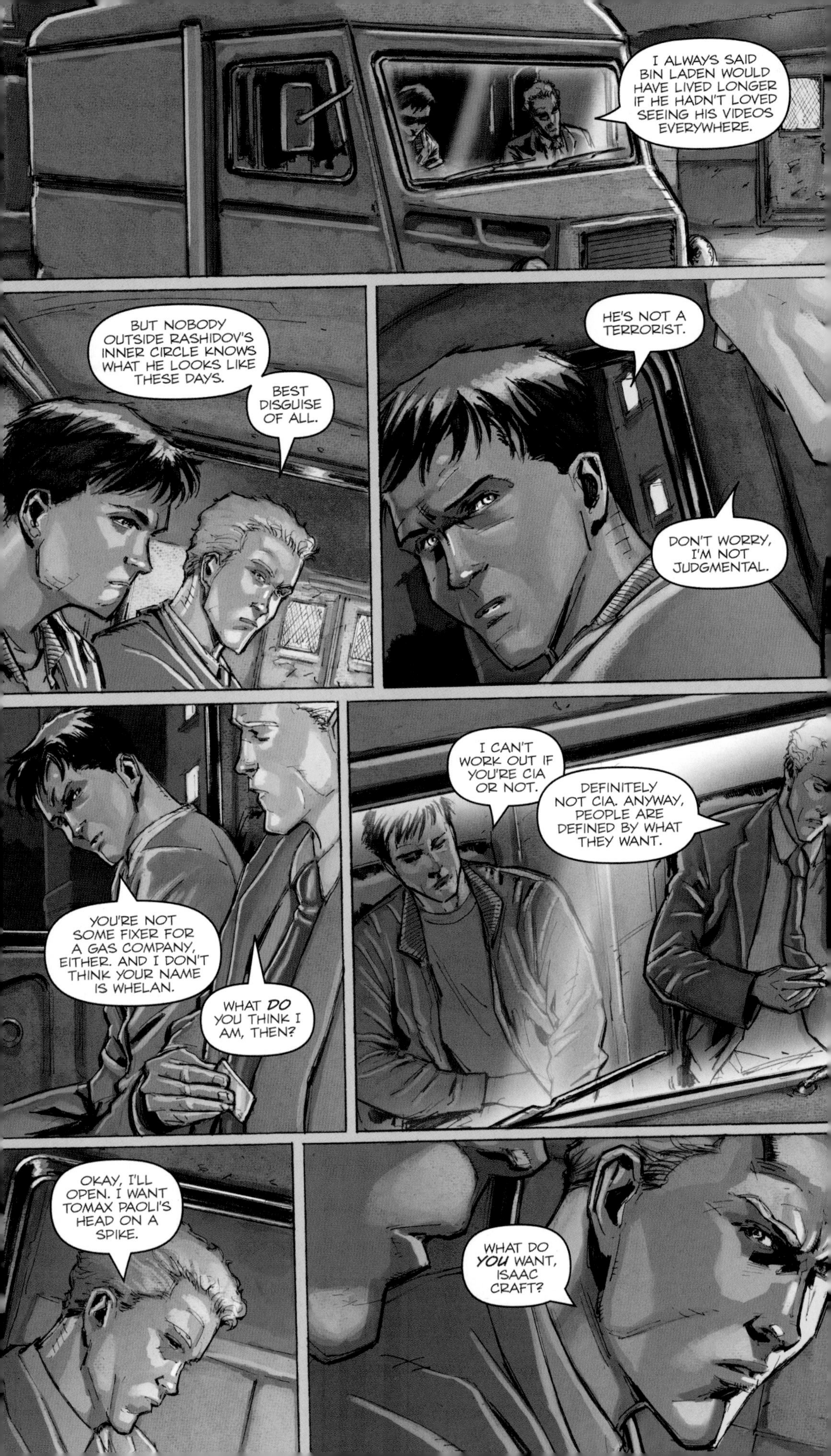
I ALWAYS SAID BIN LADEN WOULD HAVE LIVED LONGER IF HE HADN'T LOVED SEEING HIS VIDEOS EVERYWHERE.
BUT NOBODY OUTSIDE RASHIDOV'S INNER CIRCLE KNOWS WHAT HE LOOKS LIKE THESE DAYS.
BEST DISGUISE OF ALL.
HE'S NOT A TERRORIST.
DON'T WORRY, I'M NOT JUDGMENTAL.
YOU'RE NOT SOME FIXER FOR A GAS COMPANY, EITHER. AND I DON'T THINK YOUR NAME IS WHELAN.
WHAT DO YOU THINK I AM, THEN?
I CAN'T WORK OUT IF YOU'RE CIA OR NOT.
DEFINITELY NOT CIA. ANYWAY, PEOPLE ARE DEFINED BY WHAT THEY WANT.
OKAY, I'LL OPEN. I WANT TOMAX PAOLI'S HEAD ON A SPIKE.
WHAT DO YOU WANT, ISAAC CRAFT?

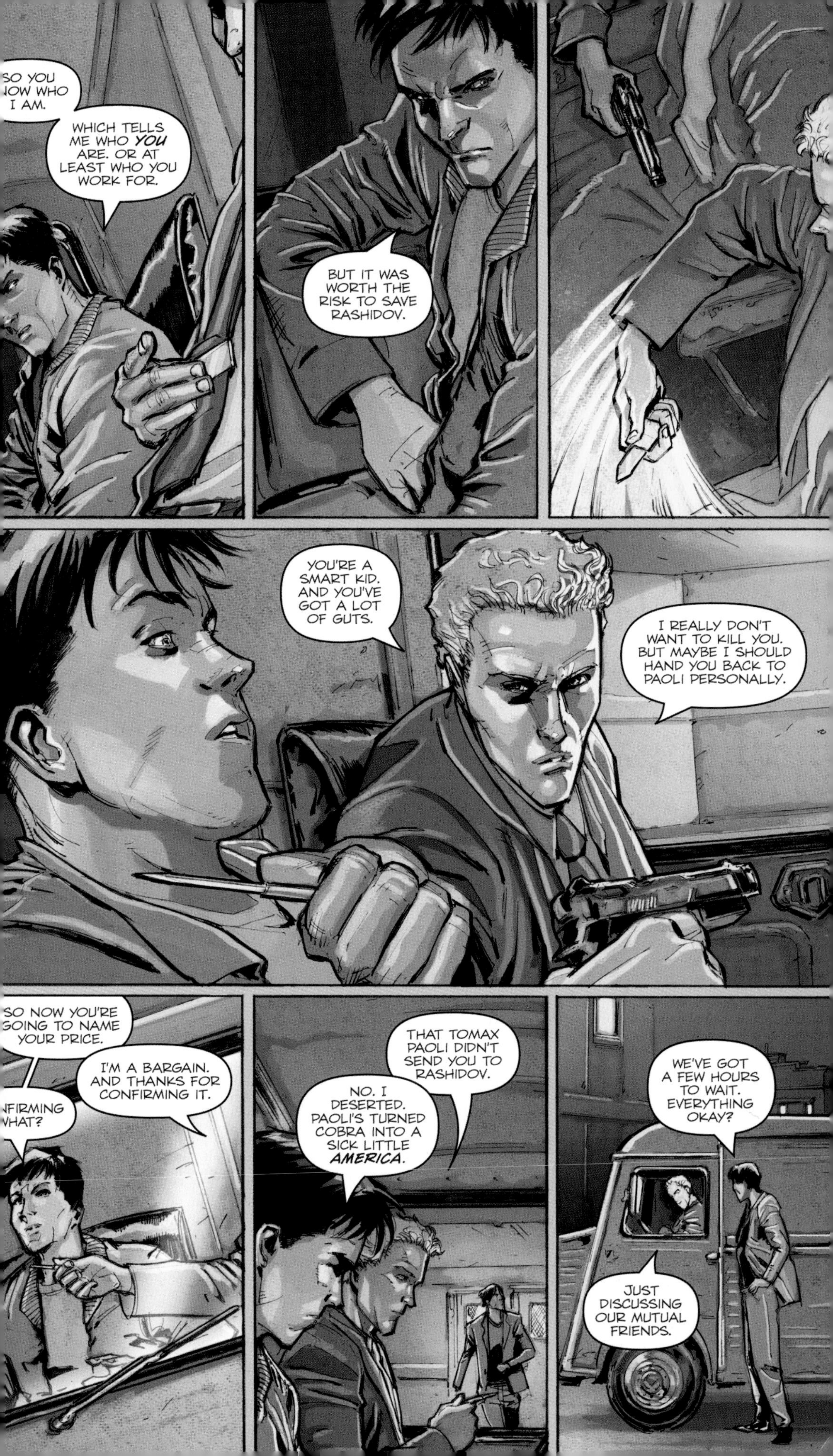
SO YOU
NOW WHO
I AM.
WHICH TELLS ME WHO YOU ARE. OR AT LEAST WHO YOU WORK FOR.
BUT IT WAS WORTH THE RISK TO SAVE RASHIDOV.
YOU'RE A SMART KID. AND YOU'VE GOT A LOT OF GUTS.
I REALLY DON'T WANT TO KILL YOU. BUT MAYBE I SHOULD HAND YOU BACK TO PAOLI PERSONALLY.
SO NOW YOU'RE GOING TO NAME YOUR PRICE.
I'M A BARGAIN. AND THANKS FOR CONFIRMING IT.
NFIRMING
WHAT?
THAT TOMAX PAOLI DIDN'T SEND YOU TO RASHIDOV.
NO. I DESERTED. PAOLI'S TURNED COBRA INTO A SICK LITTLE AMERICA.
WE'VE GOT A FEW HOURS TO WAIT. EVERYTHING OKAY?
JUST DISCUSSING OUR MUTUAL FRIENDS.

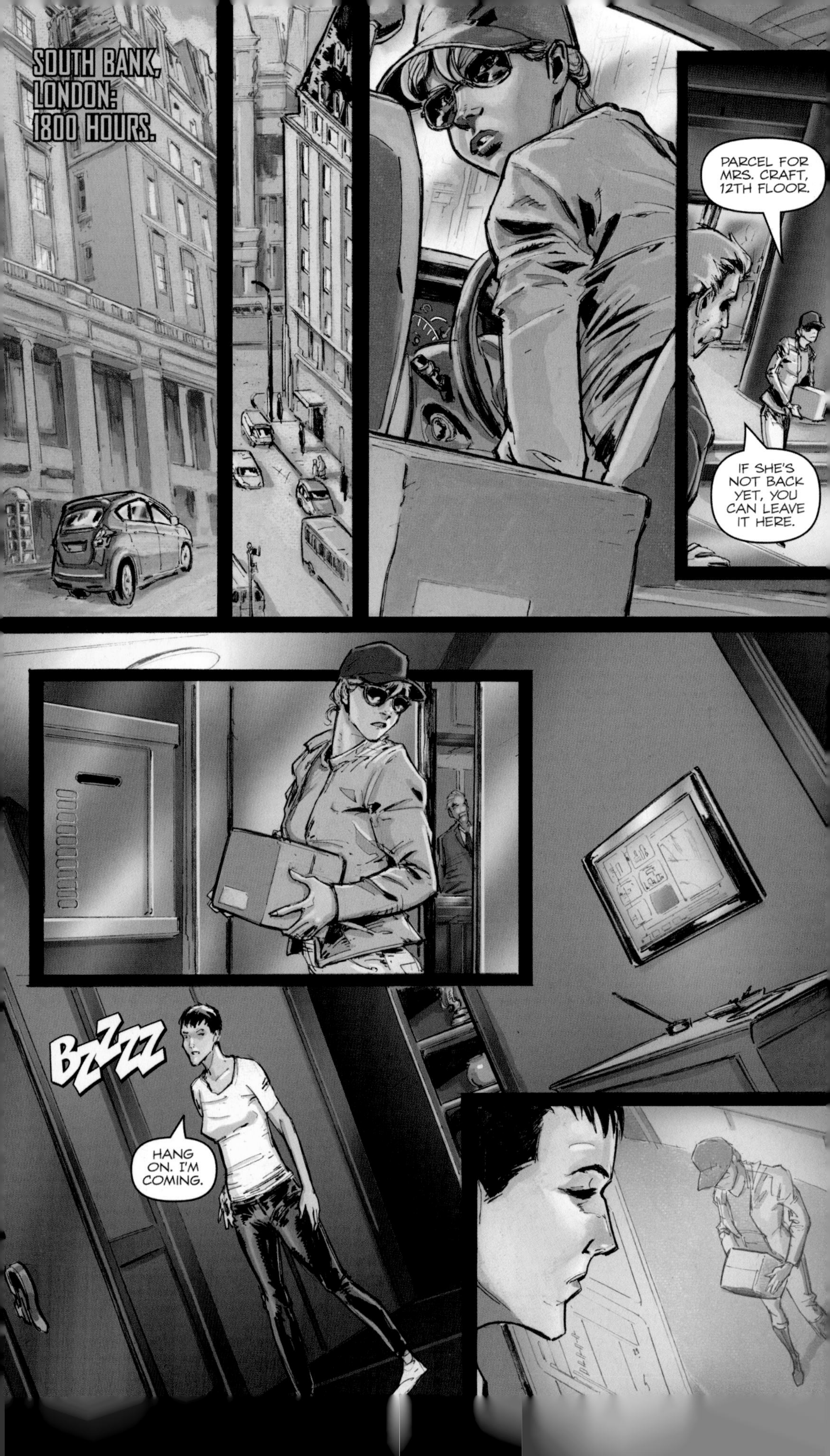
SOUTH BANK, LONDON: 1800 HOURS.
PARCEL FOR MRS. CRAFT, 12TH FLOOR.
IF SHE'S NOT BACK YET, YOU CAN LEAVE IT HERE.
BZZZZ
HANG ON. I'M COMING.

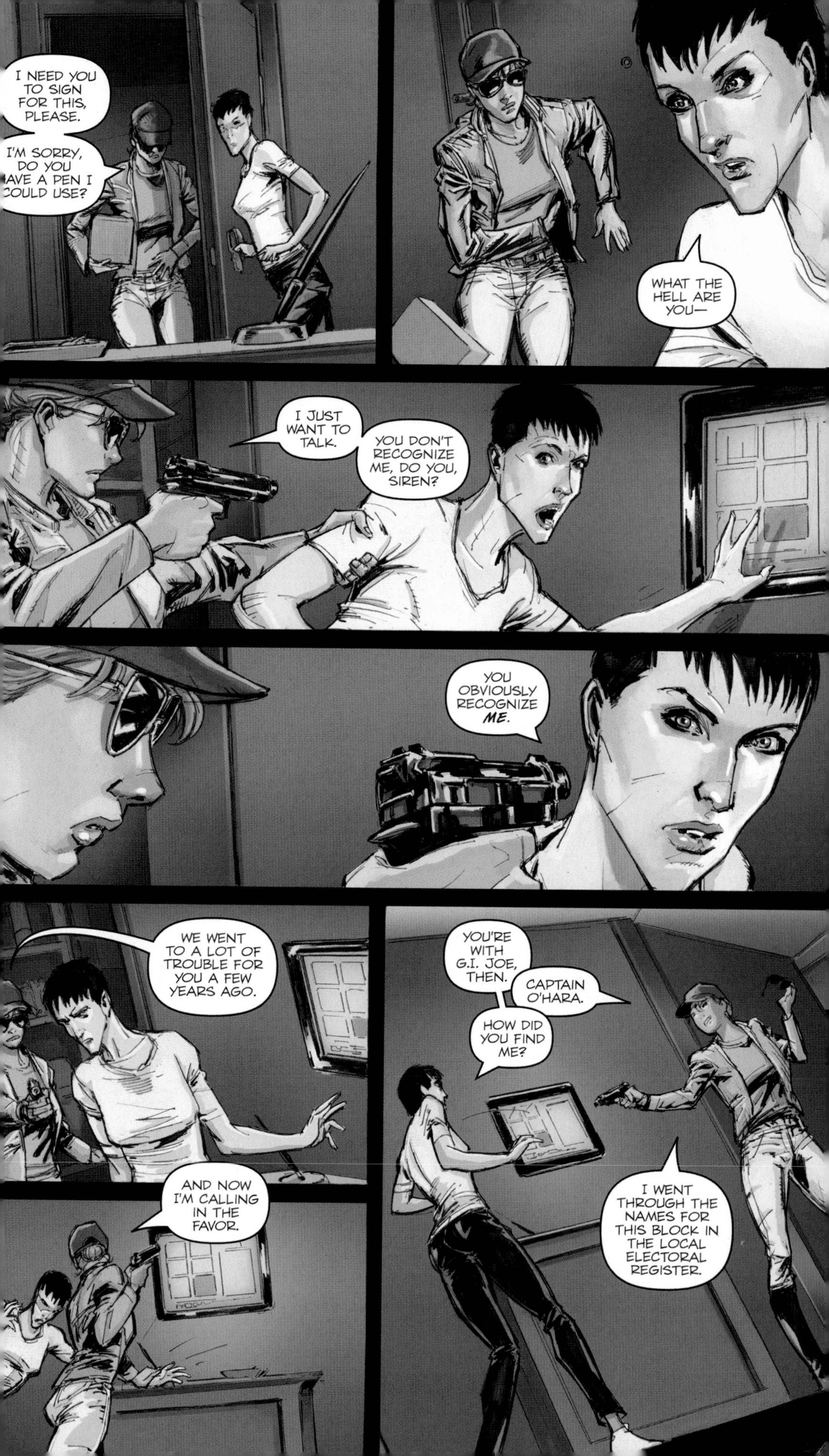
I NEED YOU TO SIGN FOR THIS, PLEASE.
I'M SORRY, DO YOU HAVE A PEN I COULD USE?
WHAT THE HELL ARE YOU—
I JUST WANT TO TALK.
YOU DON'T RECOGNIZE ME, DO YOU, SIREN?
YOU OBVIOUSLY RECOGNIZE *ME*.
WE WENT TO A LOT OF TROUBLE FOR YOU A FEW YEARS AGO.
AND NOW I'M CALLING IN THE FAVOR.
YOU'RE WITH G.I. JOE, THEN.
CAPTAIN O'HARA.
HOW DID YOU FIND ME?
I WENT THROUGH THE NAMES FOR THIS BLOCK IN THE LOCAL ELECTORAL REGISTER.

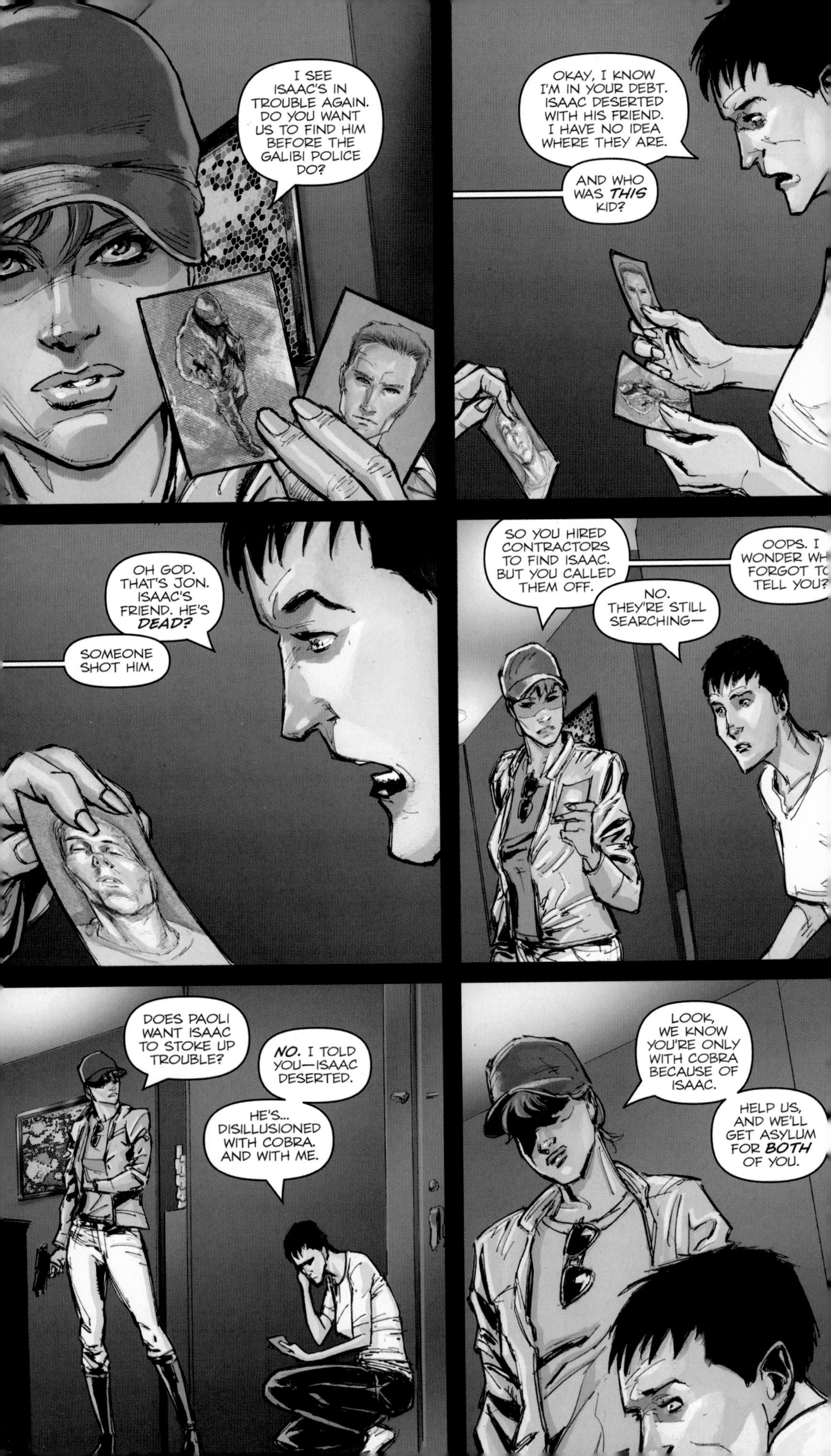
I SEE ISAAC'S IN TROUBLE AGAIN. DO YOU WANT US TO FIND HIM BEFORE THE GALIBI POLICE DO?
OKAY, I KNOW I'M IN YOUR DEBT. ISAAC DESERTED WITH HIS FRIEND. I HAVE NO IDEA WHERE THEY ARE.
AND WHO WAS *THIS* KID?
OH GOD. THAT'S JON. ISAAC'S FRIEND. HE'S ***DEAD?***
SOMEONE SHOT HIM.
SO YOU HIRED CONTRACTORS TO FIND ISAAC. BUT YOU CALLED THEM OFF.
NO. THEY'RE STILL SEARCHING—
OOPS. I WONDER WH FORGOT TO TELL YOU?
DOES PAOLI WANT ISAAC TO STOKE UP TROUBLE?
NO. I TOLD YOU—ISAAC DESERTED.
HE'S... DISILLUSIONED WITH COBRA. AND WITH ME.
LOOK, WE KNOW YOU'RE ONLY WITH COBRA BECAUSE OF ISAAC.
HELP US, AND WE'LL GET ASYLUM FOR ***BOTH*** OF YOU.

GL:OB:AL,
:RO:ROAD,
:H MYURETZ.

BRRR

VIKTOR? IT'S YEGOR.

YOU SHOULDN'T CALL ME ON THIS LINE.

IT'S IMPORTANT. I HEAR OUR *FRIEND* IS IN SKATSILI HOSPITAL WITH GUNSHOT WOUNDS.

THEY GOT TO HIM, THEN.

I HEAR THEY WERE *PEACE-KEEPERS.*

WHAT?

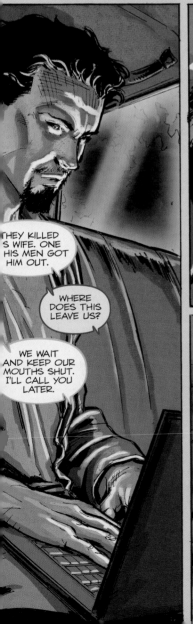

THEY KILLED :S WIFE. ONE HIS MEN GOT HIM OUT.

WHERE DOES THIS LEAVE US?

WE WAIT AND KEEP OUR MOUTHS SHUT. I'LL CALL YOU LATER.

THEY'VE GOT TO BE TALKING ABOUT RASHIDOV.

SO COBRA GOT TO HIM. BUT HE'S NOT DEAD.

WHERE IS HE NOW, MAINS?

SKATSILI HOSPITAL. IN ASTAKH.

I'M AMAZED HE CAN MOVE AROUND UNDETECTED. LET'S GO.

WELL, NOT *ENTIRELY* UNDETECTED, FLINT. HE'S GOT A HOLE IN HIM.

OKAY, SOMEONE TALKED.

OR SOMEONE'S TAPPING PHONES... HEY, I'VE GOT ANOTHER POSTCARD FROM SCARLETT.

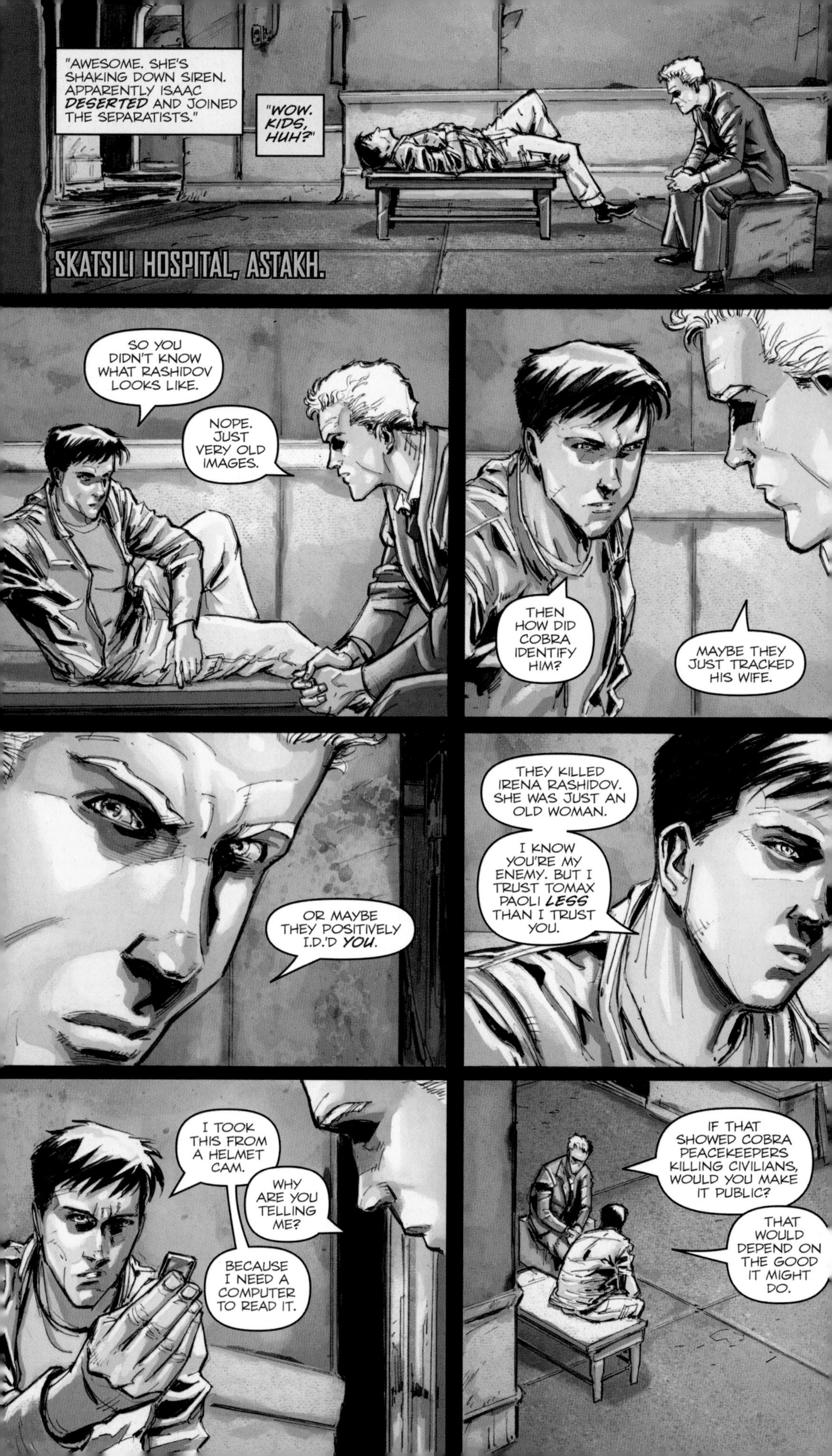
"AWESOME. SHE'S SHAKING DOWN SIREN. APPARENTLY ISAAC *DESERTED* AND JOINED THE SEPARATISTS."
"*WOW. KIDS, HUH?*"
SKATSILI HOSPITAL, ASTAKH.
SO YOU DIDN'T KNOW WHAT RASHIDOV LOOKS LIKE.
NOPE. JUST VERY OLD IMAGES.
THEN HOW DID COBRA IDENTIFY HIM?
MAYBE THEY JUST TRACKED HIS WIFE.
OR MAYBE THEY POSITIVELY I.D.'D *YOU*.
THEY KILLED IRENA RASHIDOV. SHE WAS JUST AN OLD WOMAN.
I KNOW YOU'RE MY ENEMY. BUT I TRUST TOMAX PAOLI *LESS* THAN I TRUST YOU.
I TOOK THIS FROM A HELMET CAM.
WHY ARE YOU TELLING ME?
BECAUSE I NEED A COMPUTER TO READ IT.
IF THAT SHOWED COBRA PEACEKEEPERS KILLING CIVILIANS, WOULD YOU MAKE IT PUBLIC?
THAT WOULD DEPEND ON THE GOOD IT MIGHT DO.

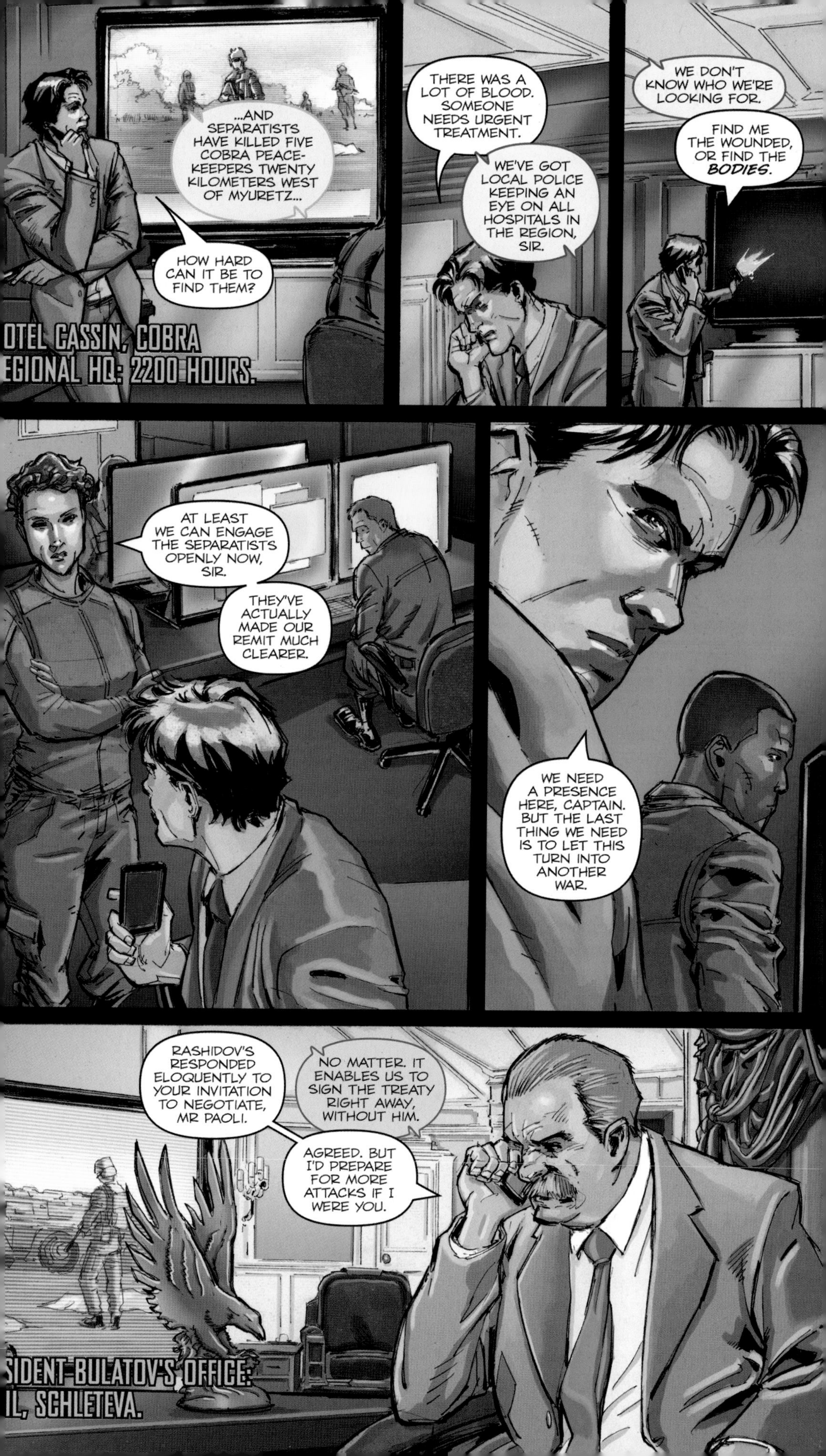
...AND SEPARATISTS HAVE KILLED FIVE COBRA PEACE-KEEPERS TWENTY KILOMETERS WEST OF MYURETZ...
HOW HARD CAN IT BE TO FIND THEM?
OTEL CASSIN, COBRA
EGIONAL HQ: 2200 HOURS.
THERE WAS A LOT OF BLOOD. SOMEONE NEEDS URGENT TREATMENT.
WE'VE GOT LOCAL POLICE KEEPING AN EYE ON ALL HOSPITALS IN THE REGION, SIR.
WE DON'T KNOW WHO WE'RE LOOKING FOR.
FIND ME THE WOUNDED, OR FIND THE *BODIES*.
AT LEAST WE CAN ENGAGE THE SEPARATISTS OPENLY NOW, SIR.
THEY'VE ACTUALLY MADE OUR REMIT MUCH CLEARER.
WE NEED A PRESENCE HERE, CAPTAIN. BUT THE LAST THING WE NEED IS TO LET THIS TURN INTO ANOTHER WAR.
RASHIDOV'S RESPONDED ELOQUENTLY TO YOUR INVITATION TO NEGOTIATE, MR PAOLI.
NO MATTER. IT ENABLES US TO SIGN THE TREATY RIGHT AWAY, WITHOUT HIM.
AGREED. BUT I'D PREPARE FOR MORE ATTACKS IF I WERE YOU.
SIDENT BULATOV'S OFFICE:
IL, SCHLETEVA.

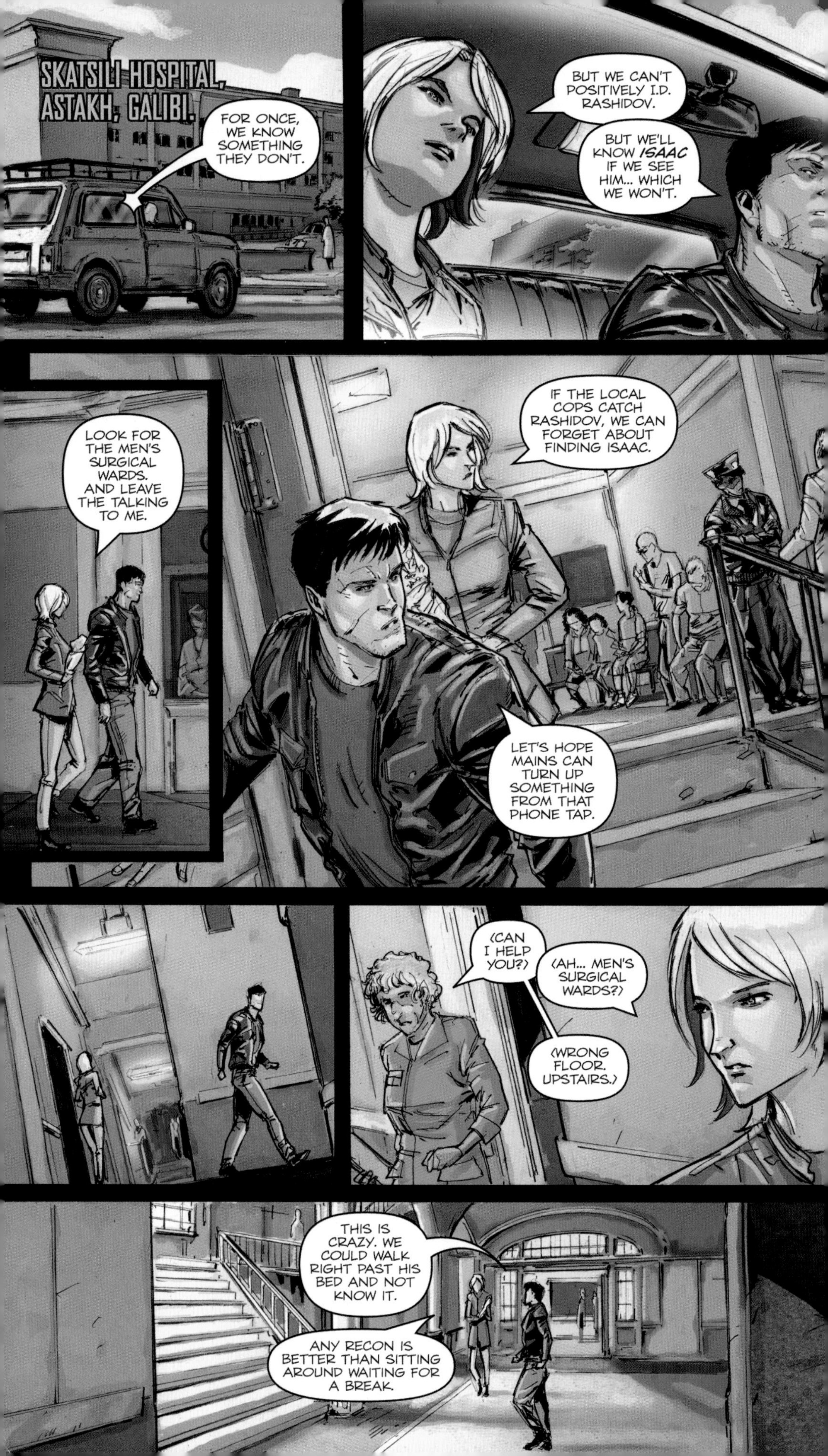
SKATSILI HOSPITAL, ASTAKH, GALIBI.
FOR ONCE, WE KNOW SOMETHING THEY DON'T.
BUT WE CAN'T POSITIVELY I.D. RASHIDOV.
BUT WE'LL KNOW ISAAC IF WE SEE HIM... WHICH WE WON'T.
LOOK FOR THE MEN'S SURGICAL WARDS. AND LEAVE THE TALKING TO ME.
IF THE LOCAL COPS CATCH RASHIDOV, WE CAN FORGET ABOUT FINDING ISAAC.
LET'S HOPE MAINS CAN TURN UP SOMETHING FROM THAT PHONE TAP.
(CAN I HELP YOU?)
(AH... MEN'S SURGICAL WARDS?)
(WRONG FLOOR. UPSTAIRS.)
THIS IS CRAZY. WE COULD WALK RIGHT PAST HIS BED AND NOT KNOW IT.
ANY RECON IS BETTER THAN SITTING AROUND WAITING FOR A BREAK.

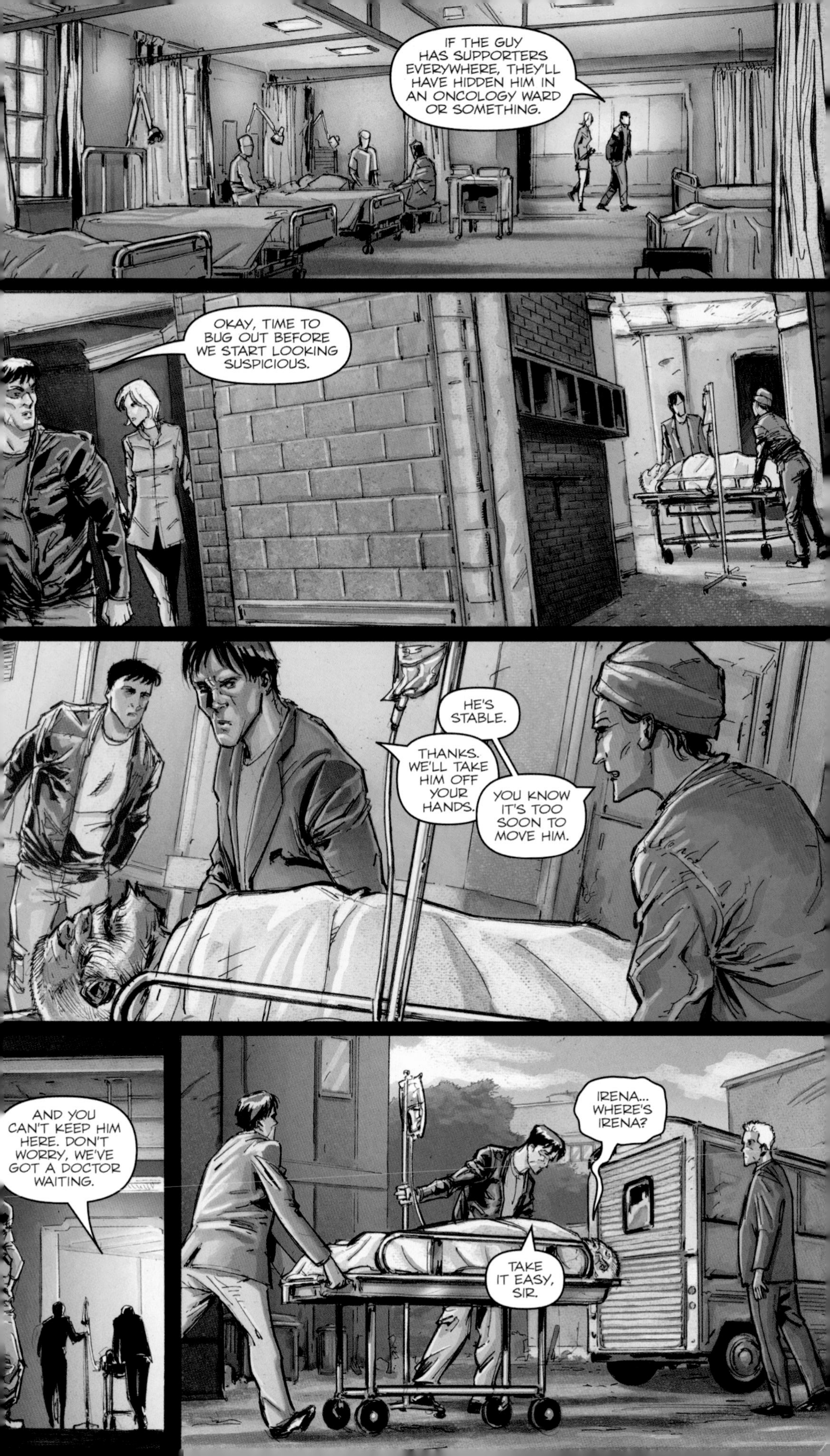
IF THE GUY HAS SUPPORTERS EVERYWHERE, THEY'LL HAVE HIDDEN HIM IN AN ONCOLOGY WARD OR SOMETHING.
OKAY, TIME TO BUG OUT BEFORE WE START LOOKING SUSPICIOUS.
HE'S STABLE.
THANKS. WE'LL TAKE HIM OFF YOUR HANDS.
YOU KNOW IT'S TOO SOON TO MOVE HIM.
AND YOU CAN'T KEEP HIM HERE. DON'T WORRY, WE'VE GOT A DOCTOR WAITING.
IRENA... WHERE'S IRENA?
TAKE IT EASY, SIR.

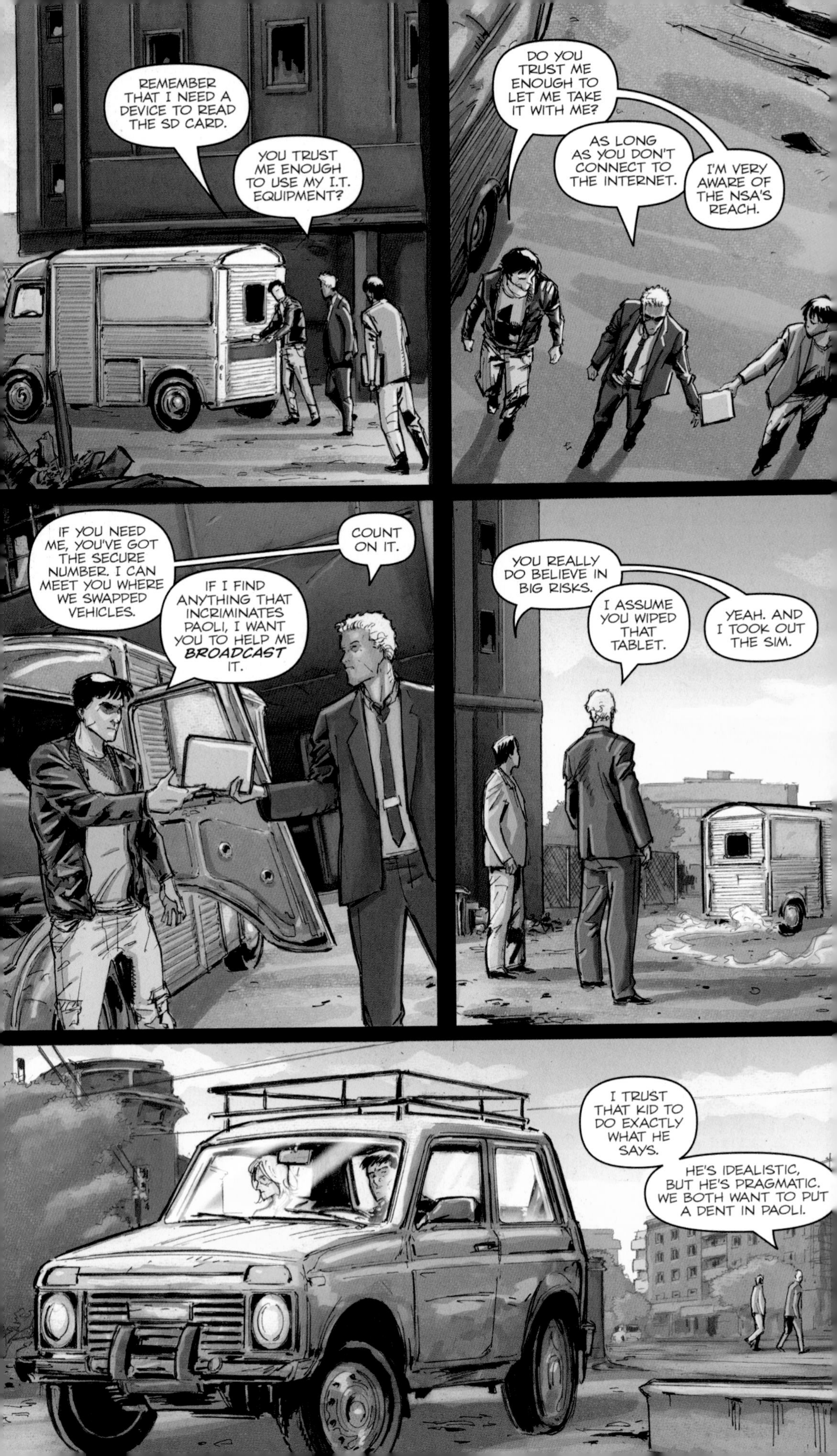
REMEMBER THAT I NEED A DEVICE TO READ THE SD CARD.
YOU TRUST ME ENOUGH TO USE MY I.T. EQUIPMENT?
DO YOU TRUST ME ENOUGH TO LET ME TAKE IT WITH ME?
AS LONG AS YOU DON'T CONNECT TO THE INTERNET.
I'M VERY AWARE OF THE NSA'S REACH.
IF YOU NEED ME, YOU'VE GOT THE SECURE NUMBER. I CAN MEET YOU WHERE WE SWAPPED VEHICLES.
COUNT ON IT.
IF I FIND ANYTHING THAT INCRIMINATES PAOLI, I WANT YOU TO HELP ME **BROADCAST** IT.
YOU REALLY DO BELIEVE IN BIG RISKS.
I ASSUME YOU WIPED THAT TABLET.
YEAH. AND I TOOK OUT THE SIM.
I TRUST THAT KID TO DO EXACTLY WHAT HE SAYS.
HE'S IDEALISTIC, BUT HE'S PRAGMATIC. WE BOTH WANT TO PUT A DENT IN PAOLI.

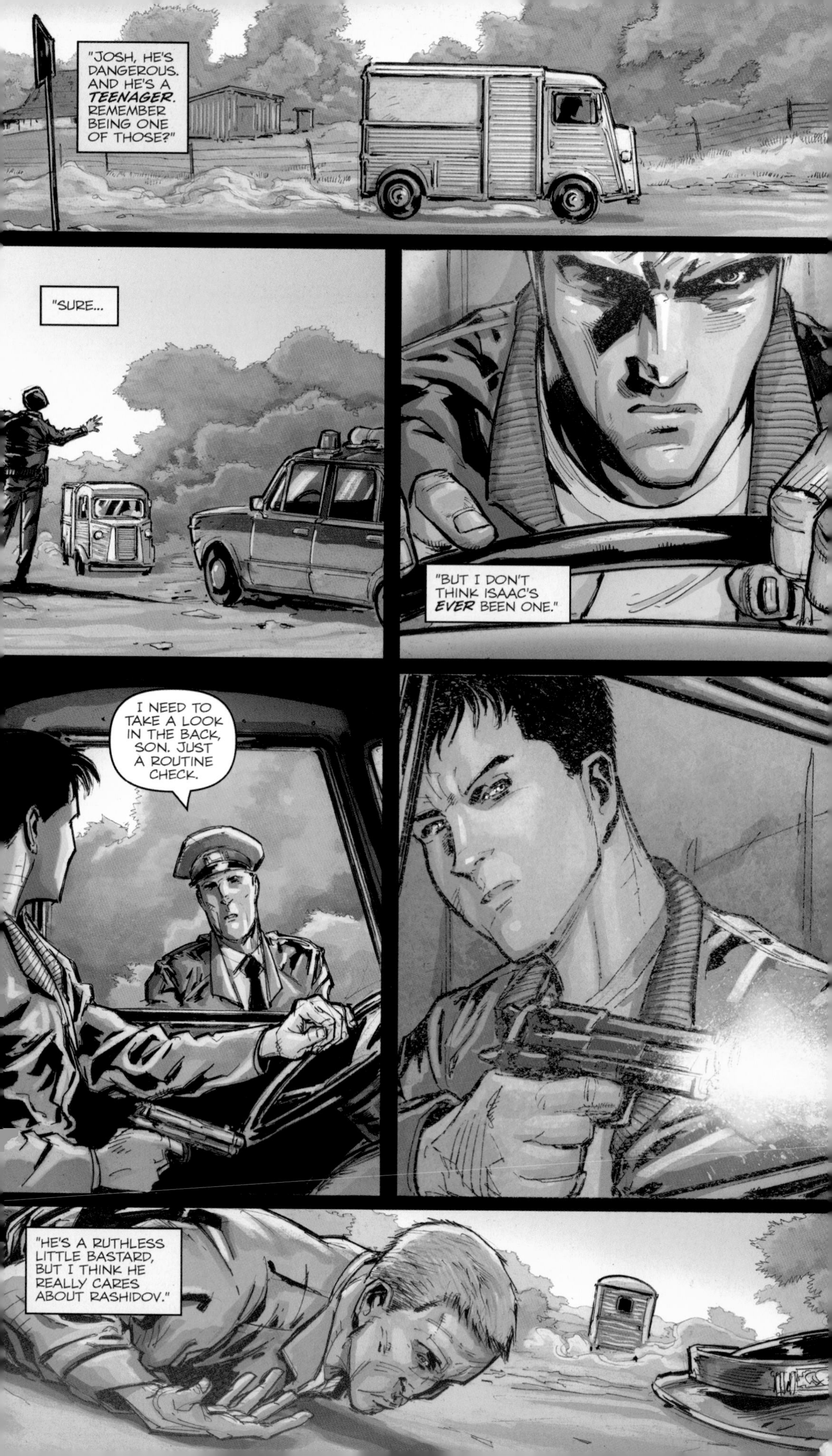
"JOSH, HE'S DANGEROUS. AND HE'S A TEENAGER. REMEMBER BEING ONE OF THOSE?"
"SURE...
"BUT I DON'T THINK ISAAC'S EVER BEEN ONE."
I NEED TO TAKE A LOOK IN THE BACK, SON. JUST A ROUTINE CHECK.
"HE'S A RUTHLESS LITTLE BASTARD, BUT I THINK HE REALLY CARES ABOUT RASHIDOV."

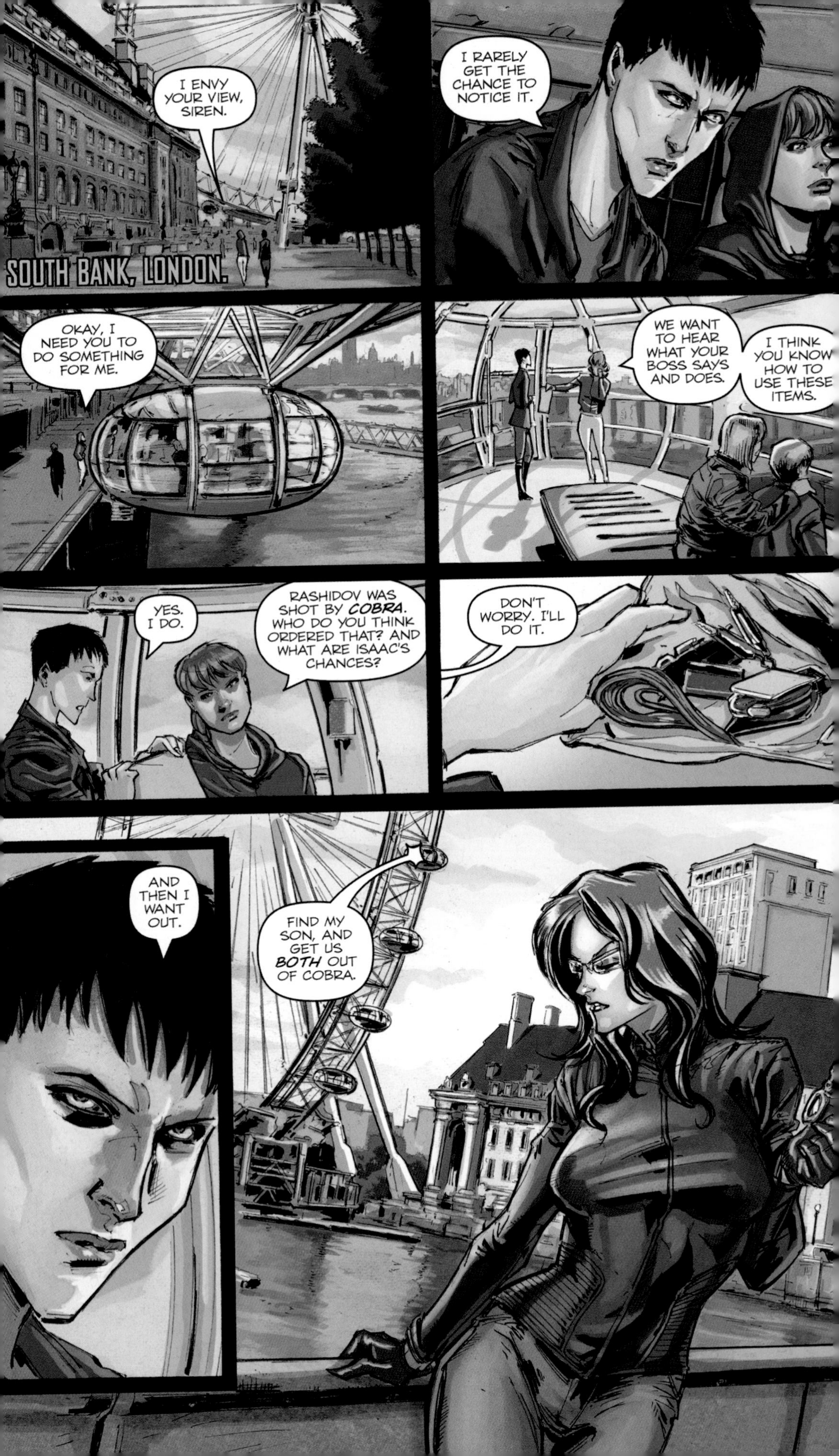

I ENVY YOUR VIEW, SIREN.
SOUTH BANK, LONDON.
I RARELY GET THE CHANCE TO NOTICE IT.
OKAY, I NEED YOU TO DO SOMETHING FOR ME.
WE WANT TO HEAR WHAT YOUR BOSS SAYS AND DOES.
I THINK YOU KNOW HOW TO USE THESE ITEMS.
YES. I DO.
RASHIDOV WAS SHOT BY COBRA. WHO DO YOU THINK ORDERED THAT? AND WHAT ARE ISAAC'S CHANCES?
DON'T WORRY. I'LL DO IT.
AND THEN I WANT OUT.
FIND MY SON, AND GET US BOTH OUT OF COBRA.

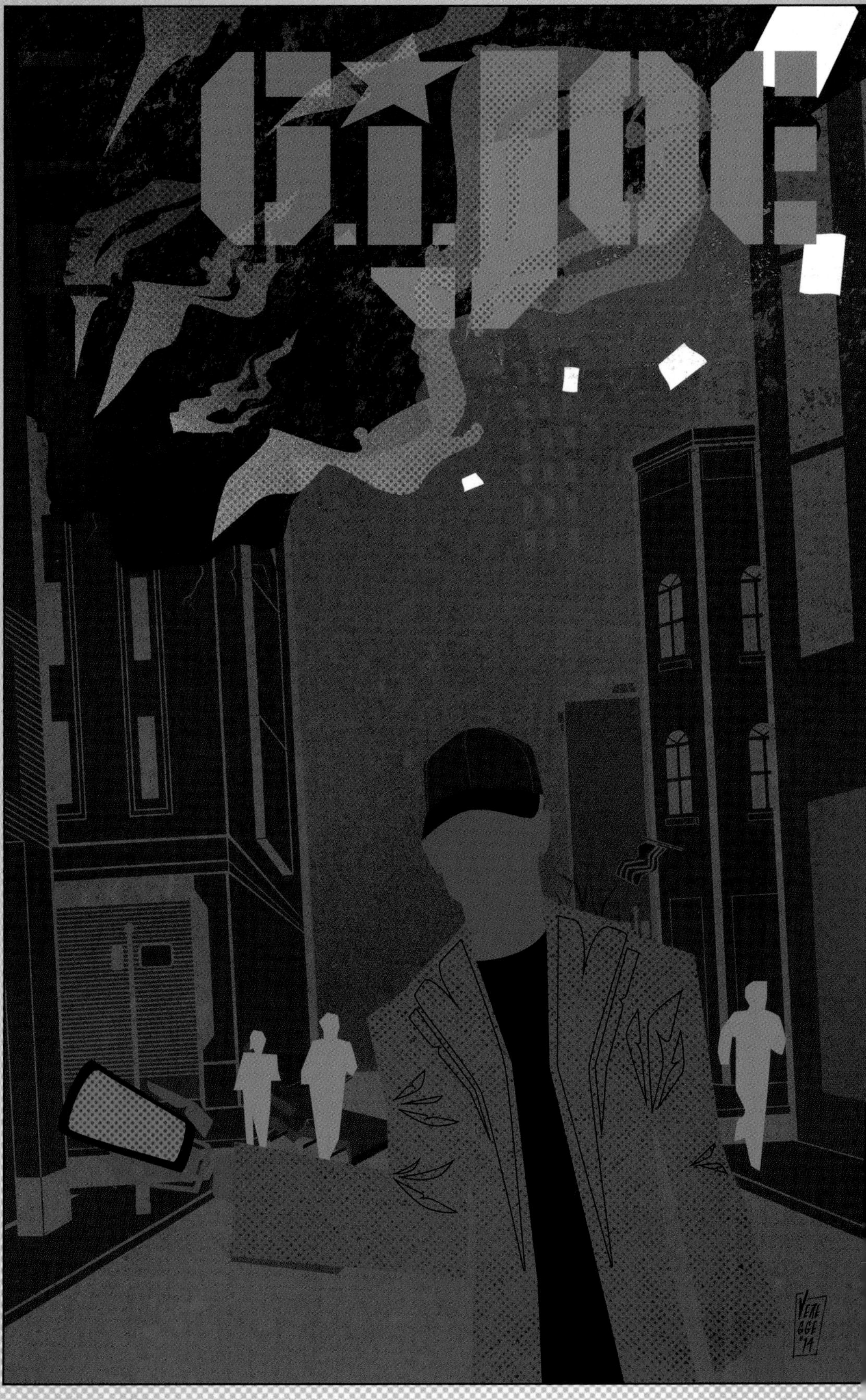
G.I. JOE
VEREGGE '14

ARTWORK BY
JEFFREY VEREGGE

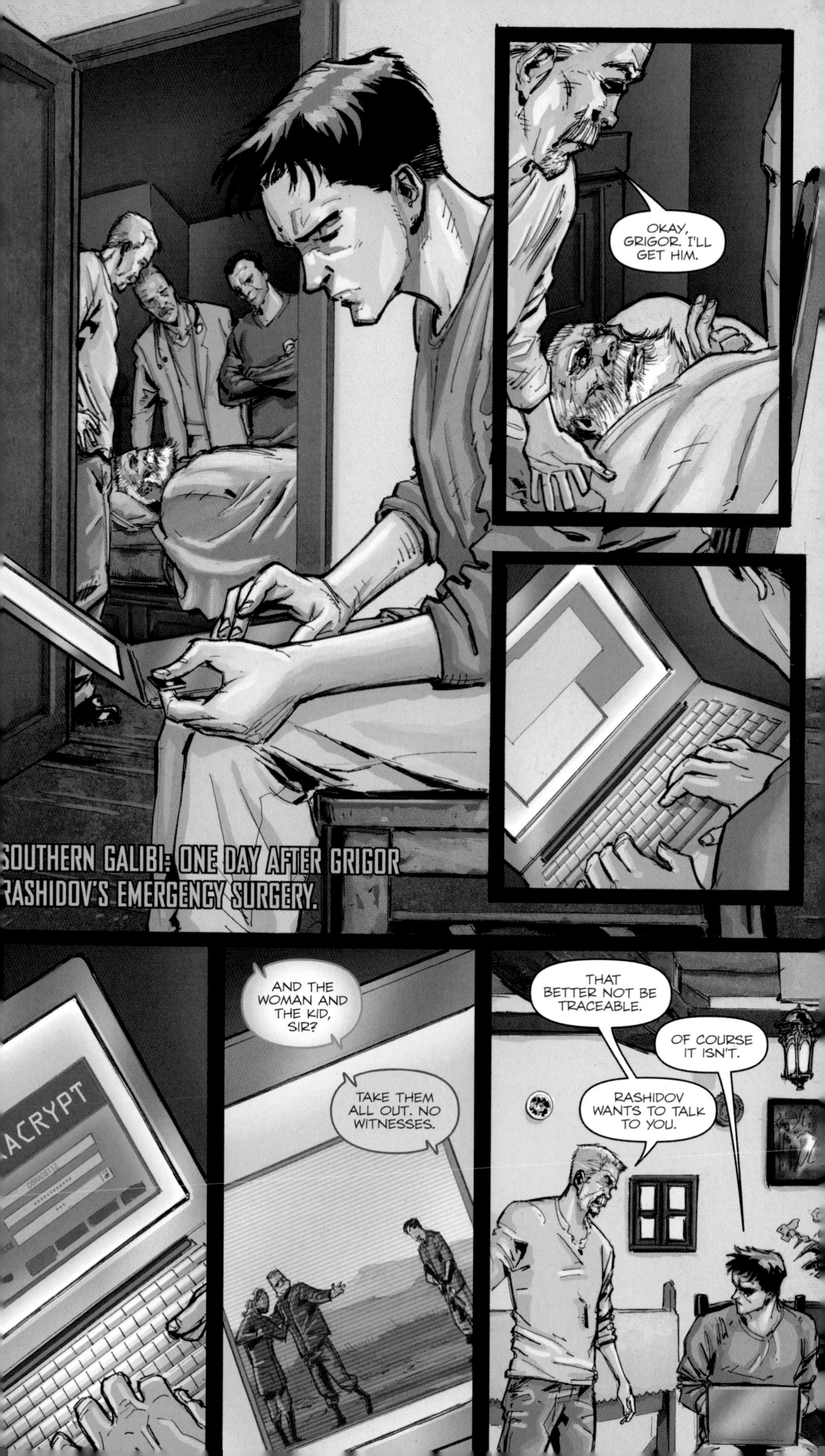
OKAY, GRIGOR. I'LL GET HIM.
SOUTHERN GALIBI: ONE DAY AFTER GRIGOR RASHIDOV'S EMERGENCY SURGERY.
ACRYPT
AND THE WOMAN AND THE KID, SIR?
TAKE THEM ALL OUT. NO WITNESSES.
THAT BETTER NOT BE TRACEABLE.
OF COURSE IT ISN'T.
RASHIDOV WANTS TO TALK TO YOU.

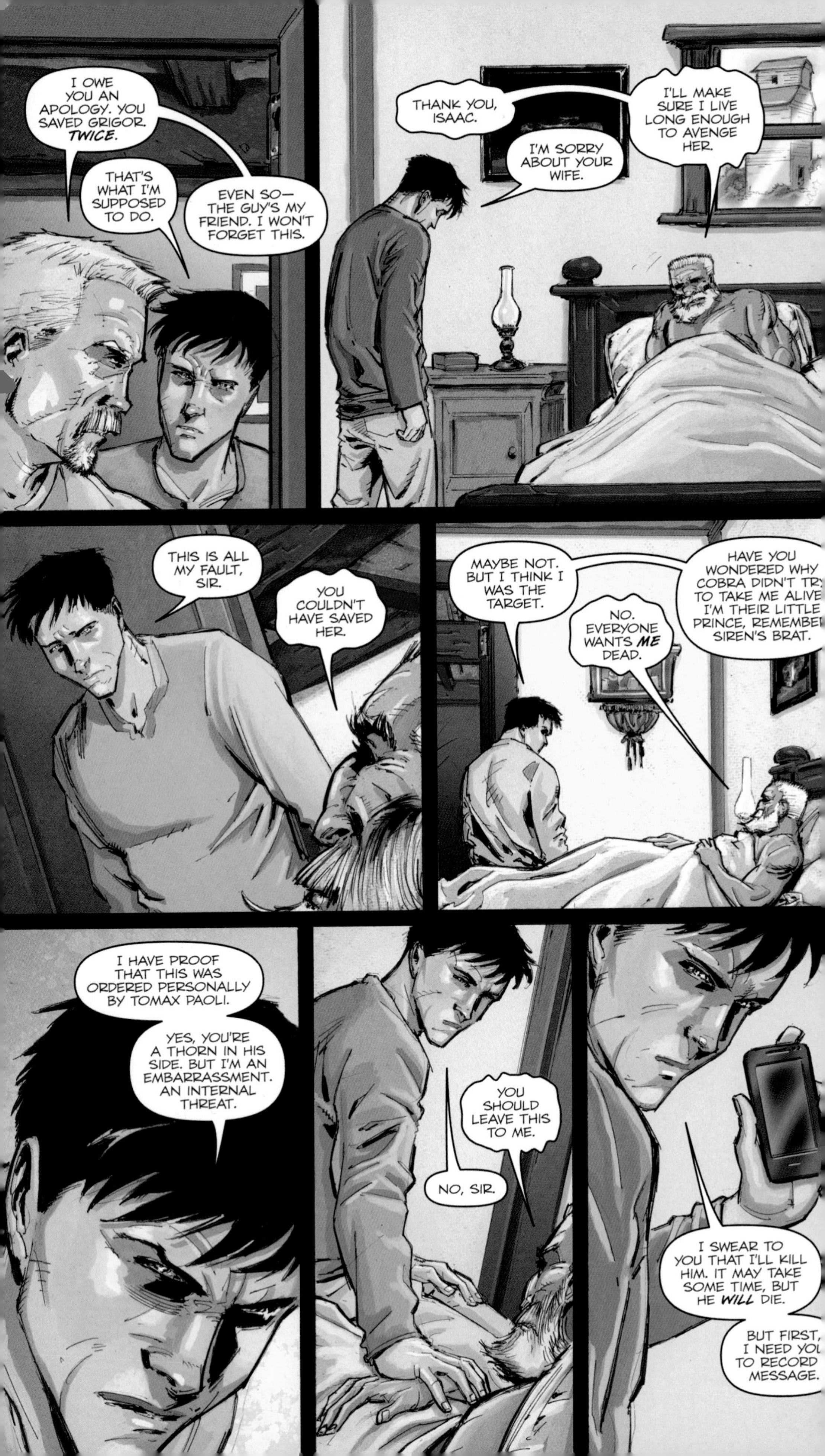
I OWE YOU AN APOLOGY. YOU SAVED GRIGOR. TWICE.
THAT'S WHAT I'M SUPPOSED TO DO.
EVEN SO— THE GUY'S MY FRIEND. I WON'T FORGET THIS.
THANK YOU, ISAAC.
I'M SORRY ABOUT YOUR WIFE.
I'LL MAKE SURE I LIVE LONG ENOUGH TO AVENGE HER.
THIS IS ALL MY FAULT, SIR.
YOU COULDN'T HAVE SAVED HER.
MAYBE NOT. BUT I THINK I WAS THE TARGET.
NO. EVERYONE WANTS ME DEAD.
HAVE YOU WONDERED WHY COBRA DIDN'T TR TO TAKE ME ALIVE I'M THEIR LITTLE PRINCE, REMEMBE SIREN'S BRAT.
I HAVE PROOF THAT THIS WAS ORDERED PERSONALLY BY TOMAX PAOLI.
YES, YOU'RE A THORN IN HIS SIDE. BUT I'M AN EMBARRASSMENT. AN INTERNAL THREAT.
YOU SHOULD LEAVE THIS TO ME.
NO, SIR.
I SWEAR TO YOU THAT I'LL KILL HIM. IT MAY TAKE SOME TIME, BUT HE WILL DIE.
BUT FIRST, I NEED YO TO RECORD MESSAGE.

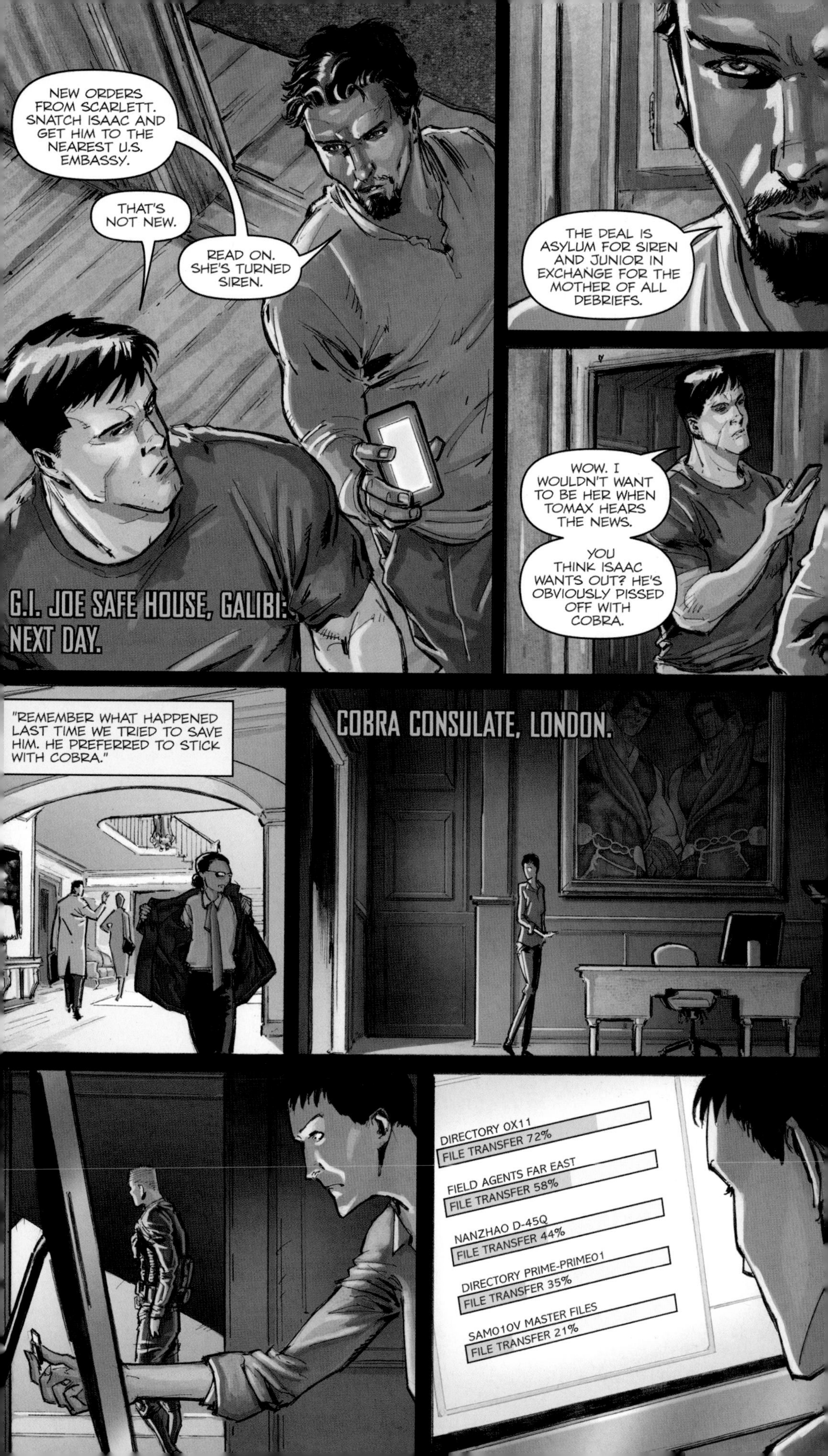

G.I. JOE SAFE HOUSE, GALIBI: NEXT DAY.
NEW ORDERS FROM SCARLETT. SNATCH ISAAC AND GET HIM TO THE NEAREST U.S. EMBASSY.
THAT'S NOT NEW.
READ ON. SHE'S TURNED SIREN.
THE DEAL IS ASYLUM FOR SIREN AND JUNIOR IN EXCHANGE FOR THE MOTHER OF ALL DEBRIEFS.
WOW. I WOULDN'T WANT TO BE HER WHEN TOMAX HEARS THE NEWS.
YOU THINK ISAAC WANTS OUT? HE'S OBVIOUSLY PISSED OFF WITH COBRA.
"REMEMBER WHAT HAPPENED LAST TIME WE TRIED TO SAVE HIM. HE PREFERRED TO STICK WITH COBRA."
COBRA CONSULATE, LONDON.
DIRECTORY 0X11
FILE TRANSFER 72%
FIELD AGENTS FAR EAST
FILE TRANSFER 58%
NANZHAO D-45Q
FILE TRANSFER 44%
DIRECTORY PRIME-PRIME01
FILE TRANSFER 35%
SAM010V MASTER FILES
FILE TRANSFER 21%

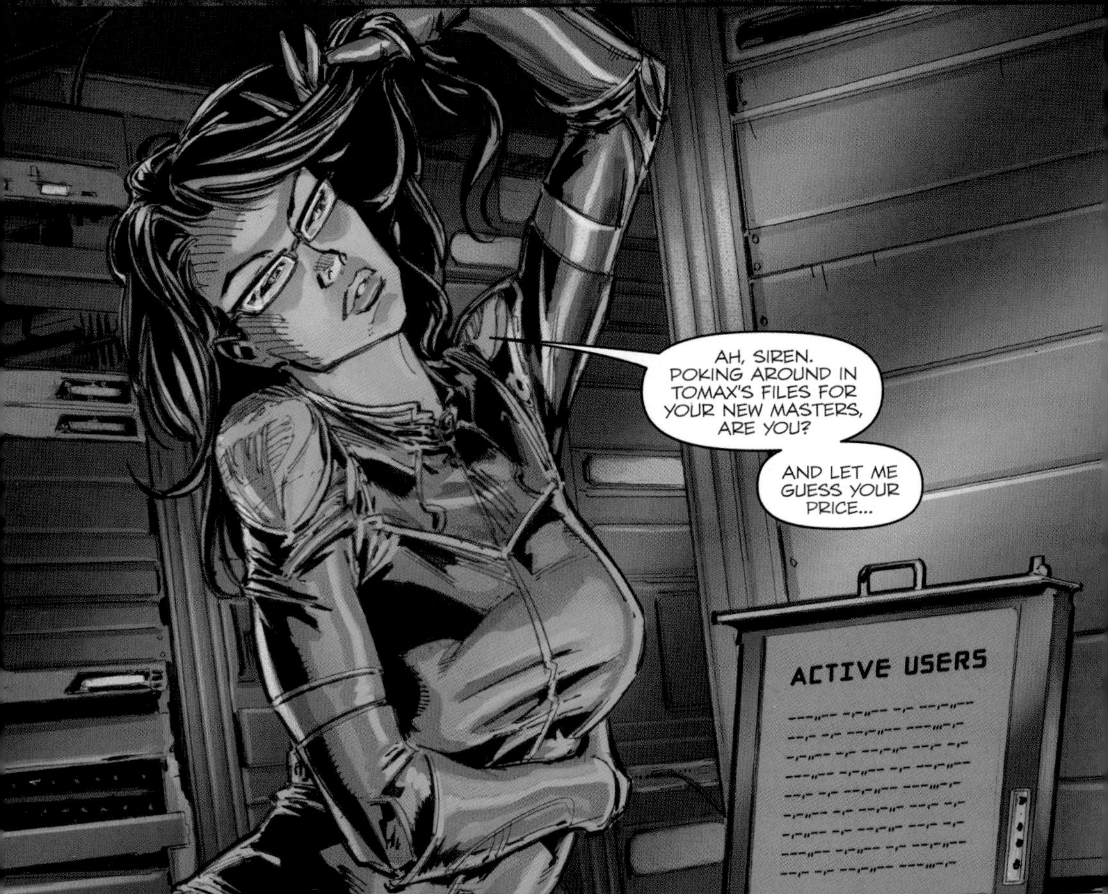
AH, SIREN. POKING AROUND IN TOMAX'S FILES FOR YOUR NEW MASTERS, ARE YOU?
AND LET ME GUESS YOUR PRICE...
ACTIVE USERS

THE FALL OF G.I. JOE
CONCLUSION

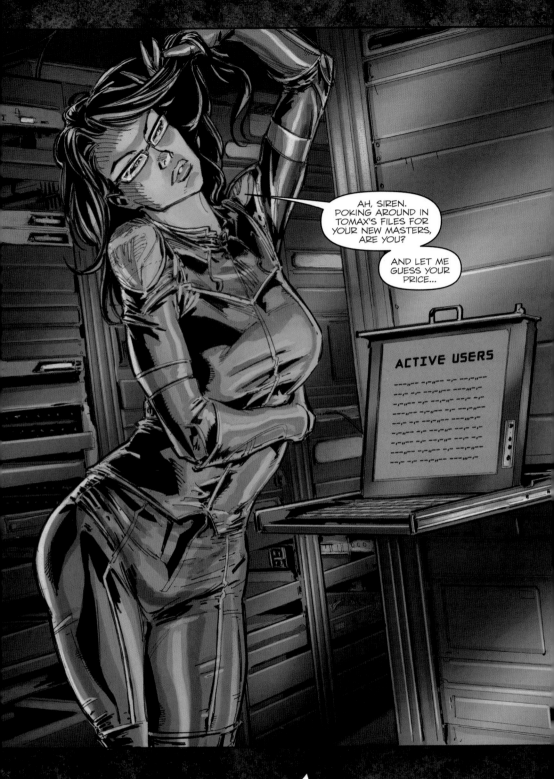

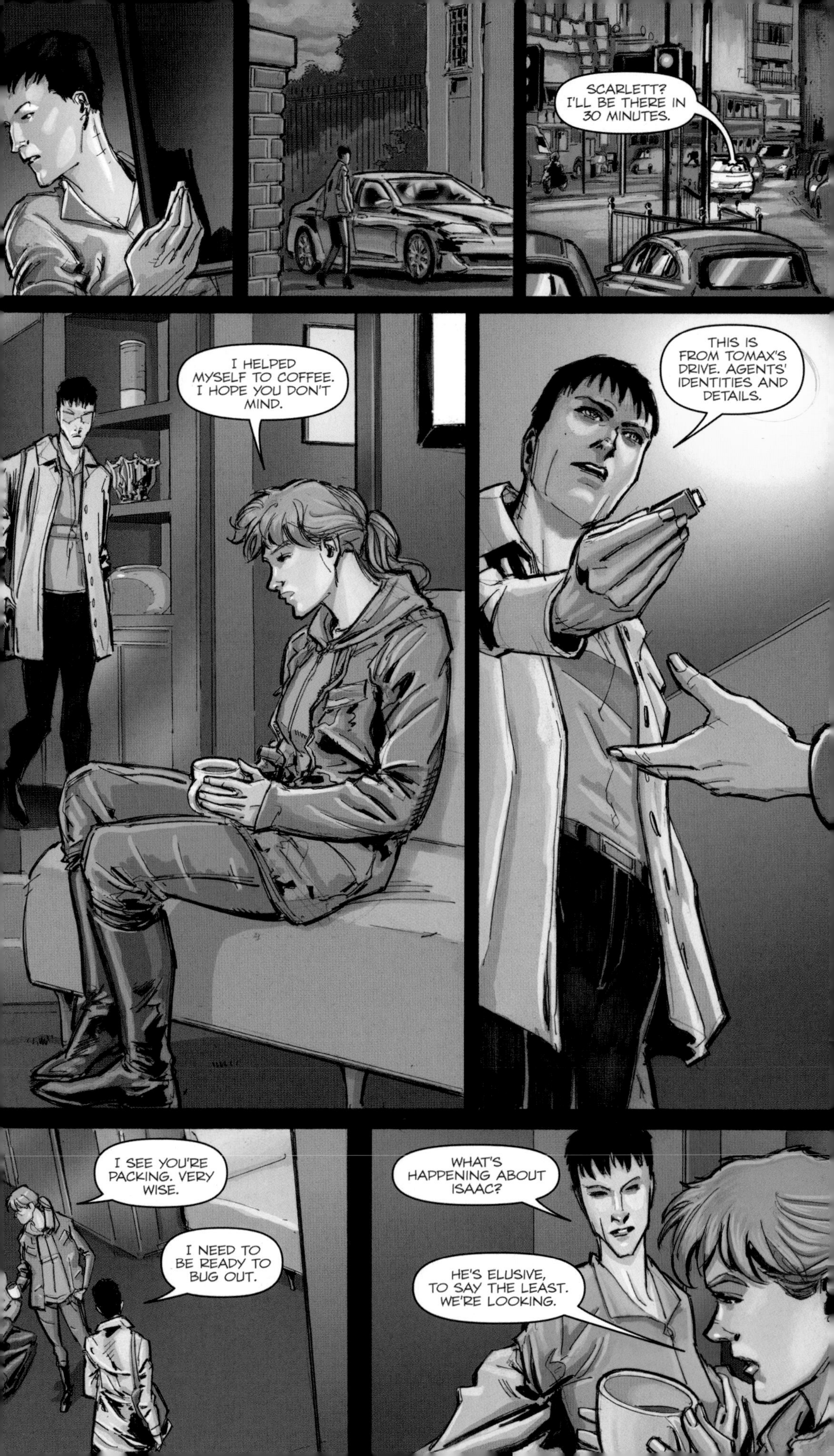
SCARLETT? I'LL BE THERE IN 30 MINUTES.
I HELPED MYSELF TO COFFEE. I HOPE YOU DON'T MIND.
THIS IS FROM TOMAX'S DRIVE. AGENTS' IDENTITIES AND DETAILS.
I SEE YOU'RE PACKING. VERY WISE.
I NEED TO BE READY TO BUG OUT.
WHAT'S HAPPENING ABOUT ISAAC?
HE'S ELUSIVE, TO SAY THE LEAST. WE'RE LOOKING.

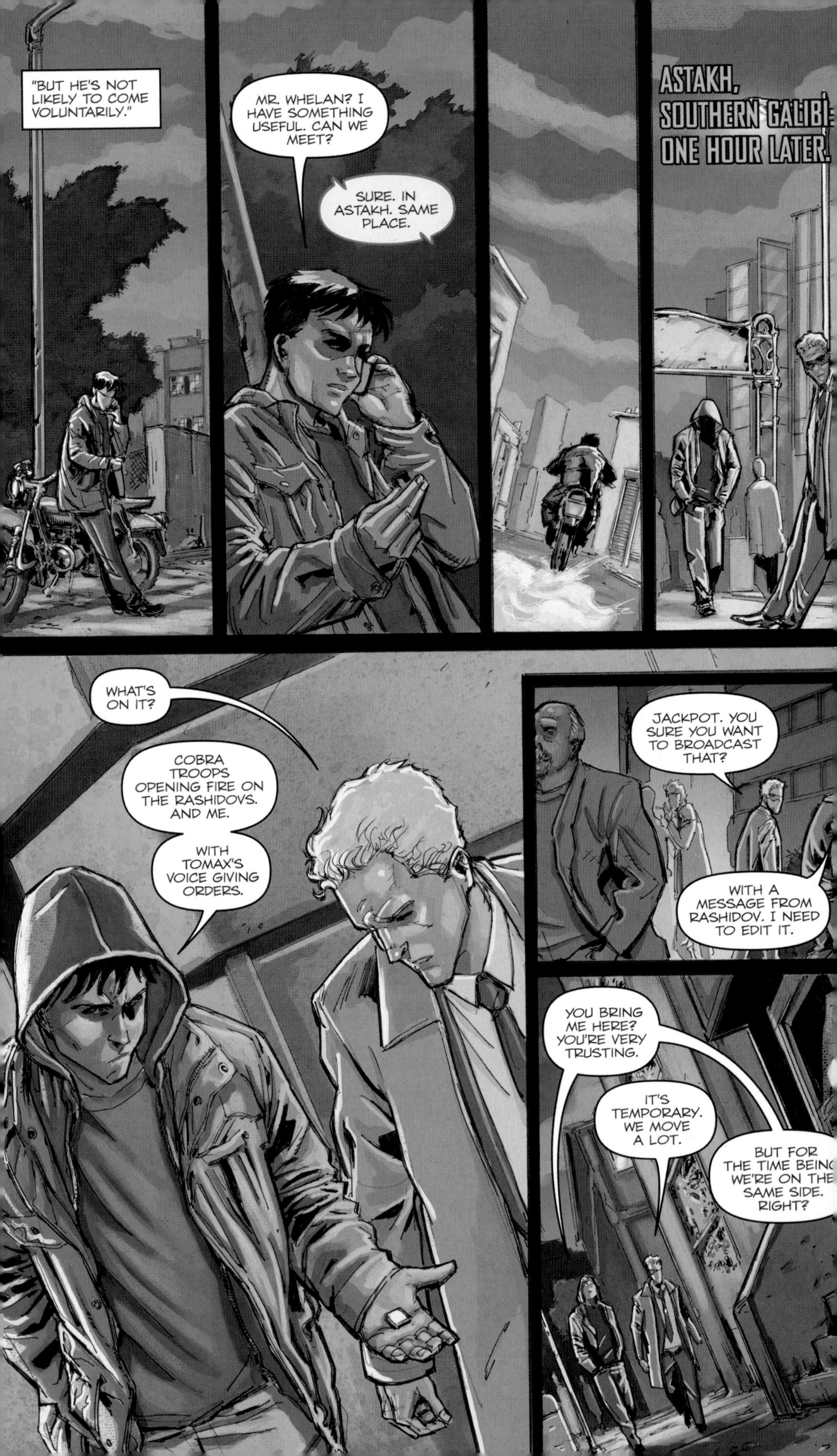
"BUT HE'S NOT LIKELY TO COME VOLUNTARILY."
MR. WHELAN? I HAVE SOMETHING USEFUL. CAN WE MEET?
SURE. IN ASTAKH. SAME PLACE.
ASTAKH, SOUTHERN GALIBI: ONE HOUR LATER.
WHAT'S ON IT?
COBRA TROOPS OPENING FIRE ON THE RASHIDOVS. AND ME.
WITH TOMAX'S VOICE GIVING ORDERS.
JACKPOT. YOU SURE YOU WANT TO BROADCAST THAT?
WITH A MESSAGE FROM RASHIDOV. I NEED TO EDIT IT.
YOU BRING ME HERE? YOU'RE VERY TRUSTING.
IT'S TEMPORARY. WE MOVE A LOT.
BUT FOR THE TIME BEING WE'RE ON THE SAME SIDE. RIGHT?

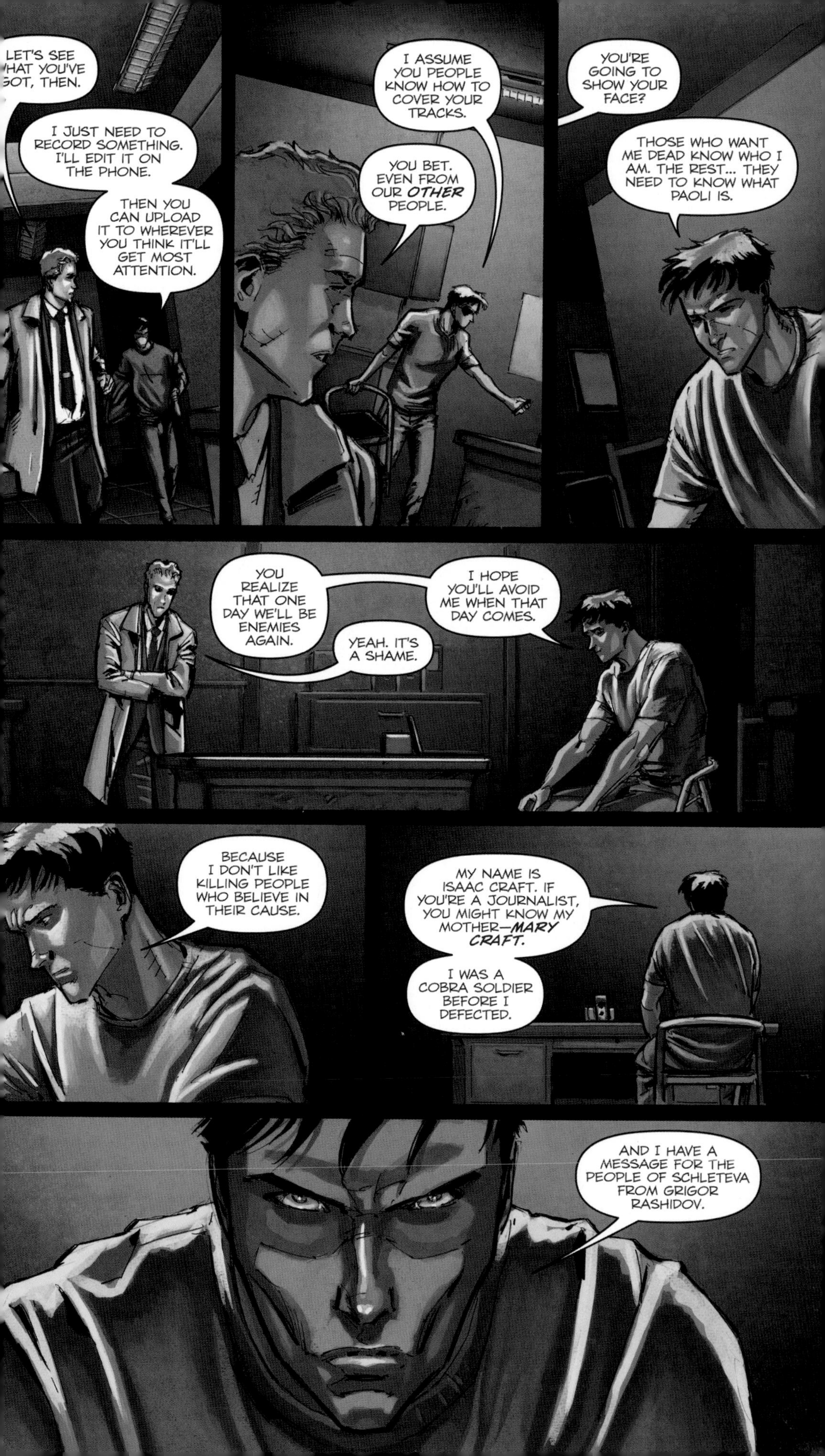

LET'S SEE WHAT YOU'VE GOT, THEN.
I JUST NEED TO RECORD SOMETHING. I'LL EDIT IT ON THE PHONE.
THEN YOU CAN UPLOAD IT TO WHEREVER YOU THINK IT'LL GET MOST ATTENTION.
I ASSUME YOU PEOPLE KNOW HOW TO COVER YOUR TRACKS.
YOU BET. EVEN FROM OUR OTHER PEOPLE.
YOU'RE GOING TO SHOW YOUR FACE?
THOSE WHO WANT ME DEAD KNOW WHO I AM. THE REST... THEY NEED TO KNOW WHAT PAOLI IS.
YOU REALIZE THAT ONE DAY WE'LL BE ENEMIES AGAIN.
YEAH. IT'S A SHAME.
I HOPE YOU'LL AVOID ME WHEN THAT DAY COMES.
BECAUSE I DON'T LIKE KILLING PEOPLE WHO BELIEVE IN THEIR CAUSE.
MY NAME IS ISAAC CRAFT. IF YOU'RE A JOURNALIST, YOU MIGHT KNOW MY MOTHER—MARY CRAFT.
I WAS A COBRA SOLDIER BEFORE I DEFECTED.
AND I HAVE A MESSAGE FOR THE PEOPLE OF SCHLETEVA FROM GRIGOR RASHIDOV.

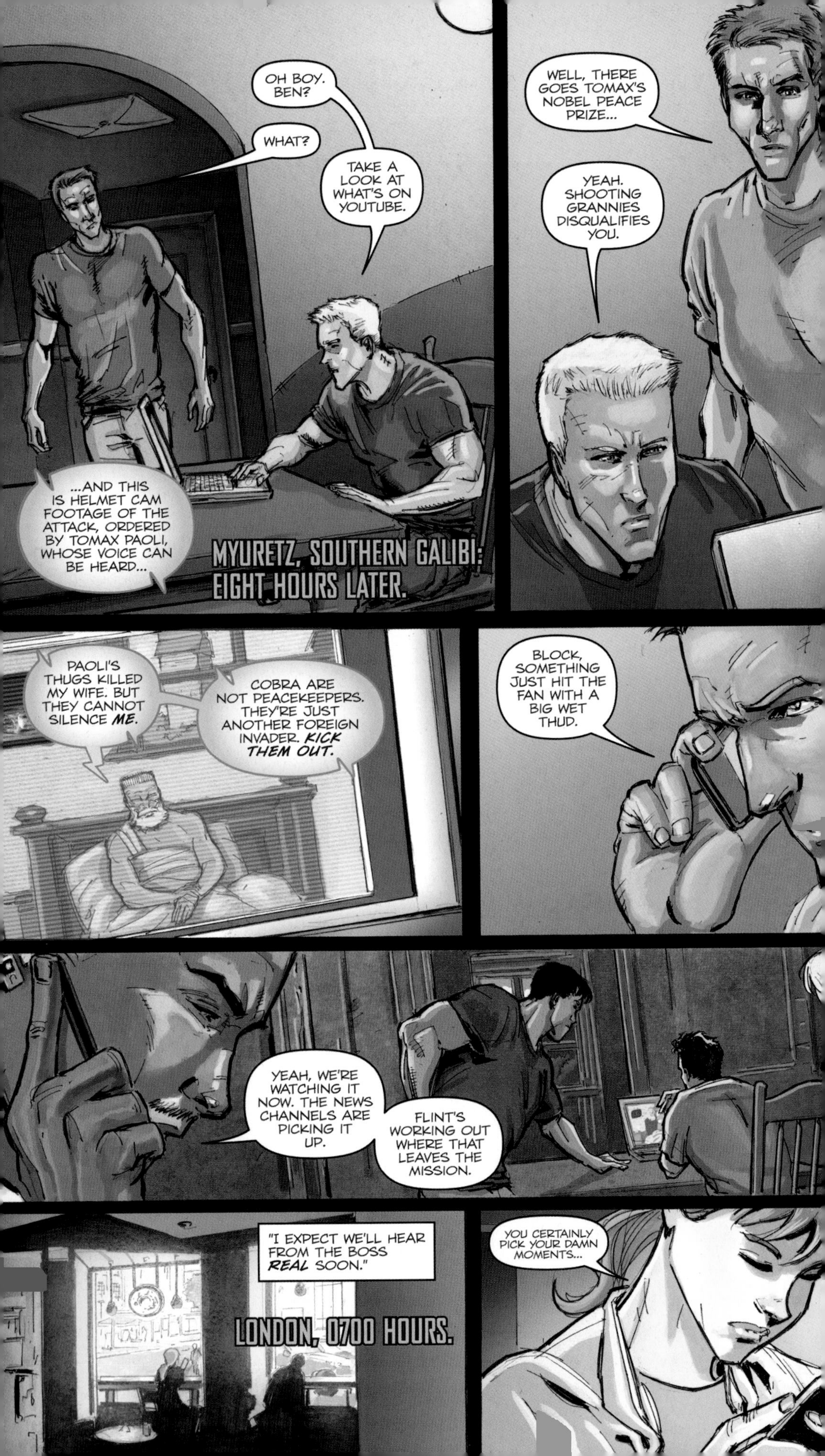
OH BOY. BEN?
WHAT?
TAKE A LOOK AT WHAT'S ON YOUTUBE.
...AND THIS IS HELMET CAM FOOTAGE OF THE ATTACK, ORDERED BY TOMAX PAOLI, WHOSE VOICE CAN BE HEARD...
MYURETZ, SOUTHERN GALIBI: EIGHT HOURS LATER.
WELL, THERE GOES TOMAX'S NOBEL PEACE PRIZE...
YEAH. SHOOTING GRANNIES DISQUALIFIES YOU.
PAOLI'S THUGS KILLED MY WIFE. BUT THEY CANNOT SILENCE *ME*.
COBRA ARE NOT PEACEKEEPERS. THEY'RE JUST ANOTHER FOREIGN INVADER. *KICK THEM OUT*.
BLOCK, SOMETHING JUST HIT THE FAN WITH A BIG WET THUD.
YEAH, WE'RE WATCHING IT NOW. THE NEWS CHANNELS ARE PICKING IT UP.
FLINT'S WORKING OUT WHERE THAT LEAVES THE MISSION.
"I EXPECT WE'LL HEAR FROM THE BOSS *REAL* SOON."
LONDON, 0700 HOURS.
YOU CERTAINLY PICK YOUR DAMN MOMENTS...

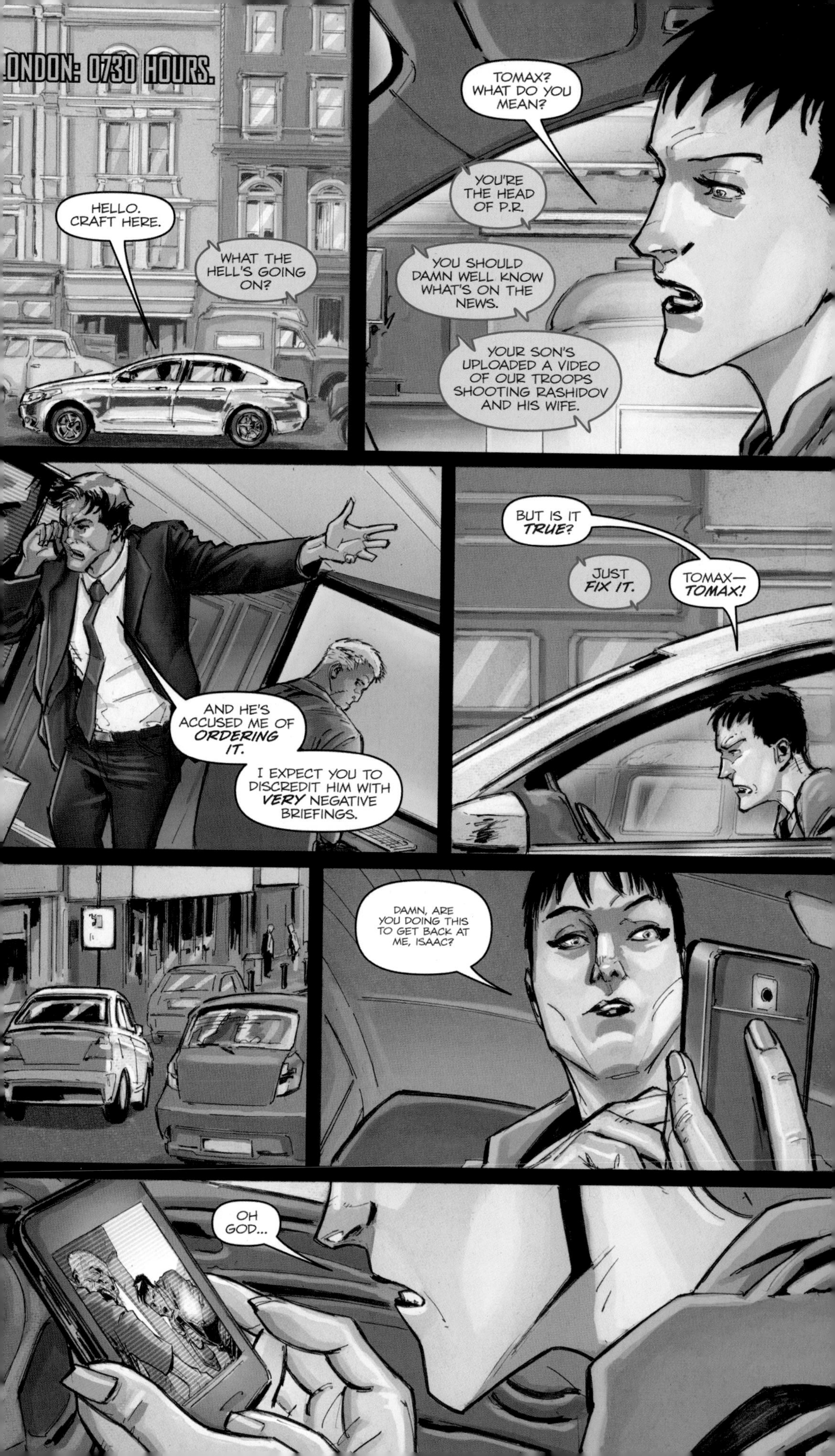
LONDON: 0730 HOURS.
HELLO. CRAFT HERE.
WHAT THE HELL'S GOING ON?
TOMAX? WHAT DO YOU MEAN?
YOU'RE THE HEAD OF P.R.
YOU SHOULD DAMN WELL KNOW WHAT'S ON THE NEWS.
YOUR SON'S UPLOADED A VIDEO OF OUR TROOPS SHOOTING RASHIDOV AND HIS WIFE.
AND HE'S ACCUSED ME OF *ORDERING IT.*
I EXPECT YOU TO DISCREDIT HIM WITH *VERY* NEGATIVE BRIEFINGS.
BUT IS IT *TRUE?*
JUST *FIX IT.*
TOMAX— *TOMAX!*
DAMN, ARE YOU DOING THIS TO GET BACK AT ME, ISAAC?
OH GOD...

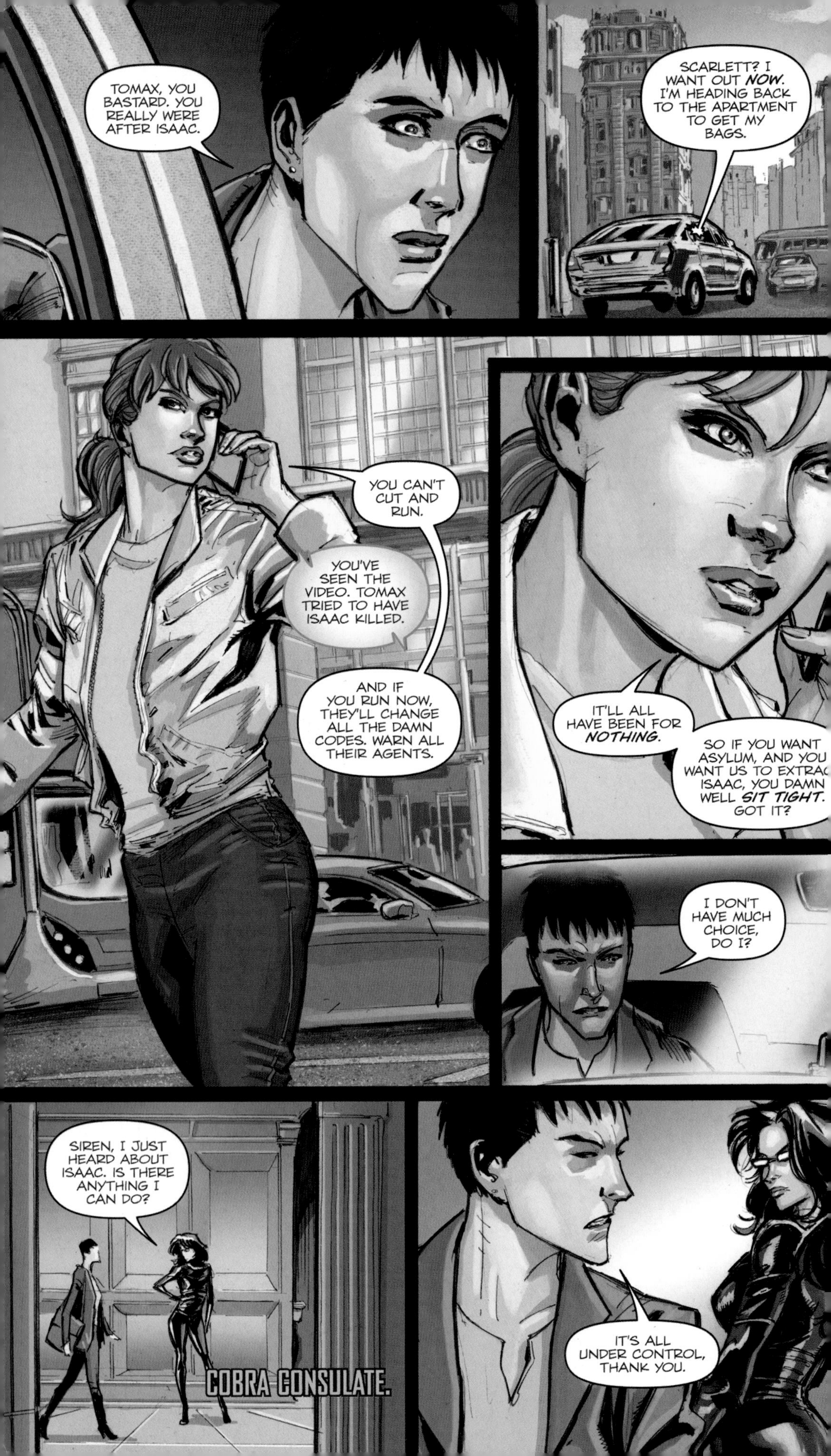
TOMAX, YOU BASTARD. YOU REALLY WERE AFTER ISAAC.
SCARLETT? I WANT OUT *NOW*. I'M HEADING BACK TO THE APARTMENT TO GET MY BAGS.
YOU CAN'T CUT AND RUN.
YOU'VE SEEN THE VIDEO. TOMAX TRIED TO HAVE ISAAC KILLED.
AND IF YOU RUN NOW, THEY'LL CHANGE ALL THE DAMN CODES. WARN ALL THEIR AGENTS.
IT'LL ALL HAVE BEEN FOR *NOTHING*.
SO IF YOU WANT ASYLUM, AND YOU WANT US TO EXTRAC ISAAC, YOU DAMN WELL *SIT TIGHT*. GOT IT?
I DON'T HAVE MUCH CHOICE, DO I?
SIREN, I JUST HEARD ABOUT ISAAC. IS THERE ANYTHING I CAN DO?
COBRA CONSULATE.
IT'S ALL UNDER CONTROL, THANK YOU.

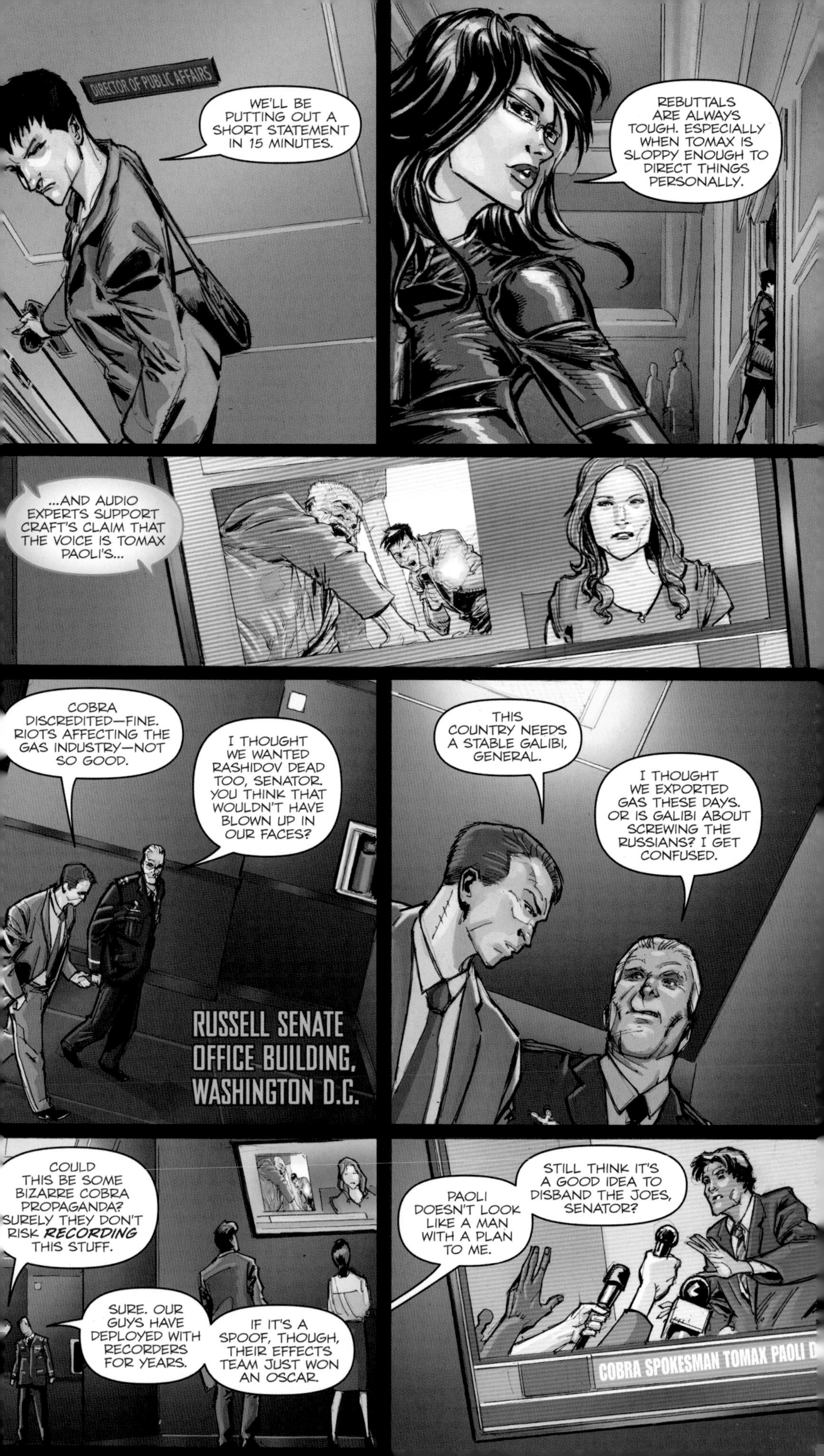
DIRECTOR OF PUBLIC AFFAIRS
WE'LL BE PUTTING OUT A SHORT STATEMENT IN 15 MINUTES.
REBUTTALS ARE ALWAYS TOUGH. ESPECIALLY WHEN TOMAX IS SLOPPY ENOUGH TO DIRECT THINGS PERSONALLY.
...AND AUDIO EXPERTS SUPPORT CRAFT'S CLAIM THAT THE VOICE IS TOMAX PAOLI'S...
RUSSELL SENATE OFFICE BUILDING, WASHINGTON D.C.
COBRA DISCREDITED—FINE. RIOTS AFFECTING THE GAS INDUSTRY—NOT SO GOOD.
I THOUGHT WE WANTED RASHIDOV DEAD TOO, SENATOR. YOU THINK THAT WOULDN'T HAVE BLOWN UP IN OUR FACES?
THIS COUNTRY NEEDS A STABLE GALIBI, GENERAL.
I THOUGHT WE EXPORTED GAS THESE DAYS. OR IS GALIBI ABOUT SCREWING THE RUSSIANS? I GET CONFUSED.
COULD THIS BE SOME BIZARRE COBRA PROPAGANDA? SURELY THEY DON'T RISK *RECORDING* THIS STUFF.
SURE. OUR GUYS HAVE DEPLOYED WITH RECORDERS FOR YEARS.
IF IT'S A SPOOF, THOUGH, THEIR EFFECTS TEAM JUST WON AN OSCAR.
STILL THINK IT'S A GOOD IDEA TO DISBAND THE JOES, SENATOR?
PAOLI DOESN'T LOOK LIKE A MAN WITH A PLAN TO ME.
COBRA SPOKESMAN TOMAX PAOLI D

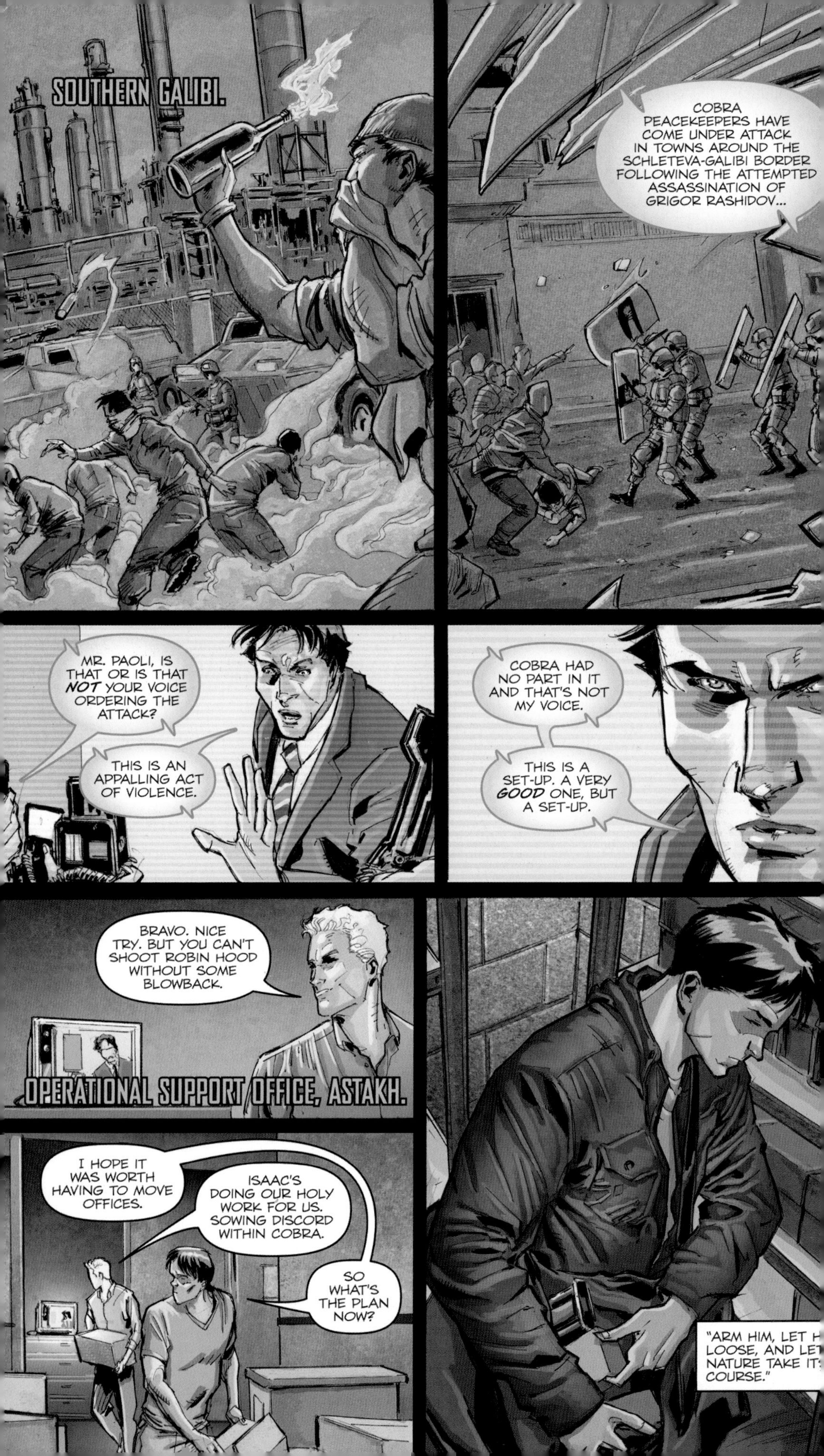
SOUTHERN GALIBI.
COBRA PEACEKEEPERS HAVE COME UNDER ATTACK IN TOWNS AROUND THE SCHLETEVA-GALIBI BORDER FOLLOWING THE ATTEMPTED ASSASSINATION OF GRIGOR RASHIDOV...
MR. PAOLI, IS THAT OR IS THAT NOT YOUR VOICE ORDERING THE ATTACK?
THIS IS AN APPALLING ACT OF VIOLENCE.
COBRA HAD NO PART IN IT AND THAT'S NOT MY VOICE.
THIS IS A SET-UP. A VERY GOOD ONE, BUT A SET-UP.
BRAVO. NICE TRY. BUT YOU CAN'T SHOOT ROBIN HOOD WITHOUT SOME BLOWBACK.
OPERATIONAL SUPPORT OFFICE, ASTAKH.
I HOPE IT WAS WORTH HAVING TO MOVE OFFICES.
ISAAC'S DOING OUR HOLY WORK FOR US. SOWING DISCORD WITHIN COBRA.
SO WHAT'S THE PLAN NOW?

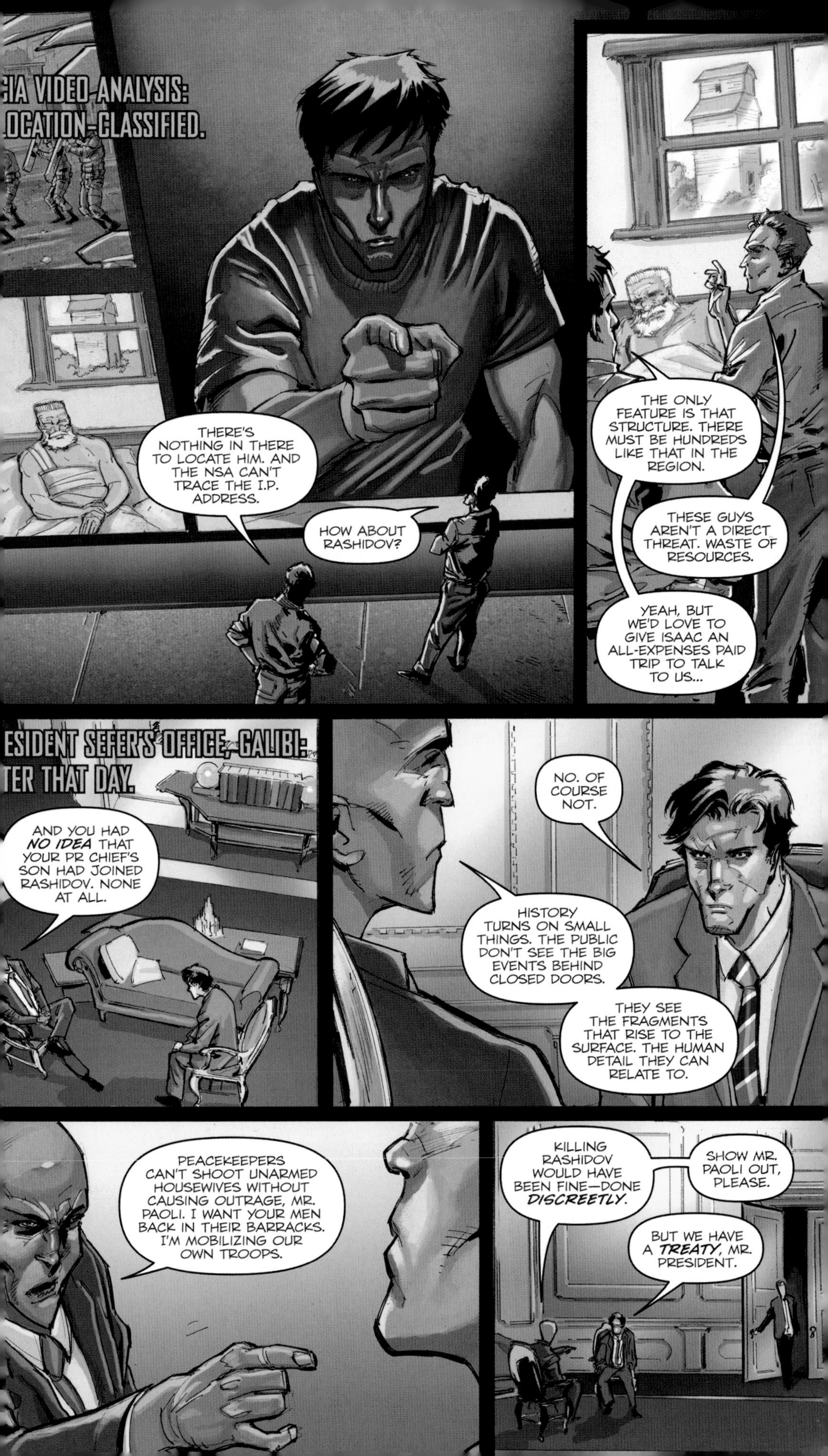
CIA VIDEO ANALYSIS: LOCATION CLASSIFIED.
THERE'S NOTHING IN THERE TO LOCATE HIM. AND THE NSA CAN'T TRACE THE I.P. ADDRESS.
HOW ABOUT RASHIDOV?
THE ONLY FEATURE IS THAT STRUCTURE. THERE MUST BE HUNDREDS LIKE THAT IN THE REGION.
THESE GUYS AREN'T A DIRECT THREAT. WASTE OF RESOURCES.
YEAH, BUT WE'D LOVE TO GIVE ISAAC AN ALL-EXPENSES PAID TRIP TO TALK TO US...
ESIDENT SEFER'S OFFICE, GALIBI: TER THAT DAY.
AND YOU HAD *NO IDEA* THAT YOUR PR CHIEF'S SON HAD JOINED RASHIDOV. NONE AT ALL.
NO. OF COURSE NOT.
HISTORY TURNS ON SMALL THINGS. THE PUBLIC DON'T SEE THE BIG EVENTS BEHIND CLOSED DOORS.
THEY SEE THE FRAGMENTS THAT RISE TO THE SURFACE. THE HUMAN DETAIL THEY CAN RELATE TO.
PEACEKEEPERS CAN'T SHOOT UNARMED HOUSEWIVES WITHOUT CAUSING OUTRAGE, MR. PAOLI. I WANT YOUR MEN BACK IN THEIR BARRACKS. I'M MOBILIZING OUR OWN TROOPS.
KILLING RASHIDOV WOULD HAVE BEEN FINE—DONE *DISCREETLY*.
SHOW MR. PAOLI OUT, PLEASE.
BUT WE HAVE A *TREATY*, MR. PRESIDENT.

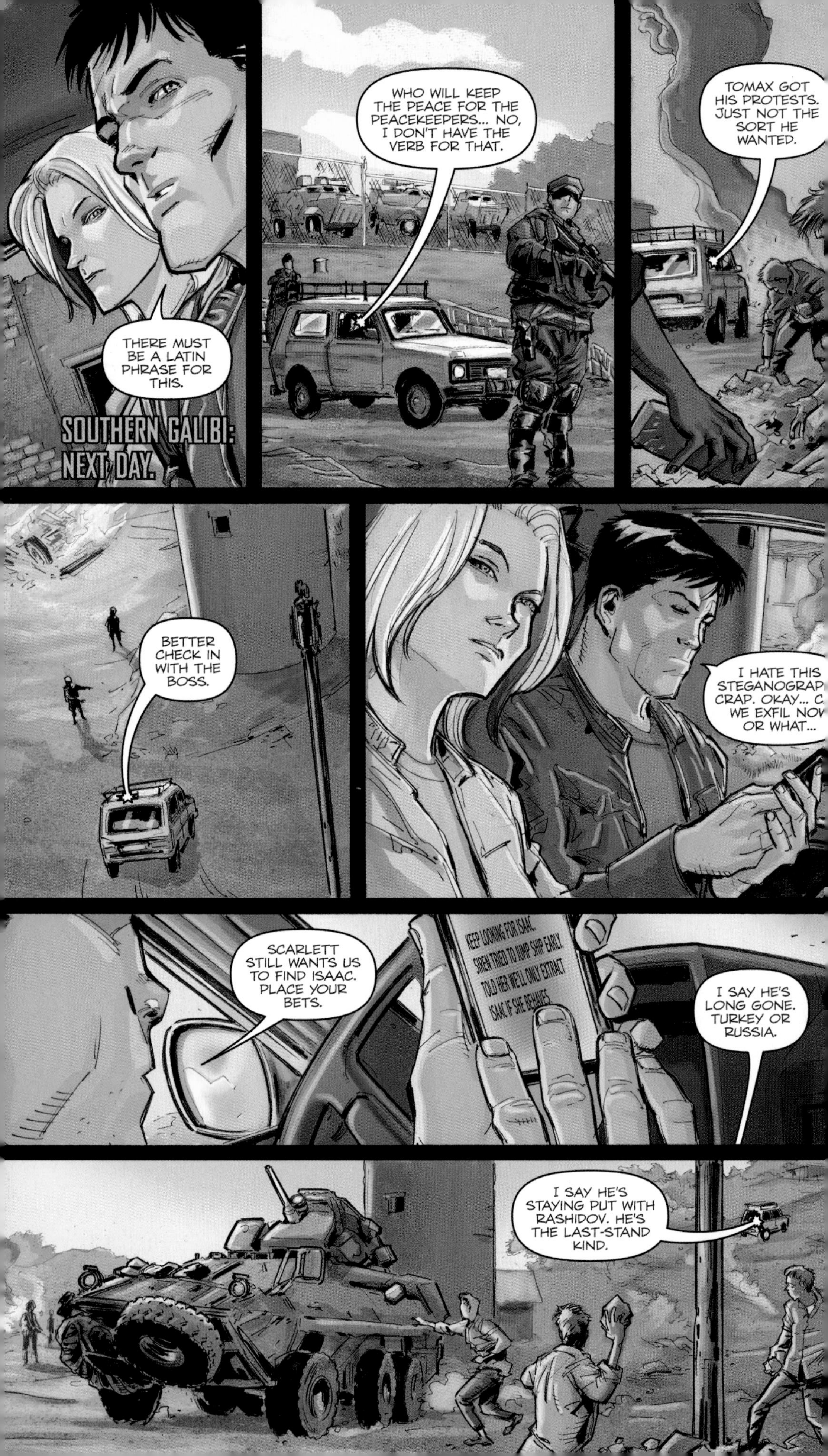
SOUTHERN GALIBI: NEXT DAY.
THERE MUST BE A LATIN PHRASE FOR THIS.
WHO WILL KEEP THE PEACE FOR THE PEACEKEEPERS... NO, I DON'T HAVE THE VERB FOR THAT.
TOMAX GOT HIS PROTESTS. JUST NOT THE SORT HE WANTED.
BETTER CHECK IN WITH THE BOSS.
I HATE THIS STEGANOGRAP CRAP. OKAY... C WE EXFIL NOV OR WHAT...
SCARLETT STILL WANTS US TO FIND ISAAC. PLACE YOUR BETS.
KEEP LOOKING FOR ISAAC. SIREN TRIED TO JUMP SHIP EARLY. TOLD HER WE'LL ONLY EXTRACT ISAAC IF SHE BEHAVES.
I SAY HE'S LONG GONE. TURKEY OR RUSSIA.
I SAY HE'S STAYING PUT WITH RASHIDOV. HE'S THE LAST-STAND KIND.

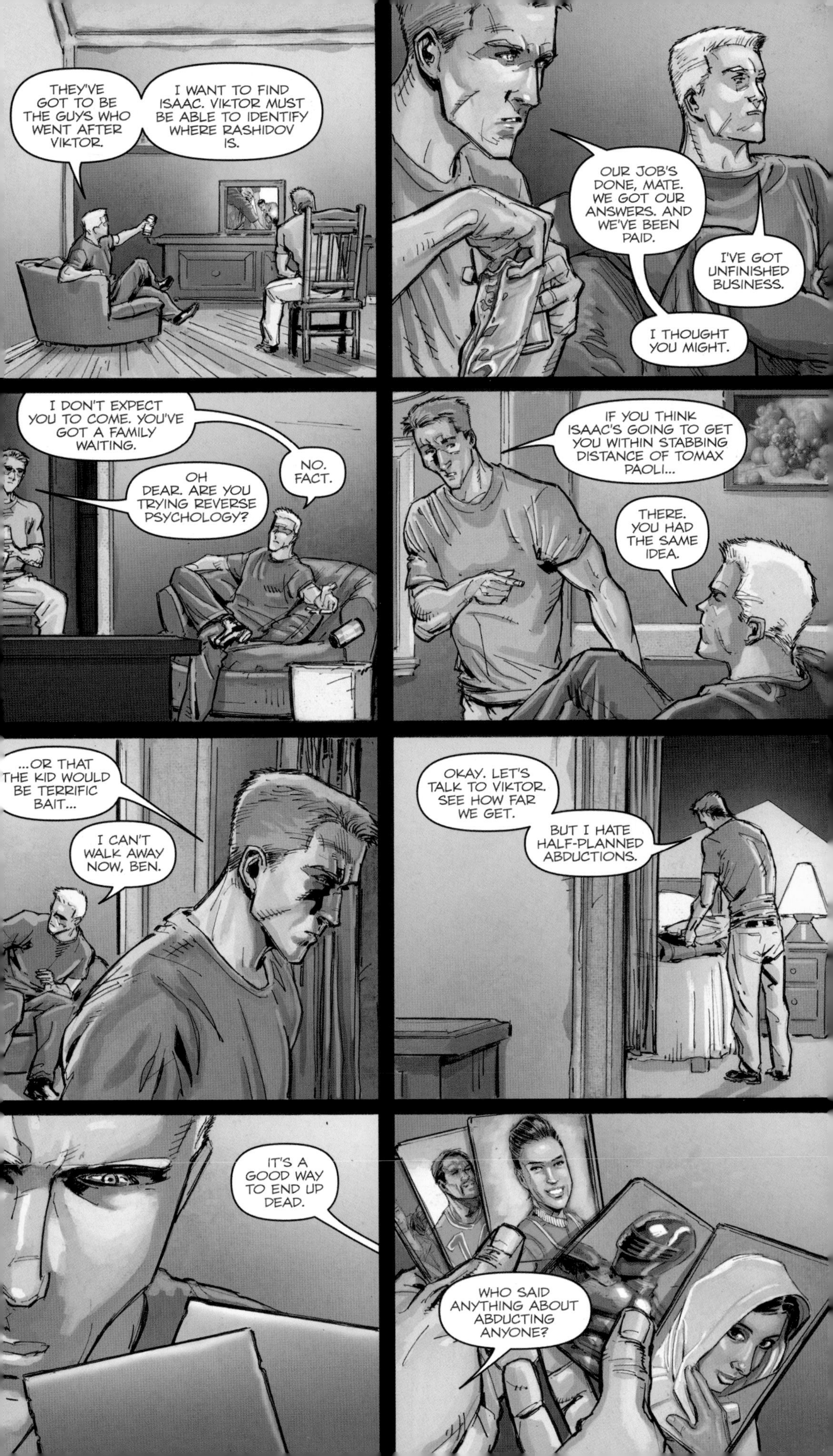
THEY'VE GOT TO BE THE GUYS WHO WENT AFTER VIKTOR.
I WANT TO FIND ISAAC. VIKTOR MUST BE ABLE TO IDENTIFY WHERE RASHIDOV IS.
OUR JOB'S DONE, MATE. WE GOT OUR ANSWERS. AND WE'VE BEEN PAID.
I'VE GOT UNFINISHED BUSINESS.
I THOUGHT YOU MIGHT.
I DON'T EXPECT YOU TO COME. YOU'VE GOT A FAMILY WAITING.
OH DEAR. ARE YOU TRYING REVERSE PSYCHOLOGY?
NO. FACT.
IF YOU THINK ISAAC'S GOING TO GET YOU WITHIN STABBING DISTANCE OF TOMAX PAOLI...
THERE. YOU HAD THE SAME IDEA.
...OR THAT THE KID WOULD BE TERRIFIC BAIT...
I CAN'T WALK AWAY NOW, BEN.
OKAY. LET'S TALK TO VIKTOR. SEE HOW FAR WE GET.
BUT I HATE HALF-PLANNED ABDUCTIONS.
IT'S A GOOD WAY TO END UP DEAD.
WHO SAID ANYTHING ABOUT ABDUCTING ANYONE?

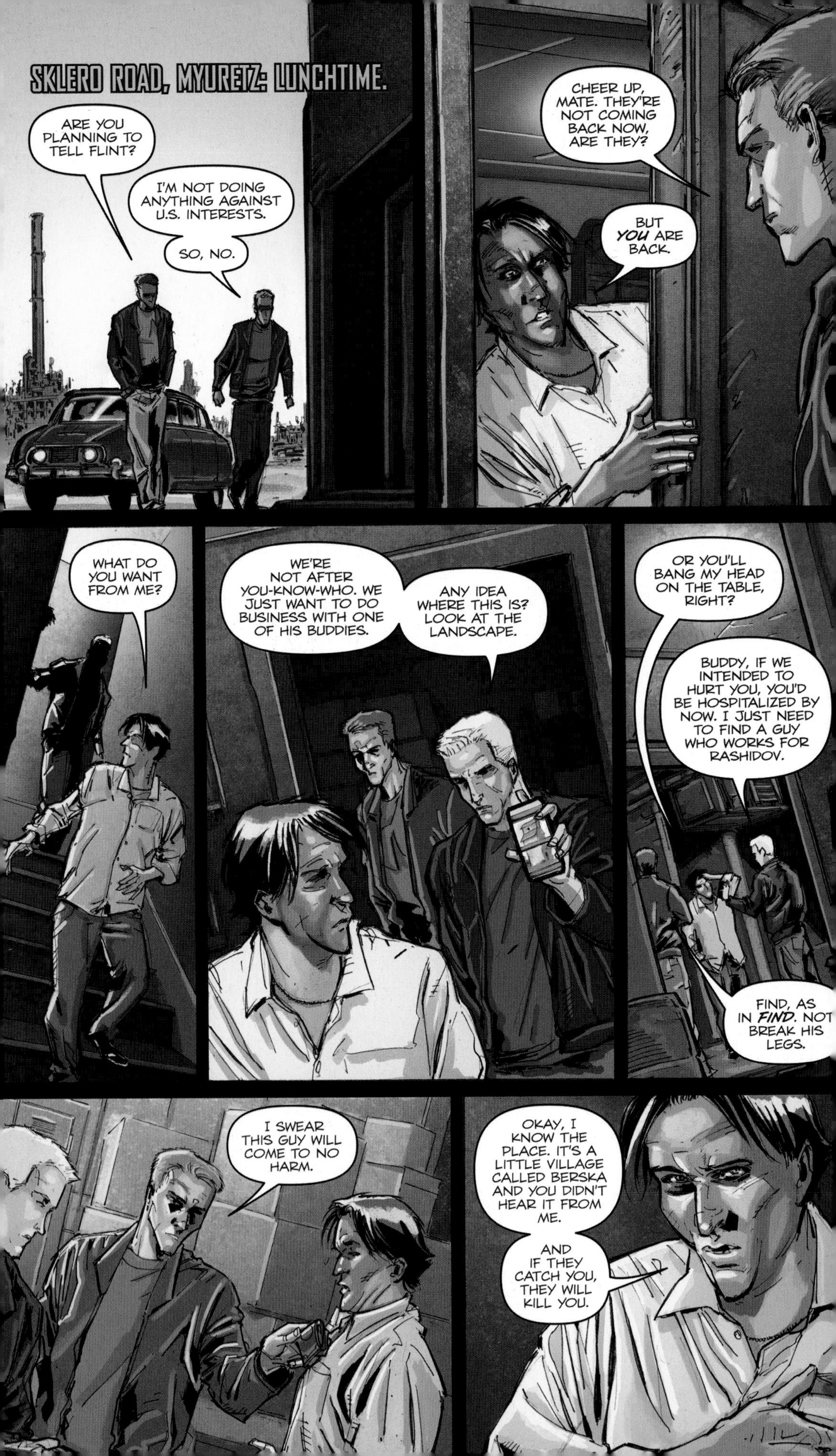
SKLERO ROAD, MYURETZ: LUNCHTIME.
ARE YOU PLANNING TO TELL FLINT?
I'M NOT DOING ANYTHING AGAINST U.S. INTERESTS.
SO, NO.
CHEER UP, MATE. THEY'RE NOT COMING BACK NOW, ARE THEY?
BUT YOU ARE BACK.
WHAT DO YOU WANT FROM ME?
WE'RE NOT AFTER YOU-KNOW-WHO. WE JUST WANT TO DO BUSINESS WITH ONE OF HIS BUDDIES.
ANY IDEA WHERE THIS IS? LOOK AT THE LANDSCAPE.
OR YOU'LL BANG MY HEAD ON THE TABLE, RIGHT?
BUDDY, IF WE INTENDED TO HURT YOU, YOU'D BE HOSPITALIZED BY NOW. I JUST NEED TO FIND A GUY WHO WORKS FOR RASHIDOV.
FIND, AS IN FIND. NOT BREAK HIS LEGS.
I SWEAR THIS GUY WILL COME TO NO HARM.
OKAY, I KNOW THE PLACE. IT'S A LITTLE VILLAGE CALLED BERSKA AND YOU DIDN'T HEAR IT FROM ME.
AND IF THEY CATCH YOU, THEY WILL KILL YOU.

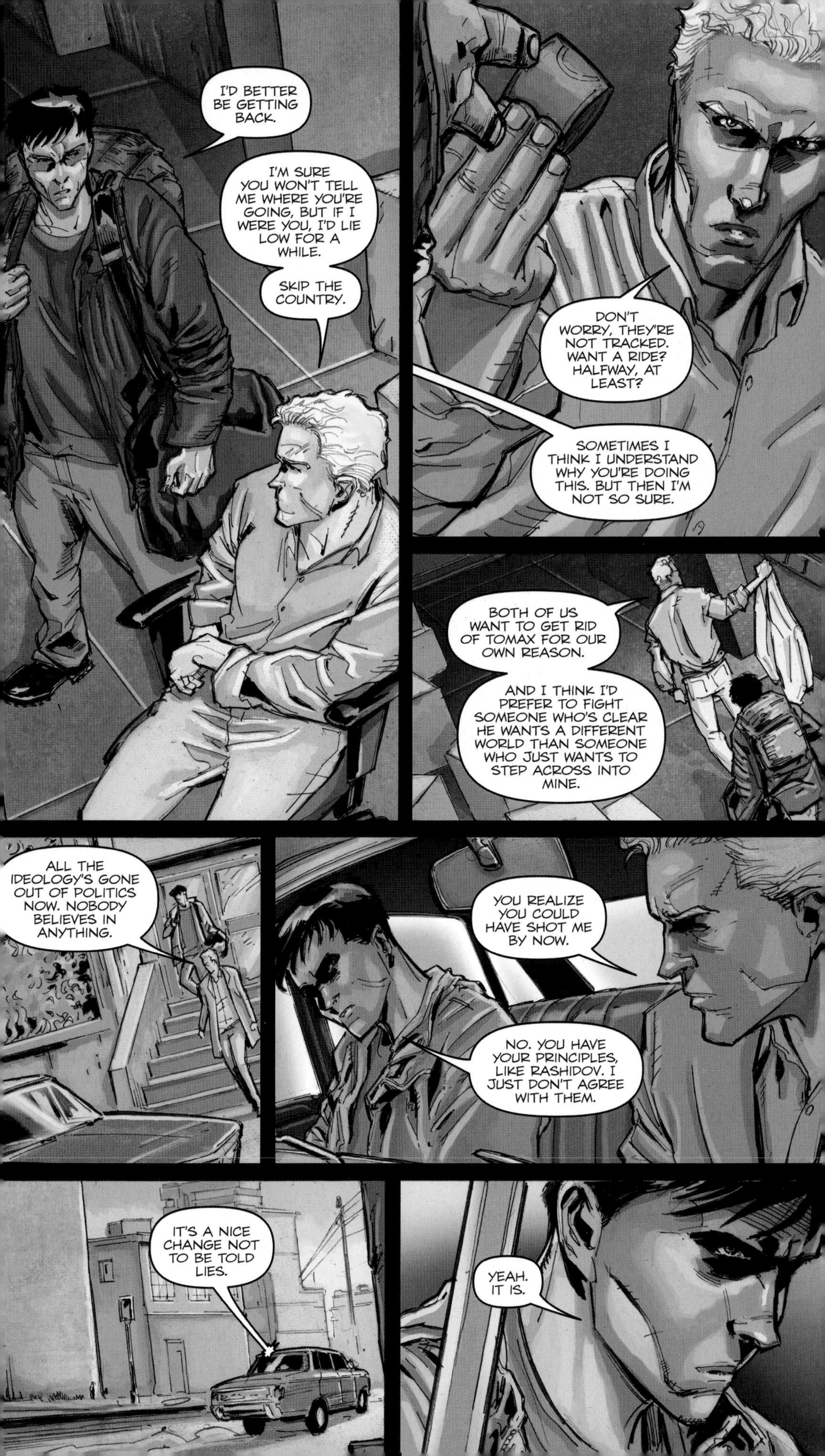
I'D BETTER BE GETTING BACK.
I'M SURE YOU WON'T TELL ME WHERE YOU'RE GOING, BUT IF I WERE YOU, I'D LIE LOW FOR A WHILE.
SKIP THE COUNTRY.
DON'T WORRY, THEY'RE NOT TRACKED. WANT A RIDE? HALFWAY, AT LEAST?
SOMETIMES I THINK I UNDERSTAND WHY YOU'RE DOING THIS. BUT THEN I'M NOT SO SURE.
BOTH OF US WANT TO GET RID OF TOMAX FOR OUR OWN REASON.
AND I THINK I'D PREFER TO FIGHT SOMEONE WHO'S CLEAR HE WANTS A DIFFERENT WORLD THAN SOMEONE WHO JUST WANTS TO STEP ACROSS INTO MINE.
ALL THE IDEOLOGY'S GONE OUT OF POLITICS NOW. NOBODY BELIEVES IN ANYTHING.
YOU REALIZE YOU COULD HAVE SHOT ME BY NOW.
NO. YOU HAVE YOUR PRINCIPLES, LIKE RASHIDOV. I JUST DON'T AGREE WITH THEM.
IT'S A NICE CHANGE NOT TO BE TOLD LIES.
YEAH. IT IS.

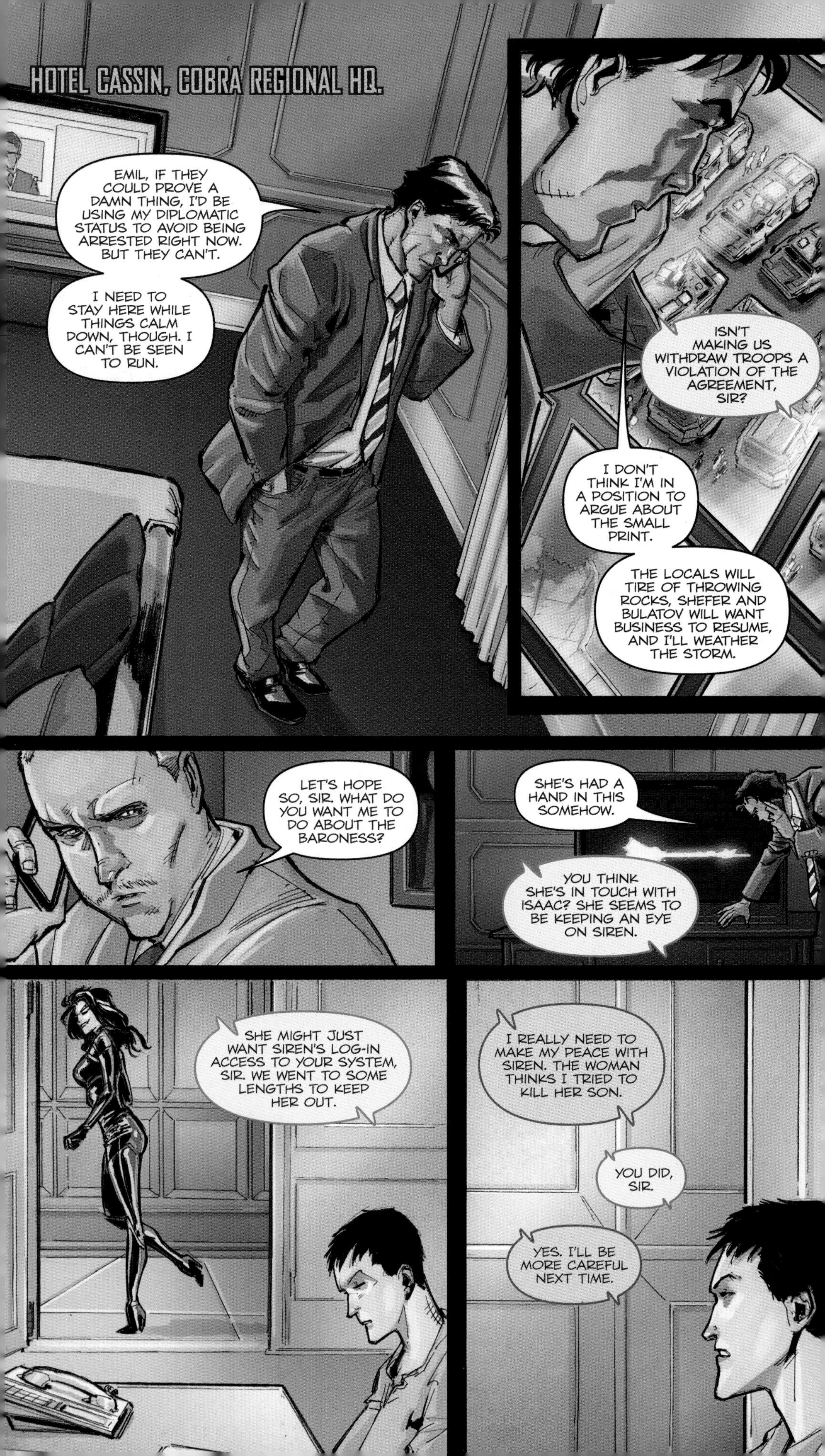
HOTEL CASSIN, COBRA REGIONAL HQ.
EMIL, IF THEY COULD PROVE A DAMN THING, I'D BE USING MY DIPLOMATIC STATUS TO AVOID BEING ARRESTED RIGHT NOW. BUT THEY CAN'T.
I NEED TO STAY HERE WHILE THINGS CALM DOWN, THOUGH. I CAN'T BE SEEN TO RUN.
ISN'T MAKING US WITHDRAW TROOPS A VIOLATION OF THE AGREEMENT, SIR?
I DON'T THINK I'M IN A POSITION TO ARGUE ABOUT THE SMALL PRINT.
THE LOCALS WILL TIRE OF THROWING ROCKS, SHEFER AND BULATOV WILL WANT BUSINESS TO RESUME, AND I'LL WEATHER THE STORM.
LET'S HOPE SO, SIR. WHAT DO YOU WANT ME TO DO ABOUT THE BARONESS?
SHE'S HAD A HAND IN THIS SOMEHOW.
YOU THINK SHE'S IN TOUCH WITH ISAAC? SHE SEEMS TO BE KEEPING AN EYE ON SIREN.
SHE MIGHT JUST WANT SIREN'S LOG-IN ACCESS TO YOUR SYSTEM, SIR. WE WENT TO SOME LENGTHS TO KEEP HER OUT.
I REALLY NEED TO MAKE MY PEACE WITH SIREN. THE WOMAN THINKS I TRIED TO KILL HER SON.
YOU DID, SIR.
YES. I'LL BE MORE CAREFUL NEXT TIME.

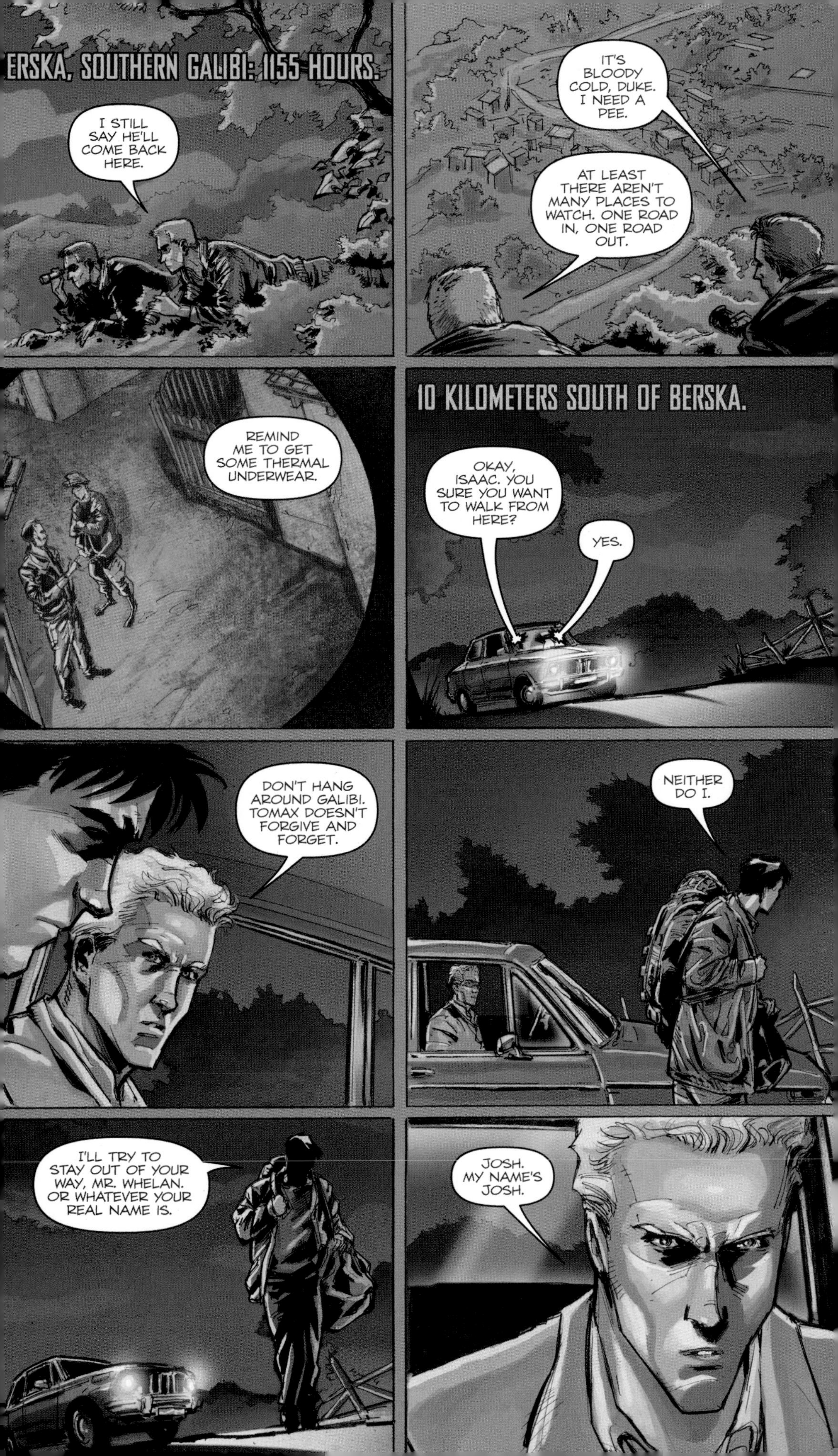
ERSKA, SOUTHERN GALIBI: 1155 HOURS.
I STILL SAY HE'LL COME BACK HERE.
IT'S BLOODY COLD, DUKE. I NEED A PEE.
AT LEAST THERE AREN'T MANY PLACES TO WATCH. ONE ROAD IN, ONE ROAD OUT.
REMIND ME TO GET SOME THERMAL UNDERWEAR.
10 KILOMETERS SOUTH OF BERSKA.
OKAY, ISAAC. YOU SURE YOU WANT TO WALK FROM HERE?
YES.
DON'T HANG AROUND GALIBI. TOMAX DOESN'T FORGIVE AND FORGET.
NEITHER DO I.
I'LL TRY TO STAY OUT OF YOUR WAY, MR. WHELAN. OR WHATEVER YOUR REAL NAME IS.
JOSH. MY NAME'S JOSH.

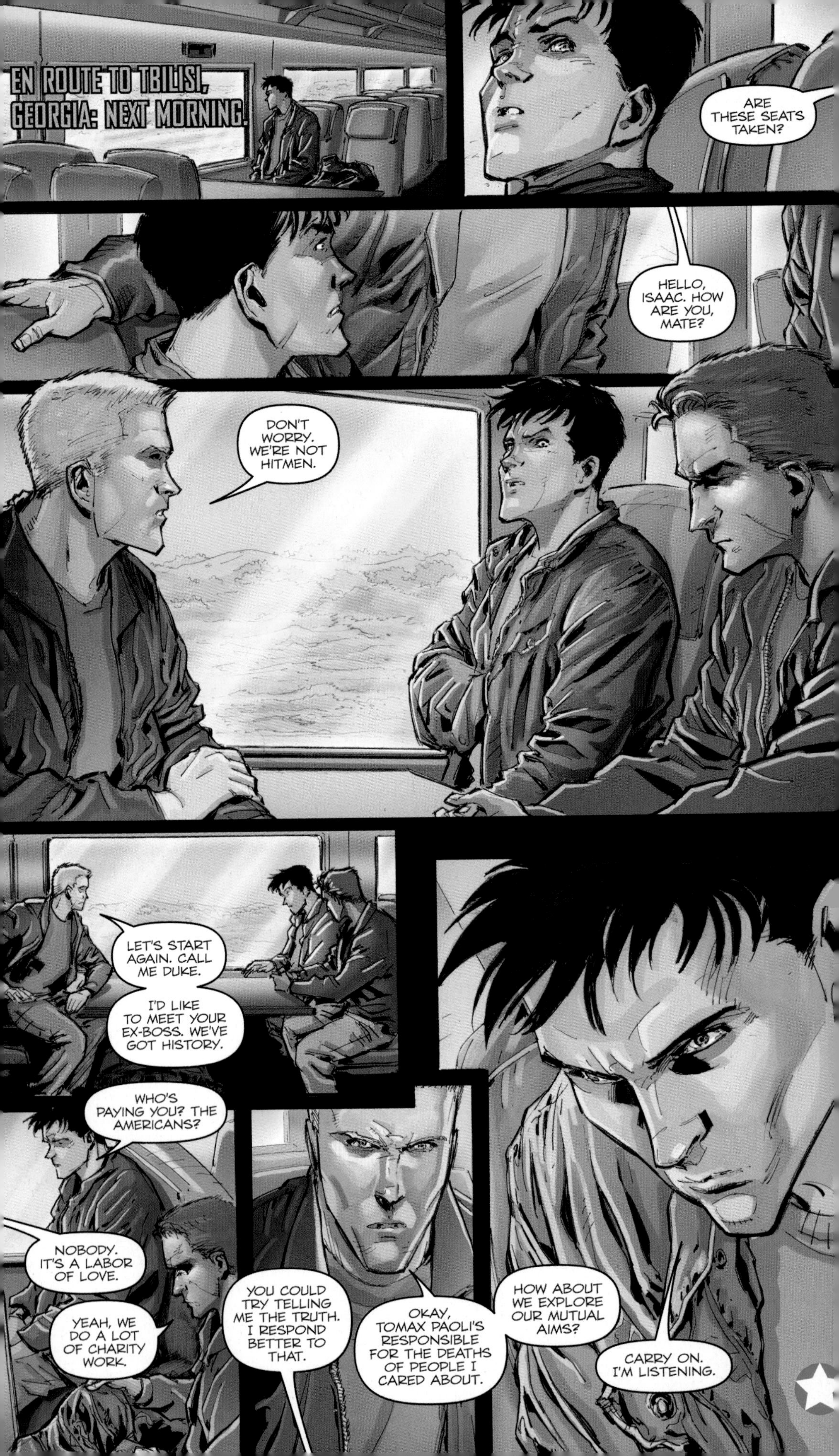
EN ROUTE TO TBILISI, GEORGIA: NEXT MORNING.
ARE THESE SEATS TAKEN?
HELLO, ISAAC. HOW ARE YOU, MATE?
DON'T WORRY. WE'RE NOT HITMEN.
LET'S START AGAIN. CALL ME DUKE.
I'D LIKE TO MEET YOUR EX-BOSS. WE'VE GOT HISTORY.
WHO'S PAYING YOU? THE AMERICANS?
NOBODY. IT'S A LABOR OF LOVE.
YEAH, WE DO A LOT OF CHARITY WORK.
YOU COULD TRY TELLING ME THE TRUTH. I RESPOND BETTER TO THAT.
OKAY, TOMAX PAOLI'S RESPONSIBLE FOR THE DEATHS OF PEOPLE I CARED ABOUT.
HOW ABOUT WE EXPLORE OUR MUTUAL AIMS?
CARRY ON. I'M LISTENING.

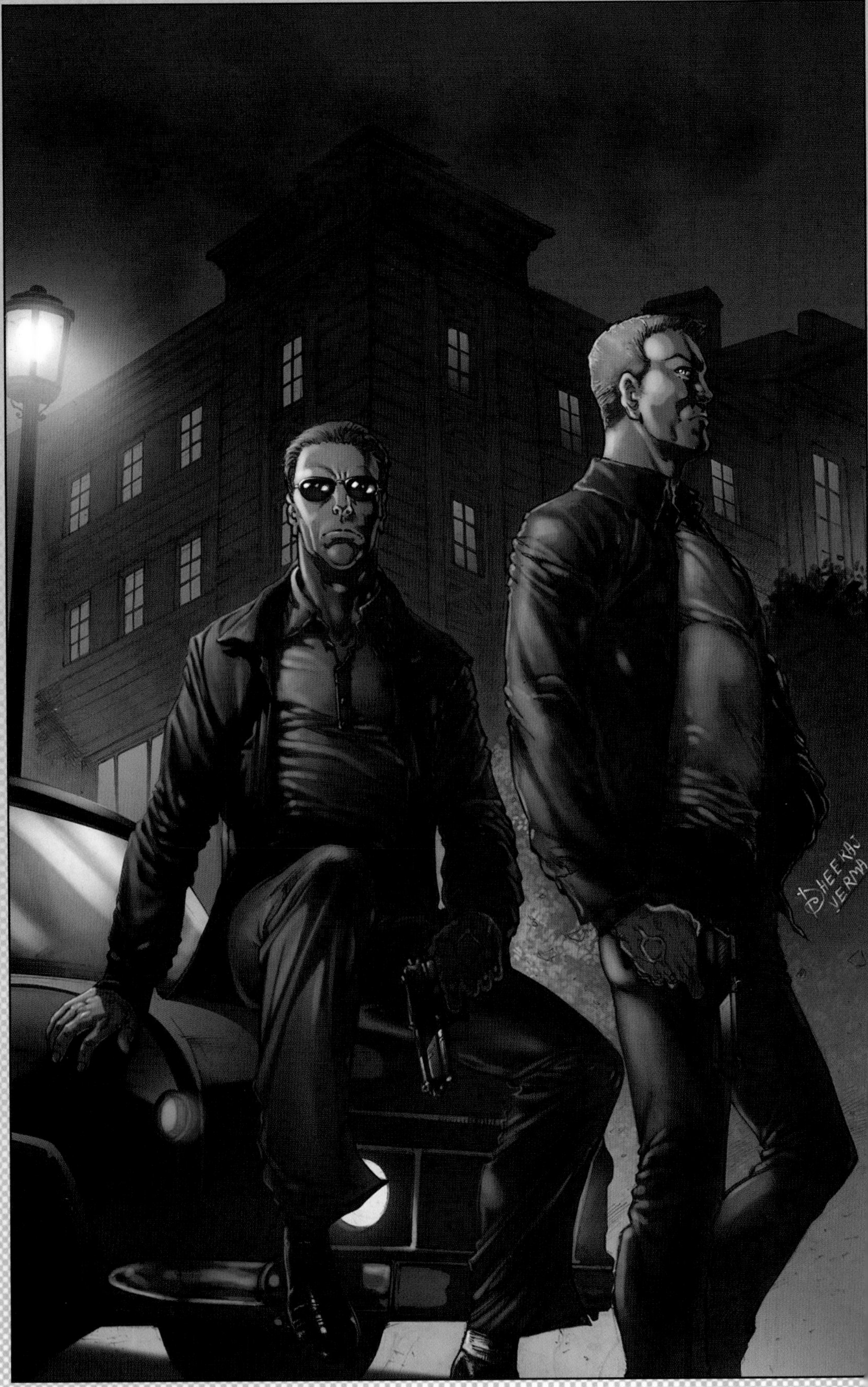
DHEERAJ VERMA

ARTWORK BY
DHEERAJ VERMA

COLORS BY
SANJAY

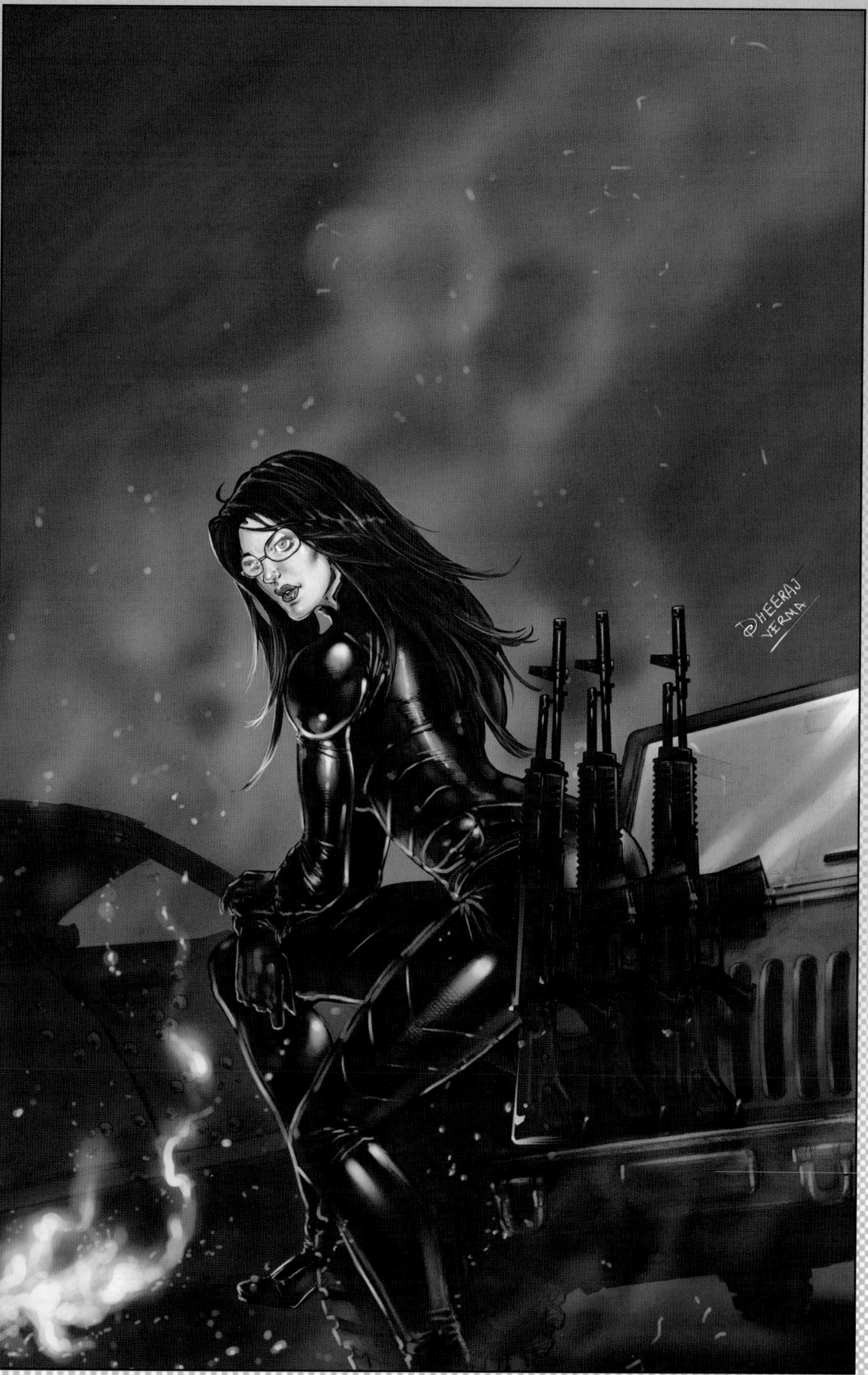
DHEERAJ
VERMA

ARTWORK BY
DHEERAJ VERMA

COLORS BY
SANJAY

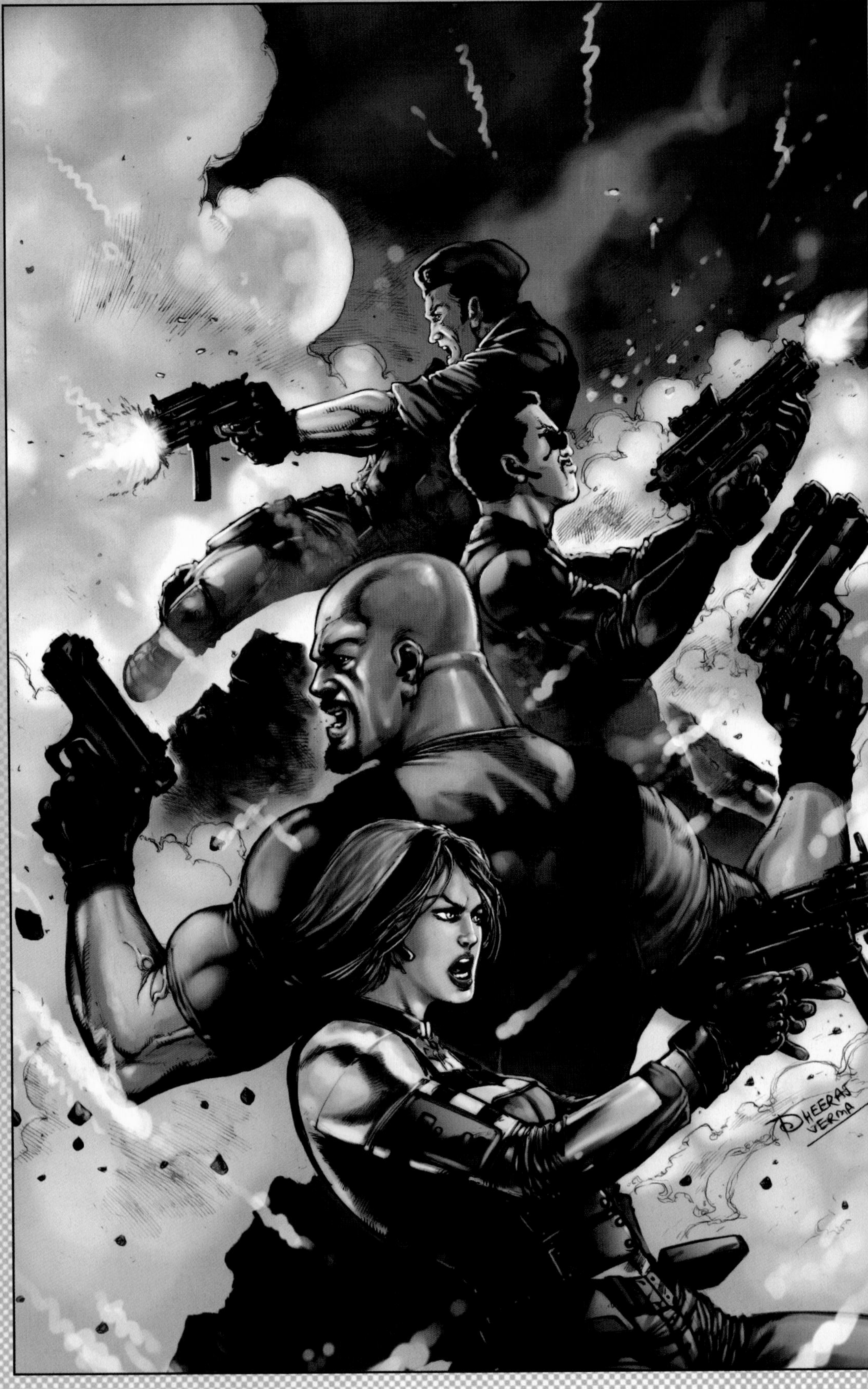
DHEERAJ VERMA

ARTWORK BY
DHEERAJ VERMA

COLORS BY
SANJAY

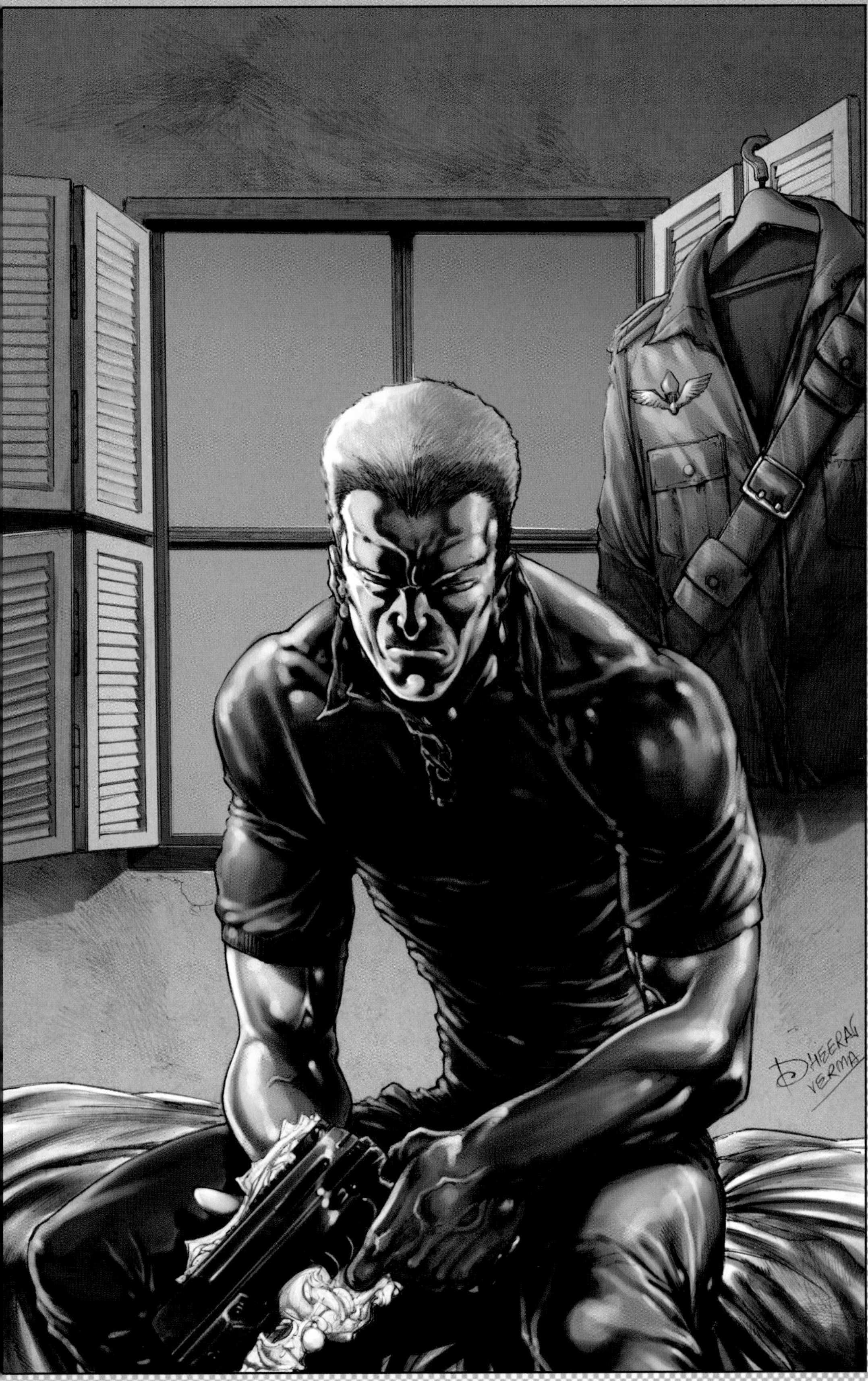
DHEERAJ VERMA

ARTWORK BY
DHEERAJ VERMA

COLORS BY
SANJAY

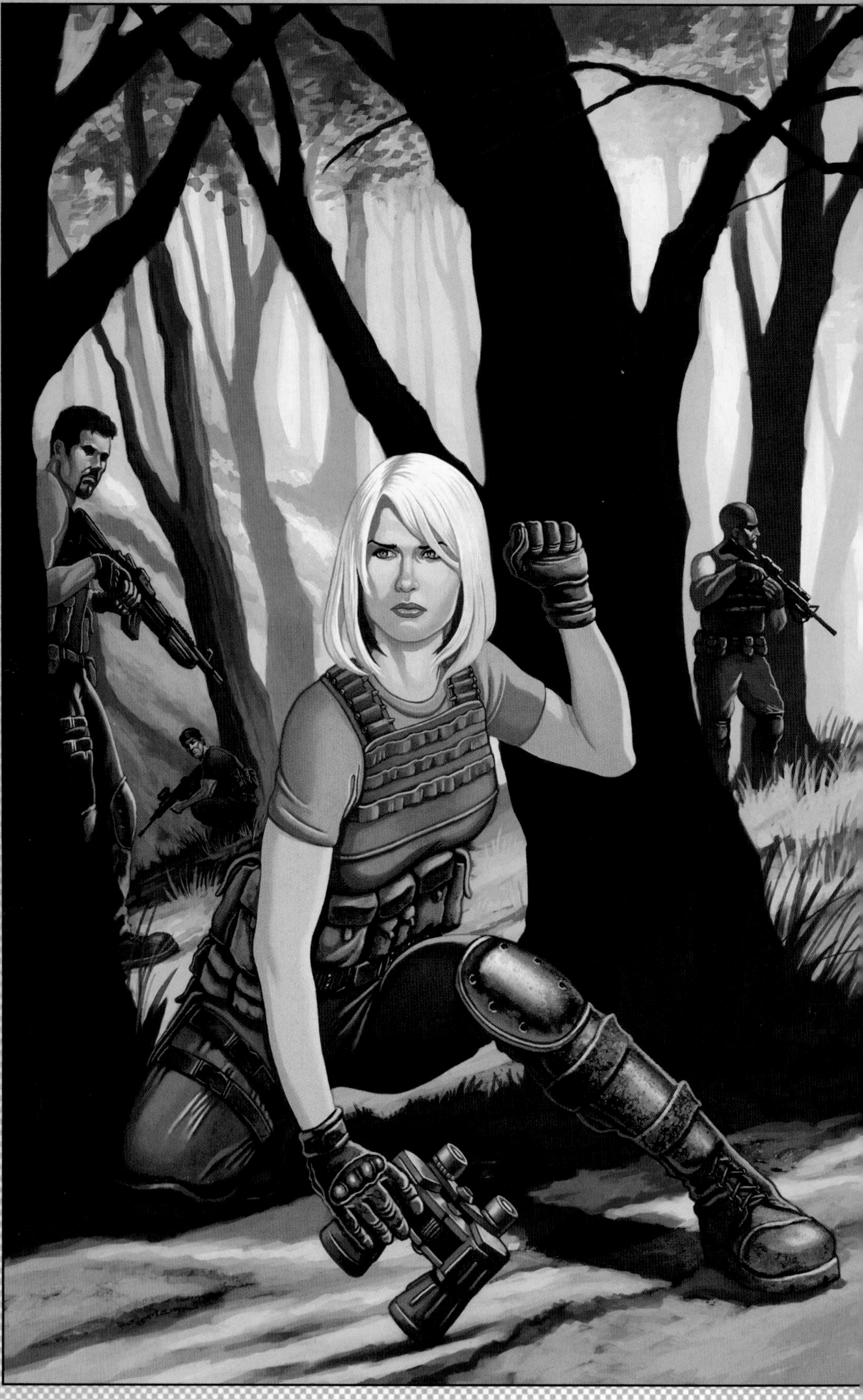

PINUP BY
KITO YOUNG

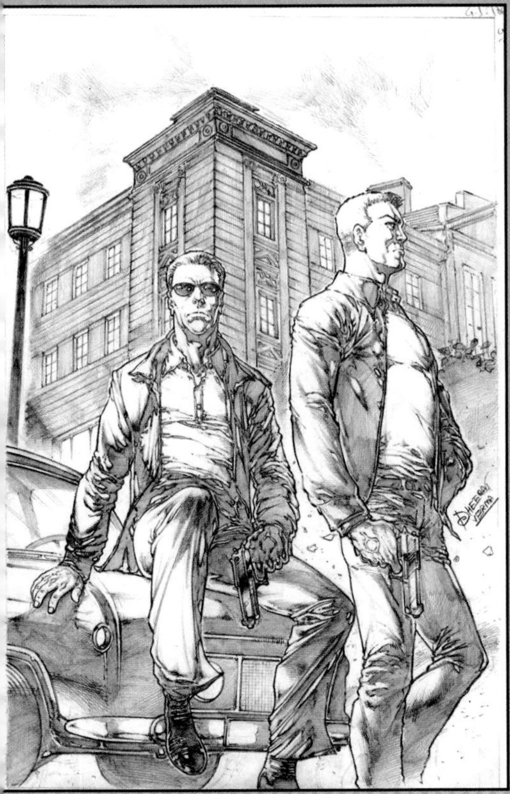

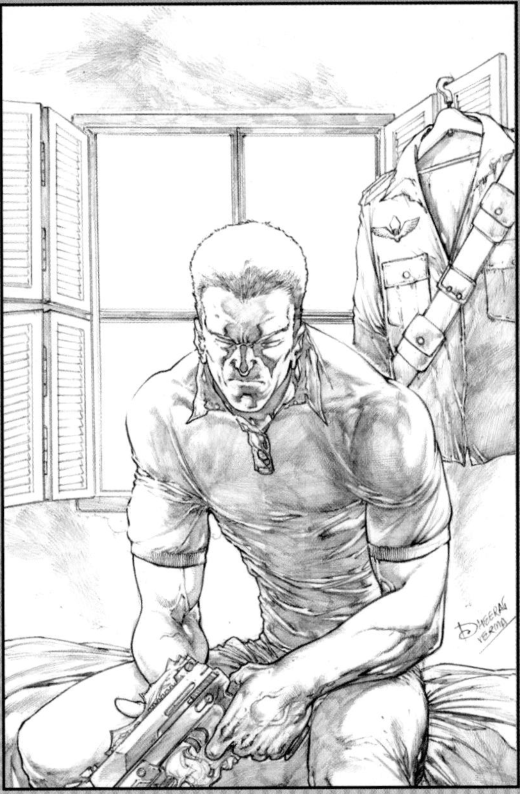

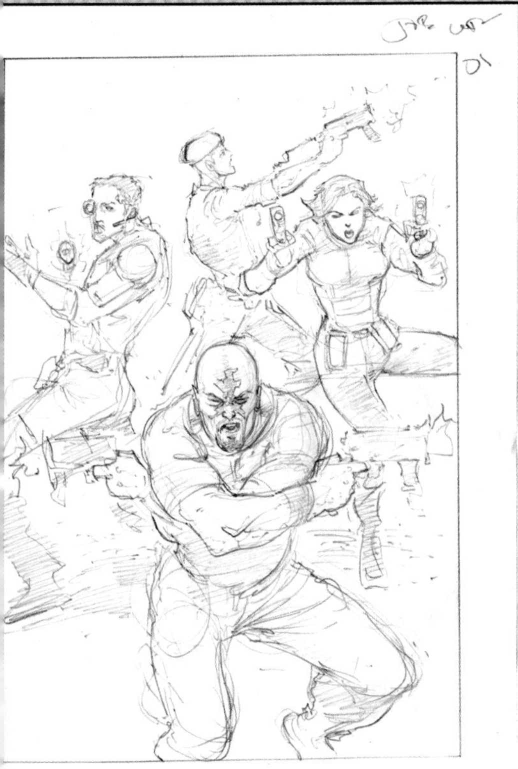

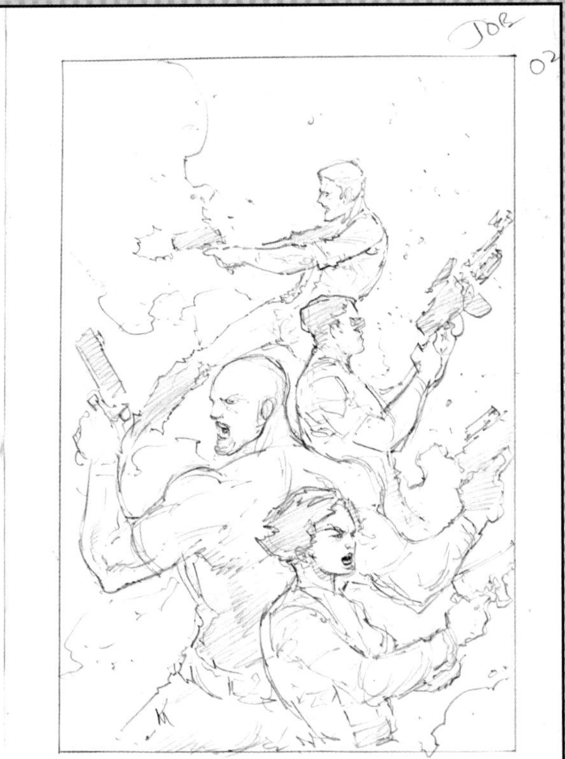

COVER PENCILS BY

DHEERAJ VERMA

THE COMIC SHOP NEWS INTERVIEW

CLIFF BIGGERS: Karen, you're a very versatile writer with some pretty impressive credentials—for readers who might not be familiar, can you tell us a little bit about your background as a writer?

KAREN TRAVISS: Okay, deep breath, and the entire career history of Karen Traviss in thirty seconds: advertising copywriter (very briefly), newspaper journalist, TV reporter and producer, newspapers again (defense correspondent), spin doctor, and now novelist and scriptwriter. I'm sorry about the spin doc bit, but I'm all better now, and it comes in very handy for fiction.

CB: What is it about military-focused fiction in particular that appeals to you as a writer?

KT: I come from a naval town, most of my family served at some time or worked in the defense industry, I was a defense correspondent, and I spent a short time in the reserves—doing a very safe, very minor job, I hasten to point out. (I've never put myself in harm's way, unless you count Royal Navy meat pies.) So I'm steeped in the culture, and I sort of fell into it with my first novel, and it stuck.

Military readers said, "Wow, your military characters are real, that's what it's really like," and suddenly I had my mission in life: I could give a voice to the man and woman in uniform so that civilian audiences got an honest view of what it really meant to serve—not so much the hardware side, because that's pretty flexible when you write a lot of SF, but the personal side, like the comradeship, the frustrations, the satisfaction, the fears, and the politics.

CB: There was a time when military fiction seemed to be very supportive of the military; then much of the fiction took a naturalistic turn that downplayed any heroic aspects in favor of a harsh view of war and the military. How do you approach military fiction thematically, and what do you hope to accomplish with your work?

KT: Well, my fiction is always realistic, because I'm basically an old journo and I can't see the world any other way, but it's also supportive of the armed forces, not because I write propaganda but because I tell it like it is. It's vital to tell the truth in fiction. Trust an old spin doc: fiction gets under people's radar way better than fact, and where the civilian population is more isolated from a shrinking military than ever, fiction ends up subconsciously shaping opinion instead.

And supporting our armed forces isn't related to supporting war as some sort of concept. It's about people, and they do the toughest job of all. Other people do dangerous work where death is a possible consequence, but no other job on earth requires you to sign up to the certainty that your job is to fundamentally to face people trying to kill you.

CB: *G.I. Joe* has walked the military fiction tightrope—while it focuses on soldiers, it has largely pit them against enemies who weren't a part of any real war... sort of a military version of James Bond. The results have allowed *G.I. Joe* writers to avoid complex politics and focus on adventure and heroism. Is your take on *G.I. Joe* more real-world?

KT: Yes, I'm real-world. I don't see the divide there, though; the real world is heroism, and it's also politics. I know folks in uniform hate being called heroes, but I often look at the incredible things guys do, the enormous risks they take and the kind of missions they pull off, and I think: if you put that in a novel, exactly as it happened, an editor would throw it back as too far-fetched. It's been true in every war, from the WWII raid on St. Nazaire to Royal Marines in Afghanistan riding into a firefight on the outside of an Apache helicopter to rescue a comrade. I really couldn't make that stuff up.

And the politics, whether it's big P or small p—you can't remove that. The armed forces go where sent, as we say in the UK, and it's the politicians we vote for who make the decisions, from budgets to getting involved in wars, for good or ill. That's where wars are really won and lost.

And in case people don't realize it, I'm English, so I approach things from another perspective. If you look at how British writers have handled American superhero comics, you'll notice it's through a different lens.

CB: What is the premise of your *G.I. Joe* series relaunch?

KT: It's five or six years from the end of the last series, and the world's changed a bit. COBRA looks like it's given up armed conflict, so the